Why the Information Highway?

Lessons from Open & Distance Learning

EDITED BY

JUDITH M. ROBERTS
& ERIN M. KEOUGH

Trifolium Books Inc.
Toronto

Why the Information Highway?
Lessons from Open & Distance Learning

First published in 1995 by
Trifolium Books Inc.
238 Davenport Road
Suite 28
Toronto, Ontario
M5R 1J6
Canada

Canadian Cataloguing in Publication Data

Main entry under title:

Why the information highway? lessons from open & distance learning

Includes bibliographical references and index.
ISBN 1-895579-39-2

1. Telecommunication in education. 2. Distance education. I. Keough, Erin M. II. Roberts, Judy.

LB1044.84.W58 1995   371.3'078   C95-930667-6

Ordering Information
Please contact Trifolium Books Inc., 238 Davenport Road, Suite 28, Toronto, Ontario, Canada M5R 1J6; tel. (416) 925-0765; fax (416) 485-5563.

Editing, Design, & Production: Francine Geraci

Printed in Canada at Hignell Printing.
Printed on acid-free paper.
Last digit is print number: 10 9 8 7 6 5 4 3 2 1

Contents

Preface

This is a timely book. It is almost a decade since the simultaneous publication of Mugridge and Kaufman's *Distance Education in Canada* and Henri and Kaye's *Le Savoir à domicile* provided a comprehensive overview of the development of open and distance learning in Canada. Much has happened in that time.

In the mid-1980s the term "distance education" was practically unheard-of in the United States, and thus Canada's vibrant distance education sector related more readily to countries farther afield. That has now changed. Due in part to the "information highway" of the title of this book, distance education is suddenly at the centre of public discourse about the electronic future. Institutions and entrepreneurs of all hues are rushing to offer new distance learning opportunities, especially by electronic mail and satellite, and especially in the United States. Distance education is now in a period of rapid evolution. Following that analogy, we can expect many new initiatives to founder and disappear while others that prove well adapted to the new environment—or a small niche within it—will survive and develop.

Canadian distance education is particularly rich in lessons and experience that can help us assess the likely fate of new mutations. This is because Canada combines a highly developed communications infrastructure, a strong tradition of the pedagogy of distance learning, and governments that have been eager to promote distance education and fund projects. Indeed, when one looks back from the 1990s to the 1970s there is a sense of déjà vu. At that time, Canadians carried out some pioneering experiments in the use of satellites in education. I well remember that in the 1970s the key issue was interaction. Would satellites be used primarily for interactive teaching or as very high broadcast towers? The answer from those experiments on the Hermes satellite suggested that broadcasting would likely be the more important application in education.

Now the role of interaction in education is back on the agenda. The Canadian experience of recent years will be very relevant to institutions around the world that are assessing the implications of the information superhighway, and all that goes with it, for their institutions. I particularly hope that reading of this experience through the issues and case studies presented in this book will lead people to make the student's experience central to their concern as they offer distance education in new ways.

I remarked, in my preface to Mugridge and Kaufman's book, that Canada is distinguished among the community of nations for its combination of opportunity and civility. Those qualities, as they emerge through the chapters in this book, are more relevant than ever. Individual access to the new technologies will vary in a way that has the potential to make the rich educationally richer and the poor poorer. Canadians take equality of opportunity very seriously in their provision of distance education, and the world can learn from them. The new media would also be the pretext for developing distance education in the direction of rampant individualism. A theme of this book is that supported open learning is the goal to strive for, that is to say, a student experience that combines independent work with authentic communication among teachers and peers.

The present exciting phase of development will change distance education in many ways. It is not just a question of new means of delivery. At the Open University we have coined the term "knowledge media" to describe the convergence of the learning and cognitive sciences with computing and telecommunications technologies. A key feature of knowledge media is that dynamic means of discovering, sharing and creating knowledge are becoming as important as the conventional notion of media "content." This issue, too, is illuminated in this book.

The contributors to this volume have a collective experience of distance education measured in centuries. Although they work *a mari usque ad mare*, most of them have known each other for many years, giving Canada a unique community of scholars in the field. I congratulate them on putting this collection together, and I commend it to readers all over the world.

JOHN DANIEL
THE OPEN UNIVERSITY
UNITED KINGDOM

Introduction

During this century, humanity has fashioned three major technological innovations: flight, automation, and telecommunications/information technology. Each has produced radical change in the existing social and economic environment. Each has also led to questions of control, that is, "Does humanity control or shape its inventions and tools, or is humanity controlled by them?"

Within 50 years of achieving sustained flight, men walked on the moon. Flight revolutionized the way that we moved goods, creating global markets for products in a way that boats and trains could not match. Companies had to reconceptualize their businesses to remain competitive. Significant numbers of middle- and working-class people travelled by air, contributing to a "new" industry called tourism. However, while we were driven to conquer space and investigate new planets, we also shaped the tools of flight to create low Earth orbiting satellites (LEOS) and mobile satellites (M-Sat) to facilitate basic inexpensive communications with remote and isolated areas, or to provide state-of-the-art truck tracking systems to ensure "just in time" delivery to market.

Henry Ford's assembly line ushered in a new, increasingly automated industrial age. Tools were invented to achieve efficiencies in task performance and to relieve workers of tedious, sometimes dangerous jobs. Robots now perform hazardous tasks such as exploring volcanos and repairing underwater structures such as oil rigs. As with flight, even during its precipitous first stages of growth, people began to shape automation to fit their needs. Housework was automated with labour-saving devices. Cottage industries grew because of the development of such technologies as automatic knitting machines.

Do these promises and challenges sound familiar now that we are faced with the third of these technological paradigm shifts? Telecommunications and information technology (IT) are said to be redefining work, leisure, education, and government. The information highway is said to be more critical to prosperity than either the asphalt highway, or the asphalt runway! We are told that education will be available at our command in the home and in the workplace. Votes on any public issues will be taken, not through sampling small numbers, but by conducting referendums by telephone or computer or through interactive home television. We appear to be at the crossroads of another major realignment of the tools that we have created. Will the pattern of change be different for this technological platform? Or, will humanity shape these tools to meet its current needs as it did in the past?

Where will distance educators fit in this process? There are some comparisons to be drawn with the tools of flight and automation. As with the former innovations, the potential benefits of telecommunications and IT will be determined by how soon and how skilfully we learn to use and shape the tools.

Correspondence courses were the first form of distance education in Canada, initiated by Queen's University in 1888. Learners' needs—for faster and more direct feedback than mail could provide, for content that could not be taught in print, for service in remote areas that challenged postal service— contributed to distance educators' use of the tools of satellite technology in the mid-1970s, a trend that continues with the adoption of computer technologies.

Distance educators quickly integrated the tool of flight into correspondence courses, using this innovation to address these learner needs for reasonable turnaround time for assignment marking and test results. Moreover, they were among the first to explore the social applications of satellites. Not only did they use the relatively easily available broadcast option to extend the reach of their teaching facilities, but they struggled to find mechanisms to deal with satellite delay so that their learners could engage in interactive computer and voice conferences. Similarly, in the area of automation, distance educators have influenced the development of that platform by requiring improved printing and faster photocopying (versus the earlier typewriter and mimeograph machines), finding educational advantages for shrinkwrapping and multiple copying of videotapes and, last but not least, being avid and innovative users of desktop publishing techniques. In sum, distance educators' experience in shaping the tools of flight and automation can be called upon in our response to the challenges of controlling the tools of this new era.

This discussion brings us to the topic of this book: the information highway, distance education and open learning, and the lessons that have been learned from shaping the tools of flight and automation, and which can be applied in this new environment. Contributors to this book, grounding their work in established research and practical experience, examine the challenges facing those who do use, or plan to use, any of these technologies in their teaching, learning, and training activities. This book can guide both experts and novices.

Part 1: Emerging Issues

In Chapter 1, Haughey reexamines the meanings, both overt and covert, of distance, explores how distance might be related to education or learning, and then links the analysis to a critique of current positions and a proposal for an alternative position for distance education. It is grounded in the conventional distance education literature.

Chapter 2, by Pacey and Penney, challenges distance educators to reexamine their perception of themselves as being flexible, innovative, creative, and empowering colleagues for learners. It points to ways in which conventional educational systems may be more flexible and creative than they used to be—and than distance educators themselves may be. It discusses principles of strategic planning used in a business environment and challenges distance educators to adapt and apply them effectively to help learners succeed.

Part 2: Case Studies

In Chapter 3, Stahmer highlights results of surveys on the use of training technologies in the workplace which reveal that usage varies by country, industrial sector, and other factors. However, case study results and a number of government and private sector planning documents confirm the benefits and opportunities offered by technology-based learning. The issues and challenges posed to the workplace, to trainers, and to the formal education system are examined.

In Chapter 4, McKinnon reviews developments at the elementary/secondary level of education. While birth rates may be declining and the size of school systems contracting, the use of distance education courses at the K–12 level is increasing. For example, distance courses are now being used extensively by school-age children, as schools do not have the teaching or scheduling flexibility to offer all the approved curricula. Moreover, adults are returning for adult basic education (ABE) offered by schools or colleges in response to changing workplace concerns about literacy and numeracy. The types of learner support, learning styles, and preferences of these diverse learners are analyzed.

In Chapter 5, Spronk notes that, like other minority groups, Aboriginals have found that distance education technologies empower them to retain and enlarge their cultural traditions. The fact that they no longer have to be sent away from their home communities to obtain a quality education permits Native children to be grounded in a sense of worth about their own heritage and still acquire the education needed to succeed in the majority culture. Training for adults is also being delivered to Native communities. Programs are being designed, in consultation with Native leaders, to synthesize traditional Native values and skills with modern job requirements.

In Chapter 6, Brindley reviews the need for learner support systems that maximize the success rate in distance education courses. For example, sophisticated computer software and hardware such as CD-ROM are making libraries more accessible to all learners. Concepts such as the "tutor/teacher as facilitator" are no longer seen as unique to distance learning. Trends and issues in these, and other, learner support systems are analyzed.

In Chapter 7, Paul addresses the management of technology—the staffing, financing, and co-ordinating—in the context of learner-centred, value-based management approaches. He compares management issues in consortia and in single- or dual-mode institutions. Issues arising from the convergence of technologies, markets (e.g., competitors as partners), and regulatory policy are also addressed.

In Chapter 8, Lamy and Pelletier set the stage for two subsequent chapters about Francophone learners. They note that Canada's Francophone citizens (26 percent report French as their mother tongue) are unevenly distributed across Canada. Although concentrated in the province of Québec, many live in other provinces and have appropriated distance education technologies as a means of enhancing and preserving their heritage through education in their own language. Various political and organizational issues are emerging at this time, as Francophone distance education is undergoing rapid growth and development. These and other issues unique to Francophones, as well as those shared with other minority groups, are analyzed and discussed.

In Chapter 9, Paquette-Frenette and Larocque extend this political philosophy to pedagogy. Although some Francophone writing on distance education parallels that in English about individualization and independent self-study, another collective theme is more central to Franco-Ontarians. Its arguments for the importance of the collective approach to learning design and delivery are examined, compared, and contrasted with sociological analyses of minority group education and adult education theories about group-based learning.

In Chapter 10, Thomas and McDonell describe technologies other than print that are emerging as central to Francophones' growing participation in distance education. Challenges arise: for example, computer software may be available only in English. But opportunities arise as well: for example, technological frontiers are expanded as Francophones create their own technologies.

Part 3: Analysis

In Chapter 11, Tobin reviews the research published in distance education in the past ten years. Comprehensive statistics about learner demographics, cost and other factors have tended to be lacking in distance education. Her chapter analyzes eight categories of research and then recommends guidelines about essential information requirements and methodologies that should be adopted to meet practitioners' needs in the current education and training environments.

In Chapter 12, Mugridge analyzes issues and models raised in earlier chapters that are emerging as central to international co-operation. For example, student retention, mobility of course materials, and funding are themes of mutual interest to the Commonwealth of Learning and the International Council for Distance Education. The Canadian historical pattern of treating national priorities first may be influenced by the prominence that international organizations are now giving to international requirements. The effect on national distance education planning of such international agencies, and the growing interest of such organizations as the OECD, are addressed.

In Chapter 13, Keough and Roberts examine the telecommunications and education policy environments that affect distance education. Many policy issues need reexamination in terms of the emerging internal and external challenges confronting distance education: transfer of educational credits, partnership parameters in the broadcast industries, the taxation and pricing of technologies. Those issues seen as particularly critical are analyzed.

Canada's Information Highway Advisory Council envisages that lifelong learning should be a key design element of the Information Highway. The Council's Working Group on Learning and Training is addressing such issues as user needs, affordability, universality and equity that have been a primary focus in the professional life of all authors of these chapters. The reader is therefore invited to read this book, and join the debate about the lessons that open distance learning may have to offer those engaged in deploying the Information Highway.

Acknowledgements

Writing and producing this book has been a team effort. Our contributors exhibited exemplary professionalism in providing significant thought-provoking content, and in never failing to meet any and all format and scheduling requirements requested of them, as did the author of the Preface, John Daniel.

Jacquie Hansford matched contributors' professionalism and more; this book would not exist without her word processing skills and her exceptional patience and flexibility.

Trifolium Books Inc. demonstrated a confidence in the need for Canadian materials about distance open learning when no other Canadian publisher would.

So to all the team, and any we have inadvertently failed to mention, our heartfelt thanks.

ERIN M. KEOUGH
JUDITH M. ROBERTS

Part 1
Emerging Issues

CHAPTER 1

Distinctions in Distance: Is Distance Education an Obsolete Term?

MARGARET HAUGHEY

Our understandings of distance education are shaped by the media with which we are most familiar. Correspondence education was meant to reflect the dependence on post office technology. More recently, some distance education institutions adopted the term *open learning,* perhaps to reflect their willingness to take students at any time and without any prerequisites, a format that implied a systems view of distance education. Now, some distance educators want to replace distance education with the terms *tele-learning* or *video-education.*

Within the North American context, the proliferation of telecommunication, and the development of technologies that can be used for communication, have brought into question the utility of the term *distance education.* Telecommunications seems to be instantaneous. This is especially true for those whose only experience of distance education is through a particular electronic medium such as audio- or videoconferencing. Naturally enough, they ask the question, "Where's the distance?" Real-time television has added to this challenge. When we can see and hear what is going on anywhere in the world at almost the moment it happens, is not the notion of distance obsolete?

In the remainder of this chapter, I would like to explore responses to this question and to argue for the retention of *distance* as a term that includes more than we might realize. This chapter, then, is focussed on a reexamination of the "distance" in distance education through an attempt to reveal the richness of the term, to explore the meanings of distance in education and in technology, and to argue that distance has still more possibilities.

Defining Distance

Geography

The most common notion of distance, and the one people most readily associate with distance education, is the idea of geographic distance. This is not surprising in North America, given the "wide open spaces" of the plains and prairies. But what do we mean by geographic distance? Evans (1989) pointed out that the idea of geographic distance depends on our identification with specific points on the surface of the ground, or in other words, with places. We give names to these places. They are our homes, our communities. They are important to us beyond their specific locations because the naming of a place is a social construct developed over time and associated not only with a physical location but also with all the aspects of the culture that created and sustains it.

Distance is the relational concept for the space between these places. "To have a concept of distance one needs a sense of place, or more specifically, places: distance becomes the space(s) between places" (Evans, 1989, p. 175). Geographic distance is therefore not just the idea that places are physically so many kilometres apart; it is also a cultural construction. The referents that anchor the physical distance are places where our hopes and aspirations have been given concrete form. When we speak of someone being from a place, we call to mind not just the dot on the map but all our connotations of the place name.

Time

Distance also connotes the passage of time. However, in this decade alone, we have become involved with telecommunications, which challenges the notion that "covering the distance," going from "here" to "there," involves bodily movement. Today, we put less emphasis on the length of time it takes to travel a distance and more emphasis on the notion that telecommunications can put us there instantly. Telephone companies try to persuade us that we can get rid of the "long-distance feeling" just by picking up the phone. We can join a celebration even if we are many kilometres away. Computer communications have linked us to a global network and promise us that, through optical fibres, the world will beat a path to our door, or that we can gain access to the world by riding the information highway without leaving home. Time, which was formerly a factor in distance, now seems irrelevant. Telecommunications has challenged the notion of time as a factor of distance, but it has also raised the question of what it means to be present at an event. In what ways does electronic presence still leave learners at a distance?

Difference

Distance connotes difference. This includes the *cultural* difference of not being from this place, the *social* differences of class, ethnicity, language, and gender, and the *psychological* differences of how we define ourselves and our apartness from others. Distance is present in our definition of ourselves as being unique, in the ways our society's definitions of our gender and class limit this definition, and in the sense we have of being rooted in a particular place and culture. We distance ourselves from others and also are distanced by the norms of our society or culture when we accept possibilities that might redefine us and our place in the world.

These competing connotations are also reflected in the etymology of the word *distance,* which comes initially from the Latin "distantia"—from *di,* meaning apart, and *stare,* to be situated, to take up a position, to stand (*Shorter Oxford,* p. 355). Embedded in its meaning are connotations of being different, separate, and independent. Distance connotes separation; in choosing to be separate, we choose to stand apart from the other, to be distant, to be uninvolved. Yet, in standing apart, we also stand *for* something, whether it is our community culture or our individual uniqueness. Together, these meanings serve to enrich the most common notion of distance as pertaining only to geography.

The Meanings of Distance in Distance Education

Why do we use the term distance education? What does it signify? How do the distances of geography, time, culture, advantage, and disadvantage relate to distance education? Discussing these questions may help us expand our understanding of the term by focussing on those aspects of distance we might otherwise ignore. In describing distance education, we often speak of distant learners, meaning the learners who are at a distance from the institution. In terms of geographical distance, we are putting all the emphasis on the space between the institution and the learners. At the centre is the institution, and the learners are at a disadvantage because they are not "here." We use terms such as *off-campus* or *extension* students but such language, while a convenient shorthand, ignores students' sense of place and may connote its unimportance in comparison with the place of the institution at the centre. Such terms can also inadvertently suggest that the only valid knowledge is that from the centre, and that students' own experiences, which are an essential part of learning, are of less worth. Further, the centralization of control that often accompanies this vision of the institution works against the autonomy of the learner who chooses to connect with others in ways not specified by the course designers.

Learner Independence vs. Learner Interaction

The "at a distance" learners are sometimes considered invisible: they are out of sight and out of mind, a statement that is itself rich in unintended meanings. In terms of temporal distance, we as distance educators have tried to find a way to overcome the tyranny of distance by arguing for both learner independence and learner interaction. Learner independence involved the advantages of distance in that the student is considered to be independent, separate, and autonomous. Learner interaction, on the other hand, was seen as overcoming a deficit in the student. Not truly autonomous, learners needed to be guided from the centre.

Few models of learner interaction are entirely peer based. Many are replications of the traditional institutional models used with students present in classrooms. In this way, the disadvantages of distance can be overcome and the "loneliness of the long-distance learner" can be relieved because, with just a phone call, he or she can join the audioconference class and feel a sense of belonging. The notion that independent learners might choose to learn in their own places, rather than be anxious to attach at the learning places decided by the institution, may be disregarded. In models where the centre is in control, place can easily connote hierarchy, and students on the margins may not speak out about their concerns. Where contact is left up to the student, the distance of difference may prevent the linking of teacher and learner. Learners who are "at a distance" are often unaware of the norms of the institutional culture, and may hesitate to become visible by asking for possibly inappropriate information or by calling at the "wrong" time.

Role of the Teacher

The definition of distance education has received attention from a number of writers. While some (Holmberg, 1985; Keegan, 1993) seek a general definition that will encompass all situations, others (Moore, 1990; Garrison & Shale, 1989; Rumble, 1986) have tried to identify the concepts that form the basis for distance education. An analysis of their work raises questions about the importance given to the notion of teacher, the preference for immediate human interaction as an aspect of instruction and learning, and the concept of autonomy as being negotiated through interaction with the teacher. In a more recent work, Moore (1993) defines distance education as not simply a geographical concept but also a pedagogical one. He suggests that transactional distance "describes the universe of teacher–learner relationships that exist when learners and instructors are separated by space and/or by time" (p. 22). He goes on to argue that, since interaction is important in reducing distance, its availability and quality can be influenced by technology:

It is obvious that the nature of each communications medium has a direct impact on the extent and quality of dialogue between instructors and learners ... . By manipulating the communications media it is possible to increase dialogue between learners and their teachers, and thus reduce the transactional distance. (pp. 24–25)

Although Moore discusses at some length the human aspects of the particular teaching philosophy of instructors, their comfort with dialogue and with a given technology, and the students' interest in interaction, he ends by suggesting that particular media of themselves are better for some instructional tasks. He goes on to note "the practical significance of this idea is that the course designers apply the idea of dividing the functions of the teacher—and delivering instruction that was assembled by a team of specialists, through numerous media" (p. 30). This idea must in turn affect Moore's concept of the teacher. In his framework, unlike the traditional notion of the teacher who uses audio-visual media as a supplement or addition to enhance classroom instruction, media are delivering the instruction. The function of the teacher is thus brought into question. If distance education can be defined as "delivering" instruction through various media, then it can be argued that, since students can cruise the Internet for information or obtain it through software programs or print materials, the teacher as a "real" person can be relegated to damage control—to solve personal difficulties and provide the social bonds considered important in motivating students to persist in their learning. The "real" teaching is in the software.

Moore also raises an important question about pedagogical distance. What would a distance of pedagogy entail? Pedagogy is not just a synonym for teaching. Rather, it involves a thoughtfulness about the learner and a tactfulness from teachers that encourage and sustain a relationship that emphasizes both learner and learning. In a pedagogical relationship, the instructor is attuned to the learner. The crucial question for many distance educators is: How essential is a personal relationship in learning? Are instructors important, or should the establishing of pedagogical relationships be the responsibility of tutor/markers? Education is based on the teaching–learning relationship. Traditionally, this has involved the teacher and the taught, and was founded on a conception of the transfer of knowledge. Those who "know" are the teachers who, through clear logical explanations, are able to transfer the information to those who do not know, the learners. Although this is now only one way of describing education, teaching strategies in many institutions have changed little from this traditional form. How, then, is the teaching–learning relationship displayed in distance education?

Clearly, the discontinuities present in traditional classrooms are also present in many distance education activities. These are partly the result of the transfer of traditional beliefs to distance education and partly the result of the ways in which distance educators have chosen to use particular technologies. Not only are learners at a distance from distance educators; we, in turn, have distanced ourselves from learners. We provide the materials, and often our expectations are such that those who fail to complete the course blame themselves rather than the institution (Conrad, 1991). Yet, even those of us who want to improve this situation often try to remove the difficulty by removing the distance and holding face-to-face seminars. Is it that simple? Is it merely a problem of geographical distance? Is there no distance in classrooms?

In addressing these questions about the place of interaction in learning, we are forced to explore our own understanding of the relationship between teaching and learning and to question our meaning for teaching. Just as distance carries within it the notion of being grounded in a particular "here-ness" for both institution and learner, and the notion of a constellation of places that are defined by their difference from other places, so also we in distance education must recognize where we are situated and seek not to reproduce the traditional form for classroom instruction, but instead to provide learning opportunities that celebrate the distances while keeping the connections to the community of learners.

The Meanings of Distance in Technology

One of the earliest and most persistent conceptualizations of distance education has involved the combination of learner independence and interaction. The independent learning happens where the student chooses to study; the interaction involves communication between the student and the institution using some combination of media, often at a particular place. Hence, distance education is mediated education, and most definitions of distance education include reference to the use of media to support communication between learner and teacher.

Defining Technology

Many authors will attest to the difficulty of defining the term "technology." It is used for items such as computers, which are also referred to as tools, and for processes such as pedagogy or instructional design. It is used so loosely that it is sometimes difficult to decide what is not a technology. The term technology has its roots in the Greek, *techné,* a mode of revealing or knowing that related to the things of this world as opposed to theoria which dealt with abstractions. Techné may initially have been used to stress the production of things according to the rules and conventions of a craft without any intention to influence the surrounding social structures, but the same root subsequently gave us *technique, technics,* and *technology.* Technology has come to mean the systematic application of scientific and other organized knowledge to a specific problem or topic. Often presented as a way to control the natural environment to help meet human needs, technology is also seen to affect social as well as physical structures.

Technology and "Isolation"

The most commonly perceived advantage of technology is its ability to overcome the "problem" of distance. It can bring the learner into the presence of the instructor, most frequently in real or synchronous time. It can link students and instructors together so that place and time become irrelevant. How is this done? Is it the technology that does these things, or do they depend on the process used? Is an audio-conference merely the technical linking of a group of people by audible telephone signals, or does it also involve a process particular to the technology? What are the difficulties that this process must address, and how do they relate to distance? To speak of one difficulty as "overcoming distance" reflects a particular view of the difficulties for learners as being isolated from the institution.

Learners, on the other hand, may not view themselves as isolated. They may be quite happy with their choice of place and, instead, view the institution as sometimes too close for comfort! Also embedded in this explanation of distance as isolation is the idea that students who are not connected to the institution and to each other lack any intellectual life. The only real learning takes place among registered members of the class.

At the same time, technology provides an opportunity that most students appreciate: the opportunity to interact with the instructor and with other learners. But we should also be aware that these linkages are an opportunity for institutions to ignore the benefits of distance and instead replicate the traditional institutional models of teaching. When students are linked together by audio- or videoconferencing, they are often considered to be "a class" and are taught from that point of view. In reality, the students are in different places and they may not want to be thought of as a group. Such a conception ignores the students' own places and the differences that are present among them. Being thought of as one class erases the differences, but not the dissonances, that this virtual reality can entail.

Technology and "Presence"

The most problematic issue associated with the use of telecommunications technologies in distance education is the assumption that learners within a network are present to each other. Videoconferencing, because of its ability to provide a visual record of the happenings at each place, is often thought to provide presence. But being present is more than being visible. In observing videoconferencing classes, I found that students seemed to be listening rather than looking at the speaker on the screen, and that instructors who had a number of students at a site differentiated among them by the sound of their voices. Students' willingness to break the social conventions of the face-to-face classroom by asides or secondary conversations, by pressing the mute and talking while someone at another site was speaking, and by getting up and moving around the room out of camera view, were examples of instances where being present to the other meant no more than it did in their own homes when they were watching television. We need to be more aware of the reasons why students choose to distance themselves from these classroom conventions and to structure these sessions in ways that acknowledge their artificiality.

The advent of computer conferencing for distance education has also challenged the silences of distance. Some users want to ensure the participation of all people who gain access to a particular conference, and they take various steps to "smoke out lurkers" on the system. In some ways, the issue of compulsory participation in computer conferencing is also about the notion of presence. In a classroom setting, student presence carries with it social responsibilities and may require participation. In a distance education setting, the same issues of control and partic-ipation are attempted through the language of student presence. In mediated communications, distance is not obsolete, but more frequently, it is silenced.

Role of Dialogue

How might technology be employed to celebrate rather than minimize distance? In a discussion of the balance between inter-action and student independence, Daniels and Marquis (1968) agreed that distance education media must provide for dialogue as an essential aspect of learning. Holmberg thought that this could be achieved through print. He considered that his study guides provided for interactivity because the insertion of ques-tions in the text and the informal nature of the language encour-aged the student to "correspond" with the text itself. Garrison and Shale opposed this view and instead stressed mediated two-way communication as an essential requirement of distance education. For Garrison (1989), the importance of two-way communication is based on a philosophy that stresses the impor-tance of the negotiation of meaning as part of knowledge making. He insisted that, unlike information, which could be transmitted through one-way communication, knowledge needed two-way communication (p. 16).

How does interaction enhance knowledge development? Gillard, for example, points out that in teaching, the instructor provides various descriptions in the process of clarifying a point.

If learning were the simple transfer of information, the first description should have been sufficient. Subsequent clarifications, which are really different descriptions, are required by students who still do not grasp what is being said. From such a viewpoint, education is considered an interpretive process where meanings are developed through talk and learners are active participants in this process. The focus of distance education is not on the "delivery" of education to learners but on the "constructing of meaning" with learners.

It is at this point that the concerns of writers for the interactivity of dialogue as an essential aspect of distance education coincide with a view of technology as extending possibilities for thoughtful practice. Today we know more about the complexity of learning, the value of discussion, and the importance of learners' previous experiences in learning (Laurillard, 1993). What remains problematic is how to encourage learning when communications take place through electronic media. We need to be aware of the issues of distance within telecommunications technologies and remember, in particular, that the ways we structure the instructional process can merely replicate the traditional models and ignore the freedom that distance can provide.

Conclusions

Further Challenges of Distance

Distance is a rich term that moves far beyond the idea of geographic distance. Earlier, I mentioned both the silences of distance and the freedom of distance. We are inclined to use distance as a pejorative term and don't seem to realize how much people value the opportunity to be alone. Being alone is an aspect of the maturity of the human spirit and, in a country like Canada, many people are drawn to the wilderness for precisely these reasons. Distance can be precious in giving us time and space to think and to be. It can mean freedom in allowing us to take charge of our own activities, a point unacknowledged when fixed-time teleconferences are held.

All of us have experienced psychological distance because it is part of the way we define whom we are. We have also used distance as we learned. We have tried simultaneously to enter fully into a topic, to be submerged in it, and at the same time, we have held it apart from us as we tried to understand what meaning to make of the idea. Both presence and distance are held in tension as aspects of learning.

The forms of distance within technology will continue to challenge us. As students use the Internet and decide to contact others all over the world, we will be faced with the issue and challenge of pedagogical distance. The complexity of our world has helped us recognize the importance of distance in respecting difference and in being more cognizant of its advantages as well as its disadvantages. Being out of sight need not mean we have forgotten those who choose to be learners at a distance.

References

Conrad, D. (1991). *Students' perceptions of studying at a distance.* Unpublished Master's thesis, The University of Alberta, Edmonton, Alberta.

Daniel, J., & Marquis, C. (1979). Interaction and independence: Getting the mixture right. *Teaching at a Distance, 15,* 25–44.

Evans, T. (1989). Taking place: The social construction of place, time and space, and the (re)making of distances in distance education. *Distance Education, 10*(2), 170–183.

Holmberg, B. (1985). *Status and trends in distance education* (2nd ed.). Sweden: Lector.

Garrison, R. (1989). *Understanding distance education.* London: Routledge.

Garrison, R., & Shale, D. (1987). Mapping the boundaries of distance education: Problems in defining the field. *The American Journal of Distance Education, 1*(1), 7–13.

Gillard, G. (1993). Deconstructing contiguity. In T. Evans & D. Nation (Eds.), *Reforming open and distance education* (pp. 182–195). London: Kogan Page.

Keegan, D. (Ed.).(1993). *Theoretical principles of distance education.* London: Routledge.

Laurillard, D. (1993). *Rethinking university teaching.* London: Routledge.

Moore, M. (1990). Recent contributions to the theory of distance education. *Open Learning, 5*(3), 10–15.

Moore, M. (1993). Theory of transactional distance. In D. Keegan (Ed.), *Theoretical principles of distance education* (pp. 22–38). London: Routledge.

Rumble, G. (1989). On defining distance education. *American Journal of Distance Education, 3*(2), 8–21.

Thinking Strategically: Reshaping the Face of Distance Education and Open Learning

LUCILLE M. PACEY
WAYNE P. PENNEY

One does not have to go beyond the media to learn that significant economic, political, and technological changes and shifts are occurring worldwide. Economic reform is reflected in approaches that reduce trade barriers and forge alliances harmonizing policy, currency, and quality standards.

Politically, some governments are collapsing while others are being formed; unexpected partnerships are being created. Countries that for years kept the rest of the world at bay are being opened; their citizens now have a window on the world that can confuse, excite, or instil any number of other emotions. People and cultures are demanding to be included in many facets of decision making that affect their lives. Impatience with governments and how they have represented citizens' needs and wants is becoming more common. The face of racial and ethnic discrimination can no longer be hidden or suppressed. Lack of access to the policy-making process is being challenged.

Borders are becoming transparent; no longer can countries pretend that influences (good or bad) outside their control will not have an impact on their citizens. The force of the media has opened the world to the public in real, unedited time, and the 500-channel universe is rapidly approaching. Indeed, some speculate that by the year 2000, this number will approach 2200! This is a time when telecommunications can eliminate or enhance the competitive advantage of critical timing. Technological advances in many spheres of activity have been rapid.

The result is that distributors of hardware and software are constantly introducing "new options" to organizations and individuals who often accept the technological "advances" as practice, thereby allowing technology to create practice. New and different partnerships, quick access to information, changes in the ways information is used, and technological advances and deployment are factors in the trend to globalization.

The linkage of education and training to the economic agenda of countries, always assumed, is now being increasingly communicated by governments, businesses, and unions. The challenge of building and maintaining a standard of living in which individuals have the opportunity to participate effectively has now become tied to a well-trained, knowledgeable population. People will need to know how to learn; indeed, they will be forced to learn throughout their lives. Political leaders have targetted education as the lifeline to economic prosperity and have recognized the need to emphasize training and education. However, while they acknowledge the need for educational reform, they continue to look back to the "old ways" to help them identify solutions.

These different realities challenge distance educators to communicate how their roles and relationships can contribute to the larger agenda of making education the anchor to a country's economic success and social health. There is a sense of urgency to this challenge, for the social and economic changes will not wait for distance education. Some of the key questions facing distance education institutions include:

• Does planning in distance education reflect the new reality of global and organizational change? Why do traditional approaches to planning offer only a partial answer?

• Are institutions flexible enough to demonstrate that they play an important and critical role in serving learners' needs and that they can alter their courses of action as the learners' needs change?

• Is there a belief that the telecommunications and technological advances will affect the work of distance learning only if allowed to do so?

Preparing distance education institutions for these rapid changes and increased expectations is forcing administrators to take a more serious look at how they plan and implement the processes appropriate to their needs. There is no best way to plan but, through observation and experience, it is possible to propose options that may help administrators work through this complex and challenging process.

We are encouraged by the readiness of institutions to participate in strategic planning, but suggest that the complexity of the global scene requires a more holistic and organic approach. This need for "fuzzy boundaries" tends to create tension in an organization, which is disruptive and seen to be dysfunctional. We propose that this state of "fuzziness" is the only state that promotes organizational creativity and provides the way to healthy distance education institutions in the future.

Issues

Traditional Approaches to Strategic Planning

There are many strategic planning models, but it is fair to say that the component parts of the process, if not identical, are very similar in nature.

Strategic planning is the process by which the guiding members of an organization envision the organization's future and develop the necessary procedures and operations to achieve that future. The vision of the future provides both a direction and the energy to move in that direction ... successful strategic planning is characterized by organizational self examination, confronting difficult choices, and setting priorities. (Pfeiffer, Goodstein, & Nolan, 1989, p. 56)

Today most organizations, including distance education units, are involved in some form of strategic planning. Even if the model adopted is often the one most expedient to the nature of the organization, there is a common understanding that the intent behind the process is to ensure that the organization can indeed envision its future, can influence the direction the future will take, and most importantly, can create its future.

It has been natural for distance educators to accept, and even to welcome, the principles of strategic planning. Distance educators have typically defined themselves as the innovators who take up the challenge of breaking new ground in delivering education and improving access to learners, and have considered themselves to be both politically and organizationally progressive thinkers. Conventional strategic planning models have adapted reasonably and readily to their world. Such models have been helpful in reducing complex issues into manageable component parts for analysis and resolution, and have provided a framework for organizations to monitor progress and to use that information for the process of envisioning a future. Distance educators have been very good at picking up these models and struggling with their various component parts. One has only to review the approaches used in planning for course development, delivery, and student support to see the similarities.

Pfeiffer, Goodstein, and Nolan (1989) propose nine important steps for strategic planning (see Figure 2.1).

Stage 1: Metaplanning, or Planning to Plan
The commitment to planning is communicated to the organization, and adequate resources are identified to ensure a successful outcome. Typically, this is also the time when an external environmental scan is undertaken to ensure that the organization is aware of the factors that could have an impact on the eventual successful implementation of the strategic plan. Scanning occurs throughout all stages of the process.

Stage 2: Values Audit
A review and validation of the individual and organizational values is conducted as a means of explicitly linking the behaviour and actions of individuals and the organization to more traditional plans and actions.

Stage 3: Mission Formulation
This anchor of the strategic plan typically answers three primary questions:

- What does the organization do?
- Whom does the organization serve?
- How does the organization carry out its task?

**Figure 2.1
The applied strategic
planning model.**

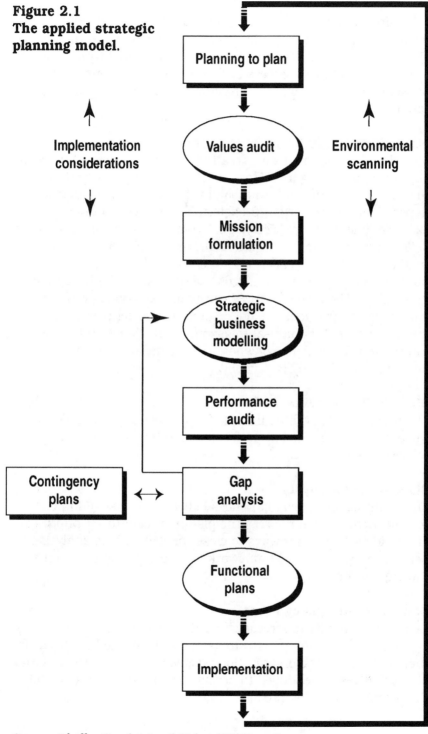

Source: Pfeiffer, Goodstein, & Nolan (1989), p. 6.

Unfortunately, in distance education it is often difficult to devise a single important phrase that describes the work succinctly and clearly. Not to be dissuaded, many institutions do struggle through the process and eventually come forward with a mission statement, which is promulgated throughout the organization.

Stage 4: Strategic Business Modelling

Modelling is concerned with creating a definition of the business objectives, including indicators of success and a description of the way the organization will look in the future. These descriptions usually span certain predetermined periods of time; for example, one, two, or three years. Typically, as the organization defines its objectives, it begins modelling itself, using information that it has collected reflecting the recent performance of the organization and those key standards that it has chosen to measure its success. The model ensures clarity and consistency of measurement and provides the opportunity to project past trends into the future. It is natural to assume that the vision for the future, and the evidence of where the organization is now, will not always be directly in "synch."

Stage 5: Performance Audit

The performance audit is intended to establish benchmarks of the organization's current performance in terms of growth, quality, service, etc.

Stage 6: Gap Analysis

This analysis identifies differences between the vision and current performance, and forces the planning team to set priorities and to identify creative ways to close the gap(s). This analysis becomes the core of the framework for the strategic direction of the organization.

Stage 7: Contingency Plans

Because the ability to forecast the future accurately is limited, contingency planning is used to assess some of the key "what-ifs" that could affect the organization positively or negatively. A series of alternatives is developed to provide a fuller understanding of the potential range of impacts.

Stage 8: Functional Plans

Functional and operational plans are based on information gleaned from the preceding stages and shared throughout the organization. These operational plans usually focus primarily on the "how" now that the "what" has been described, and include appropriate references to new resources and to the redeployment of resources as appropriate.

Stage 9: Implementation

The most important phase is implementing the plan and evaluating that implementation against the success factors that have been articulated earlier.

Strategic Thinking and How It Is Different

A systematic, highly disciplined approach to planning (as articulated in the preceding section) provides a very neat, tidy model. It promotes consultation and participation, builds on past history and knowledge, incorporates the necessary checks and balances key to monitoring progress, and allows for timely adjustments. Theoretically, distance education institutions involved in this or similar processes could ensure that they are at the leading edge of the development of open learning, and are positioned properly to demonstrate the contribution that they make to fostering access to learning, contributing to the love of learning, and participating in the all-important economic agenda. So, you might ask, why are we taking the time to review what seems to be an important process that most distance educators are committed to and are practising?

Over the last decade, we have witnessed changes throughout the world that none of us anticipated or ever believed could occur. Few of these changes appeared to emerge in a carefully planned way; rather, many appeared to run counter to logic. Almost nothing in the real world is rational, yet there is a tendency to use reductionist, linear models for strategic planning. The work of scientists in chaos theory readily illustrates that reductionist thinking does not work when looking at complex systems. We need to learn new skills that will help us address complex issues in a holistic fashion. The difference between reductionist and holistic approaches is the quintessential difference between strategic planning and strategic thinking. Until we achieve this goal, we will never succeed in promoting the concept of lifelong learning in the world today. As leaders in education, we cannot continue to tinker with the edges of what are much bigger, more complex issues.

Two important principles are embedded in a holistic approach:

• A strategic mind set is more important than a well-articulated plan.

• Vision and values are the key to adaptive, responsive decision making and action planning.

If there is a high degree of variability in an organization's operating environment, it becomes less important *what* its plans are, and more important *how* its planning decisions are made. Strategic decision making that is aligned with the organization's vision of the future and consistent with its guiding values is what we are advocating. It should be an organic process based on a collective vision of the future and driven by shared values. Planning should be a highly collaborative and interactive process, promoting meaningful dialogue among the stakeholders and building consensus on key issues and concerns. The process of developing the plan is sometimes more important than the plan itself, because it *stimulates* and *reinforces a strategic mind set.*

An effective approach, therefore, generally involves a creative challenge to managers and other stakeholders to develop a collective vision of the future of the organization. In particular, it is necessary to articulate the values, beliefs, or principles that people feel should guide decision making. Sometimes these can best be expressed in the form of a corporate "credo" or similar document. Specific issues, such as the structure, goals, strategies for change, and allocation of scarce resources, become much easier to resolve as a result of this groundwork.

Such a process can contribute to team building. Participants gain insight into their own beliefs and assumptions and those of their colleagues. Better interpersonal communications, more focussed decision making, and improved use of collective resources usually result. In addition, this process enhances the probability that the output of the planning cycle will be viewed as credible, and will be supported in its implementation.

The Changing Global Context

With this concept of strategic thinking in mind, what are some of the major external trends and challenges facing distance education institutions today?

Changing Concepts of Knowledge

Peter Drucker (1993) views knowledge as the new competitive advantage for individuals and society.

The change in the meaning of knowledge that began two hundred fifty years ago has transformed society and economy. Formal knowledge is seen as both the key personal and the key economic resource. In fact, knowledge is the only meaningful resource today. The traditional "factors of production"—land (i.e., natural resources), labor, and capital— have not disappeared, but they have become secondary. They can be obtained, and obtained easily, provided there is knowledge. And knowledge in this new sense means knowledge as a utility, knowledge as the means to obtain social and economic results. (p. 43)

Drucker postulates that individual knowledge will catapult society into a new phase of development rivalling the industrial revolution in scope and impact. He is not optimistic about the ability of the existing educational system to provide the opportunities for individual learning without widespread, systemic change. This is not a radical argument. Much has been written, both in the educational field as well as in other spheres of activity, about this fundamental shift. Unfortunately, little has been done from a systemic perspective to make this transition.

Additionally, there is a continuing debate about what actually constitutes knowledge. Concepts of holistic thought are colliding with more traditional views of knowledge as discrete and distinct blocks that can somehow be separated into cognitive, affective, and behavioural components. Chaos theory and systemic thinking, popularized by such writers as James Gleick (1987), John Briggs and David Peat (1989), Peter Senge (1990), and others, are being advocated as the newest panaceas for humankind's salvation. Only time will tell if these concepts prove to have lasting substance.

Different World Views

In an era when rapid transport and telecommunications are making the global village a reality, undercurrents of differing world views held by individuals of differing cultures have increasing impact on all educational institutions. In recent years, many Western institutions have created international studies divisions to offer programs to developing countries. To their dismay, many of these programs have been less than successful, while others have been abysmal failures. These failures are sometimes attributed to poor instructional design or delivery problems. Is this necessarily the correct diagnosis?

Edwin Nichols has developed a model for understanding the philosophical aspects underlying cultural differences, which is summarized in Table 2.1.

Samuel Huntington (1993) puts forth the argument that culture represents the fault line for civilization and its continued survival and prosperity. In discussing the differences between Western concepts and those of other cultures, he argues that "Western ideas of individualism, liberalism, constitutionalism, human rights, equality, liberty, the rule of law, democracy, free markets, the separation of church and state, often have little resonance in Islamic, Confucian, Japanese, Hindu, Buddhist or Orthodox cultures" (p. 40). He goes on to observe that a recent review of comparative values in different societies concluded that "the values that are most important in the West are least important worldwide" (p. 41).

Unless educators develop an in-depth understanding and empathy for cultural differences, attempts to work with other cultures will be sadly undermined. Indeed, even strategic thinkers need to assess their conceptual models carefully when working in a cross-cultural context, to ensure an appropriate fit.

The Changing Organizational Context

While the broad global context represents real challenges to the future growth and development of our distance education

Table 2.1
Philosophical aspects of cultural differences.

Ethnic Group/ World View	Axiology	Epistemology	Logic	Process
European Euro-American	The highest value lies in the object or the acquisition of the object.	One knows through counting and measuring.	Either/or	All sets are repeatable and reproducible.
African Afro-American Native American Hispanic Arab	The highest value lies in the inter-personal relationship between men.	One knows through symbolic imagery and rhythm.	The unity of opposites	All sets are inter-related through human and spiritual networks.
Asian Asian-American Native American Polynesian	The highest value lies in the cohesive-ness of the group.	One knows through striving toward the transcendence of thought and mind.	The objective world is conceived indepen-dent of the universe.	All sets are indepen-dently interrelated in the harmony of the universe.

Source: Nichols, E., as cited in LeBaron

institutions, many administrators are facing daunting challenges at home.

Shrinking Resources

Certainly one of the most pressing problems in the public educational system is shrinking financial, physical, and human resources. Previously unthinkable levels of budget cuts threaten the very existence of institutions as the various stakeholders fight for survival. Institutions are often confronted simultaneously with the need to recraft their vision of the future, and a budget deficit massive enough to cause immediate bankruptcy if they were a private sector entity. The level of trust and openness necessary to move collaboratively toward a new future in such situations may well be undermined by financial threats.

Multiple Stakeholders

Public- and private-sector organizations alike are overwhelmed by demands for stakeholder involvement in decision making. Internal and external groups, various ethnic and culturally unique student communities, and more traditional representatives, such as boards of directors and senior levels of government, all clamour for support of their own points of view. In many respects, this trend reflects a fundamental shift in North American society from a hierarchical to a flatter, consultative model.

Rapidly Developing Technologies

Drucker, among others, notes that "knowledge is power," and that increased access to advanced computer and telecommunications technology by the end user (those whom we have traditionally defined as "the student") is fast becoming a reality. No longer will traditional institutions be able to retain control over the educational process, and define how, when, or where knowledge acquisition will occur.

New Competitors

In British Columbia, there are in excess of 800 private post-secondary institutions competing with publicly funded colleges and universities. While publicly funded institutions might hope that the private institutions will go away if they are ignored, many of these latter organizations are aggressively embracing the new technologies as a means of achieving "competitive advantage," and are relatively unfettered by the historic constraints of their public sector counterparts. Survival in the future, for both public and private sector institutions, will depend on their ability to respond to the increasingly sophisticated demands of students.

Faculty/Staff/Administration Skeletons

Many distance education institutions are also victim to the accumulated history of poor relationships between faculty, staff, and administration. Like many professional service organizations (health care being another key example), trust and allegiance often fall along disciplinary lines. At its worst, a hornet's nest of warring Balkan states exists within an institution, with continual skirmishes and guerrilla sorties between departments. The departments will unite briefly when the "shifty administrators" make one of their rare appearances from the vaunted heights of their ivory tower. The prevailing attitude in this worst-case scenario is a battle for survival, and each independent "guerrilla squad" has to grab and hoard what it can of the scarce resources, because no one else in the institution can hope to understand their unique needs!

This is not to suggest that distance education institutions are alone in suffering from such poor relationships. Both union and non-union, public and private sector organizations have all been subjected to varying degrees of such pressures. However, their widespread nature does not diminish the urgent need to address them constructively.

Strategic Thinking in Practice

Moving from Linear to Holistic Planning Approaches

Developing a plan, however, is only part of the challenge. It is not unusual to find a carefully crafted statement of mission and vision adorning an organization's reception area. Annual reports or promotional material may proudly refer to a set of shared values, as an indication of their organization's commitment.

Frequently, however, these impressive products of the strategic planning process are not internalized, and fail to guide decision making on a day-to-day basis.

Ross Paul (1990) describes a strategic planning exercise that was initiated in an orderly, participatory fashion, following the advice of experienced and published organizational strategists. The process was not unlike the Pfeiffer model described earlier. Paul writes: "My attempts to oversee a democratic process, seeking consensus as to ... mission, mandate and planning almost met with disaster" (p. 180). He goes on to describe the corrective action taken when the strategic planning process was "left in the lurch" with Paul on a "tightrope." Interestingly enough, Paul's corrective actions, which included revisiting respective roles and "shifting the decision from what ought to be done to how it will be done" (p. 180), resulted in a plan that was realistic and achievable. Paul did not argue in support of this change in process; rather, he was illustrating the difficulties of using a rational, linear model for planning that does not provide for flexibility to accommodate change owing to changing circumstances.

Planning is a dynamic process, requiring constant review, consultation, and flexibility. Most contemporary planning models are reductionist in theory and practice. By breaking down the complex challenges into ever smaller, containable and manageable envelopes, institutional leaders lose sight of the whole. They are very good at data collection and analysis, review of trends and extrapolating those trends into the future in logical, linear ways, but lose sight of the forest for the trees. "...[L]inear models are notoriously unreliable as predictors, which is their usual function ..." (Briggs & Peat, 1989, p. 175).

One reason for this unreliability is the impossibility of reassembling the whole after the complex component parts have been analyzed in their separate units. The linear models cannot help us understand how the elements interact. Organizations, including distance education institutions, are not made up of separate, unrelated forces that can be managed piecemeal. Rather, educators have to work at breaking down this illusion and learn how to provide leadership in addressing the whole— regardless of how complex this may be. Peter Senge argues that "we will have to move through the barriers that are keeping us from being truly vision-led and capable of learning" (Senge, 1990,

p. 5). Scholars of organizational development are now beginning to refer to "non-linear futures," or a "systems approach to reality" (Briggs & Peat, 1989, p. 174).

If distance educators are to create a powerful vision for the future, they have to view the open learning system as a subtle whole with dynamic and complex interrelationships. They can no longer assume that what happens in institutions, states, or countries will not have an impact upon the contiguous regions. As distance learning organizations evolve, they have to ensure that their connectedness to the whole is understood by the heads of state and political decision makers, as well as by their respective colleagues and staff.

It is no longer good enough to use such descriptors as single-mode and dual-mode institutions and to argue the merits and challenges faced by each. Instead, individuals need to understand their roles and relationships within systems of learning and education, their connectedness to economic development and wealth generation, as well as their influence on the learner and the culture of learning.

The systems approach is relatively young. It still has to prove itself as a more effective way of examining organizational issues than the traditional strategic planning model. Yet, we have suggested that there is a need to try it. It hypothesizes that we can learn to deal with complex organizational and management problems through non-linear modelling. "The development of the systems model exemplifies the shift that the science of chaos and change is making from quantitative reductionism to a qualitative holistic appreciation of dynamics" (Briggs & Peat, 1989, pp. 175–176). The challenge is ours.

Increasing Flexibility through Partnerships

Distance teaching institutions based on the industrial model suffer from the disadvantage that their whole organization, and especially their management and decision-making process, is built around the requirements of the mass production of "one way" teaching materials. Consequently, innovation is extremely difficult ... (Bates, 1990, p. 4).

The above statement is interesting when one considers the principles of access, flexibility, and learner centredness, which are the cornerstones of open learning. In the struggle to promote distance education and open learning, institutions were forced to make choices, such as how to develop courses, how to deliver them, how to support the learner, and how to demonstrate a quality product. These choices were backed by procedures, staffing decisions, labour unions, and capitalization of such resources as hardware, software, and printing presses. Gradually, these institutions, which were founded on flexibility, found themselves increasingly locked into rigid operational patterns that tend to lose sight of the learner. An excellent example is the fact that publicly funded institutions are obliged to operate within the regional boundaries set down by the funding agency. This restriction is reasonable when the public purse of a province or state is concerned, but less logical if the borderless world is considered.

Like major countries, businesses, and corporations, distance learning institutions need to consider partnerships and alliances that cross borders. Although this may seem to be a risky venture because it requires harmonization of standards, we need to trust our colleagues and accept that the quality of their work is as good as or better than ours. Acceptance of competition as the norm, protection of turf, and fragmented approaches to accountability limit our potential. If solid partnerships are to be established that will benefit learners and the countries they live in, educators have to come to the table ready to share visions and resources, and committed to new ways of working together in a different, expanded context.

Good practice is not a universal, transferable commodity. What may work in one context may be dysfunctional in another. The context is the most important factor in determining appropriateness and effectiveness. Peter Drucker has cautioned that it is not good enough just to do things right (efficiency); we need to be sure we are doing the right things (effectiveness).

Embracing Technology

The impact of technology on society and on the practice of distance education is another important element for consideration. In particular, the role of telecommunications and information technologies has continued to be debated. Areas of debate have included:

• whether technology should be allowed to set work agendas;

• how robust the technology is in helping to create interaction with students;

• how to decide which technologies will work best and which will not work well; and

• how to frame policy recommendations about using technologies most effectively.

Distance educators have not come to any resolution or agreement in this debate, and it is doubtful that they ever will. What is becoming evident is that while they agonize interminably over these important questions, the world is passing them by. The accepted and expanded use of technology in everyday life is rendering protracted consideration of these issues meaningless. Individuals of all ages are involved in day-to-day activities employing a variety of technologies that are increasingly accepted as common practice. These individuals are not challenging the role of technology in their personal lives; they are using it!

Ursula Franklin defines technology as a system involving "organization procedures, symbols, new words, equations ... and most of all a mind set." "Technology, like democracy, includes ideas and practices; it includes myths and various models of reality ... and like democracy, technology changes the social and individual relationships between us. It has forced us to examine and redefine our notions of power and of accountability" (Franklin, 1990, p. 12).

Franklin's concerns about society's willingness to accept technology without question are based on her comparison of "growth" models and "production" models. She describes a production model (earlier described by Bates as an industrial model) as one where things are made, with the goal of attaining total control and predictability of the process and results. Her thesis is that, to date, technology has been used in ways where the production model is promoted and enhanced—a highly undesirable situation. Growth, on the other hand, can occur only with nurturing. It happens, is not made, and therefore is unpredictable. Schools and universities are operated under production models, where procedures and rules will deliver a predictable commodity. "If there ever was a growth process, if there ever was a holistic process, a process that cannot be divided into rigid predetermined steps, it is education" (Franklin, 1990, p. 29).

In trying to deal with the complexity of the issues that technology raises, distance educators have adopted production model thinking, which reduces the components to their smallest manageable parts. For example, they have packaged, or fragmented, the issues into such areas as the learner and appropriate use of technologies; the creation of telecommunications networks; the acquisition of hardware and the development of software. This packaging has tended to result in marginalizing the role of technologies in distance education. Technologies are treated as an add-on that results in high costs and demonstrates little evidence of payoff to the learner. A growth model would consider distance education as an organic whole that includes technology as an integral part of the open learning system. Accepting technology as here to stay and shifting the planning and development processes to integrate technology have the potential to move distance educators closer to the real challenge—promoting and fostering learning and the learner.

There is another reality that cannot be overlooked when the acceptance of technology is being considered, and that is the move of conventional educational institutions toward technology to extend the boundaries of the physical campus. The distinction between the work of distance educators and of conventional educators is blurring as both move to serve students beyond the boundaries that were originally defined in terms of campus and classroom. A recent article in *Time* magazine described the educational institution of the future as one with no clearly defined campus, with open access to information for the learner, with a fully networked electronic learning environment, and a flexible time schedule (Elson, 1992). While distance educators have reason to feel vindicated, even smug, about conventional institutions' starting to recognize the wisdom of their ways, they also need to recognize that they are in danger of being "leapfrogged"—that is, they may become redundant, perhaps extinct. In this changing world, nothing is sacred, including the role of distance education and how technologies are used.

It would be ironic should distance education (a system that has always seen itself as innovative, flexible, and on the cutting edge of change) be leap-frogged by mainstream education, a system accused of being rigid, inflexible, bureaucratic, and resistant to change. Is there a message here? Is anyone listening?

Distance educators (indeed, all educators) have cause to heed James Burke, acclaimed author of the best-selling book and television series, *The Day the Universe Changed*, and his strong, clear statement on the impact of technology and information.

A late-21st century complex individualistic networked informed community may look back and smile at the way that, up to the end of the 20th century, we simple hicks with our closed institutionalized inflexible traditional monolithic hierarchical slow-response bureaucratic way of doing things never seemed to know what was happening until it hit us. ("Business re-engineering," 1992, p. 2A)

Learning to Learn

Public policy makers have been very busy trying to link the issues of economic and social change to the provision of more relevant education: for the young, for those who are unemployed or under-employed, as well as for those who are employed but whose jobs will be changing radically. Institutional policy makers have been equally busy discussing such needs as organizational flexibility, responsiveness to learners, rapid introduction of new curricula, and the development of creative thinkers and doers. No longer is it appropriate for education to be seen to stop once one acquires a job. "Education must be for a lifetime of living, learning, and personal growth through discovery" (Kenney-Wallace, 1992, p. 8). Kenney-Wallace argues that educators need to match "access, quality, equity, and needs with institutional missions and mandates" (ibid.).

In Canada, there is a growing awareness of the need for our educational system to help individuals "learn how to learn." The focus is on young preschool children, based on the premise that, if children learn how to learn, they will continue learning throughout their lives. However, the theme "learn how to learn" typically assumes that these skills will be applied in a conventional classroom, where children study as a group under the direction of a professional teacher. Few challenge the assumption that formal learning occurs only in the classroom, and even fewer question that the focus should be on the young. What about the unemployed adult, the marginalized adult, or the professional adult who does not know how to learn (or, at least, lacks the confidence to do so)? In the production or industrial model of education, the learner is viewed as the product and is therefore adapted to fit curricular goals and outcomes. These practices remain entrenched in conventional institutions, and the production model persists in our education system. Thus, students are forced to fit the system rather than the system adapting to fit the learner. Interestingly, distance educators have fallen into the same trap because of their need to conform with traditional practices in order to be credible.

Opportunities to foster learning and the learner do not appear to be increasing in distance education. Distance educators must take responsibility here because, like conventional educators, they have emphasized content and examination of content. As information grows, it is impossible and foolish to believe that any educational system can continue to identify and package the explosion of information into credit courses forever. Effective educators have to rethink the process of learning and education, so that the product of education becomes a curriculum that is designed and modified to meet the needs of the learner. Content-based, discipline-driven approaches are being challenged at the primary and elementary school levels and should soon have an impact on the secondary and post-secondary levels. Perhaps the greatest contribution of distance educators in the future will be to help individuals gain confidence in their ability to learn, to communicate measures of success, and to facilitate ways in which learners can demonstrate and realize their ability to meet those measures. Distance educators should never use the production model as their excuse. As progressive educators, their agenda must be to enable the learners and learning rather than to cover content and process students.

Practical First Steps to Strategic Thinking

Can Distance Education Institutions Make the Shift?

The road to effective organizational change is littered with the corpses of good intentions, short-lived enthusiasm, and management fads and panaceas: total quality management, quality circles, quality assurance, zero-based budgeting, value-for-money audit, customer-driven organizations, self-managed work teams, participative management. Within the next couple of years, society will likely witness the same fate for continuous learning, learning organizations, liberation management, and intellectual capital, among other buzzwords.

Why have such apparently well-meaning initiatives seemingly failed, and what does this trend mean for distance learning organizations and society?

• Are there really no effective ways of coping with the difficulties faced by organizations today?

• Are none of the seemingly promising concepts and approaches of the past 20 years capable of achieving lasting success?

• Do management ideas all have a shelf life of less than three years?

• Are distance educators condemned to search continuously for the next "silver bullet" and, in the process, to cause untold damage and harm to their organizations and society through a never-ending series of quick fixes?

There is no quick fix to the challenges facing distance education institutions and society. At any moment, the issues facing an organization are the sum of its cultural history for the previous 15 to 20 years (perhaps even longer). To expect that the organizational path defined by this collective history can be easily changed by developing a strategic plan is highly unrealistic. A period of three to five years, at a minimum, is needed to foster cultural realignment effectively and to bring about sustained improvement, especially in large, complex, and traditional organizations. Fortunately, there are a number of steps (not all of which are painless!) that can be taken in the short term to yield results.

Create a Vision

As simple as it seems, many organizations do not have a clear vision of their preferred future. The process of creating a vision should not be confused with strategic planning as it is widely practised. Creating a vision focusses on what the organization (and its people) truly wants instead of what is thought to be possible given current constraints and competitive pressures.

Focus on Critical Issues

Once the organization visualizes what it truly wants then, by all means, use some of the available analytic tools to assess current reality, but always in relation to the preferred future. Effective change will occur when efforts are firmly anchored in "real time" issues facing the organization. In other words, focus on solving real organizational concerns, rather than adopting the latest program.

Mobilize the Total Team's Resources

Today, more than ever, people are an organization's only real competitive advantage. Global events are changing far too rapidly, technology is becoming obsolete before it is installed, and financial stability is an unfortunate oxymoron. Only its people know the detailed workings of an organization (whether it provides services or products, is profit or non-profit). Unless their collective expertise, energy and enthusiasm, and willingness to collaborate are effectively engaged and aligned with a common purpose, an organization is likely doomed to mediocrity or worse.

Anchor Change in Sound Organizational Development Principles

A systemic view of the organization must be developed that incorporates the principles of successful organizational development.

When linked to appropriate concepts of knowledge and different world views, organizational development can be a powerful tool to avoid the pitfalls of fragmenting the perceived problem, which often leads to partial solutions. For example, the introduction of a new educational strategy also affects organizational structure, power relationships, communication patterns, learner support, and all other aspects of the organization's functioning.

Conclusions

Distance education and open learning have always promised and delivered easier access to quality education for learners. This result has been achieved through painful analysis, self-criticism, and comparison with benchmarks established by conventional educational institutions. It would be tragic for leaders in distance learning to allow themselves to be overtaken by the conventional systems, while believing they were improving access to education, and identifying creative, innovative ways to empower the learner. Clearly, they are faced with increasing challenges today and in the future.

These challenges, which have the potential to become barriers to change, are bound by commitments to particular methods of delivery, to existing means of course production, and to current ways of providing student support services. Massive investments in capital, staffing, and procedures have made it difficult for distance educators to understand, accept, and adapt to changing realities, especially the imperative need to plan for, and implement, change. Conventional strategic planning models will not suffice. They need to be supplemented or replaced by non-linear, intuitive, creative approaches that help define the organization for the future. Linear models can help with the analysis of current reality but they do not help institutions get beyond those conventional, self-imposed boundaries that reduce the ability of organizations to adapt. If institutions of open learning and distance education do not create a new vision, they run the risk of being replaced by new and different institutions or by conventional institutions that have made the necessary changes.

References

Bates, A.W. (1990, November). *Third generation distance education: The challenge of new technology.* Presentation to the 15th World Conference on Distance Education, Caracas, Venezuela.

Briggs, J., & Peat, F.D. (1989). *Turbulent mirror: An illustrated guide to chaos theory and the science of wholeness.* New York: Atheneum.

Business re-engineering: What, why and how. (1992, June 8). *Information Week,* pp. 1A–8A.

DELTA (Developing European Learning through Technological Advance) Project. (1990). *Priorities for new training and learning technology in the 1990's—A strategic review of flexible learning technology.* Brussels: Commission of the European Communities Directorate.

Drucker, P. (1993). *Post-capitalist society.* New York: Harper Business.

Dunham, E.A. (1992, February). *Educational reform: The critical role of information technology.* (Occasional Paper #14). Washington: Institute for Educational Leadership.

Elson, J. (1992, April 13). Campus of the future. *Time,* pp. 52–58.

Enchin, H. (1992, April 9). Dwindling funds force new order on universities. *The Globe and Mail,* p. C1.

Franklin, U. (1990). *The real world of technology.* CBC Massey Lectures Series. Toronto: CBC Enterprises.

Gleick, J. (1987). *Chaos: Making a new science.* New York: Penguin Books.

Huntington, S. (1993). The clash of civilizations? *Foreign Affairs, 72*(3), 22–49.

Kenney-Wallace, G. (1992, May 22–24). Plato, cartels, and competitiveness policy: How to shape a new educational paradigm. In R. Dobell & M. Neufeld (Eds.), *Proceedings of the North American Institute Conference Live and Learn, Learn and Live* (pp. 8–13). Ottawa: Oolichan Books.

Naisbitt, J., & Aburdene, P. (1990). *Megatrends 2000.* New York: William Morrow & Co.

Nichols, E., as cited in LeBaron Duryea, M. (1992). *Conflict and culture.* University of Victoria, Institute for Dispute Resolution.

Moore, M.G., Thompson, M.M., Quigley, B.A., Clark G.C., & Goff, G.G. (1990). *The effects of distance learning: A summary of literature.* Number 2 in the Research Monograph series. Toronto: Pergamon.

Paul, R.H. (1990). *Open learning and open management: Leadership and integrity in distance education.* New York: Nichols Publishing.

Pfeiffer, J.W., Goodstein, L.D., & Nolan, T.M. (1989). *Shaping strategic planning: Frogs, dragons, bees and turkey tails.* London: Scott, Foresman & Co.

Rumble, G. (1986). *The planning and management of distance education.* New York: St. Martin's.

Senge, P.M. (1990). *The fifth discipline: The art and practice of the learning organization.* New York: Doubleday.

U.S. Congress, Office of Technology Assessment. (1989). *Linking for learning: A new course for education.* Washington, DC: U.S. Government Printing Office.

Part 2
Case Studies

CHAPTER 3

Learners in the Workplace

ANNA E. STAHMER

This chapter focusses on open and distance learning in the workplace. It sets the stage by looking at trends in learner characteristics and needs, by examining the providers of this training, and by situating workplace training in terms of expenditure patterns. On the basis of survey information and case studies, the chapter then identifies the status and trends of open and distance learning and the use of technology in workplace training (Conference Board of Canada [Conference Board], 1991, 1992, 1993). The implications of these trends are discussed from the perspective of workplace learning systems, the organizations, the people in the system, and budgeting and costs. The chapter concludes with reflections on steps to accelerate open and distance learning that is accessible to a wide range of adult learners, in small or large organizations.

Training in the Workplace

A Look at Trends

Increasing numbers of adults will need access to learning opportunities and continuing training in order to do their jobs, and to be ready to adapt to changes in their work. The fact that these learners are working adults establishes the parameters for ways in which this learning should be conceived and delivered. Advances in learning technologies and the proliferation of technologies in the workplace provide a certain synergy with the needs of adult learners, which is being recognized in the corporate world. A cursory glance at the providers of workplace training will draw a picture of the supply side and how it is poised to deliver open and distance learning. Lastly, and very importantly, the financing of such training is a vital factor in the use of open and distance learning in the workplace.

Who Are the Learners?

The characteristics of future adult learners, the reasons why they need access to learning, and the conditions under which they must find such access encompass a large group of people who will greatly benefit from open and distance learning. These learners typically include:

• Working adults who usually have family responsibilities. For example, in the Toronto area, almost 70 percent of women with children under 16 were in the labour force in the late 1980s (Social Planning Council, 1988).

• Older workers. Demographic projections show that, contrary to traditional patterns, youth can no longer be expected to provide the new skills needed by the labour force.

• People who are currently in the workforce and who will need to upgrade their skills and knowledge (Moses, 1991). It is reported that most adult Canadians may change careers and jobs every five years (Advisory Council on Adjustment [Advisory Council], 1989).

• Workers who need higher levels of skills within existing occupations. Use of sophisticated technologies in the workplace will mean that, by the year 2000, over 64 percent of jobs will require 13+ years of education. However, one in four Canadian adults is reportedly functionally illiterate, and 30 percent of Canada's young people leave school before they achieve a high school diploma (Advisory Council, 1989).

• Highly skilled professionals, such as engineers or technologists. These workers require continuing access to new knowledge and skills, because the half-life of knowledge in technological fields can be as short as three years.

• Managers and supervisors who need new organizational skills as a result of changed work and business environments.

• Workers and professionals at all levels who are looking for career advancement.

• Employees of small firms. Most firms in Canada are small. Only 37 percent have formal training programs, and only 13 percent have a training budget. In contrast, nearly all large firms (1000+ employees) and 64 percent of medium-sized firms (100–999 employees) have training programs.

What Is Important to These Learners or Their Employers?

Workplace trainers and trainees indicate that learning opportunities should exhibit some of the following characteristics to be suitable to this group of adults, who have family and other commitments:

• provide convenient access, in terms of place and time;

• deliver flexible and self-paced learning to allow for differences in learning styles;

• be modular in design, so that learning can be integrated with work and family obligations;

• be curriculum based, or progression oriented, to avoid duplication or knowledge gaps;

• provide some form of certification or accreditation;

• support learners in pursuing a personal continuous learning plan;

• use work environments and adult learning principles as reference points; and

• be time efficient to reduce costs of trainee wages,[1] or to manage the investment of time required by individual learners.

Open and distance learning systems exhibit many of these characteristics.

What Are the Sources for Workplace Training?

Broadly speaking, six different sources offer formal workplace training. The list includes:

• In-house training departments, which account for the majority of training expenditures in larger companies, and which are increasingly sophisticated in their use of technologies for this purpose.

• In-house training departments in large companies that are set up as revenue centres, and sell their generic courses to other companies.

• Colleges and universities with services ranging from company-specific contract training to continuing education and part-time studies. They are increasingly looking at technologies to support their work.[2]

• Not-for-profit organizations or school boards, which are principally active in the areas of adult basic education. The use of technologies by these groups is not extensive, but increasing.

• Professional and trade associations, some of which are known to make active use of training technologies.

• Commercial courseware and training providers, a few of whom are very sophisticated in the development and use of technology-based training.

These providers co-operate with each other, through, for example, contractual arrangements, as well as with other organizations, such as provincial education communication authorities. They also purchase off-the-shelf training technology products, or subscribe to teleconference services from other suppliers. Of this list of providers, company in-house training departments may well be the most active users of technology, and of open and distance learning techniques. Their flexibility in budgeting and ability to address cost issues squarely may be principal reasons for this.

What Are the Sources of Financing?

Numerous studies and reports outline the need for continuous adult, professional, and workplace training to maintain national prosperity. The need is expressed in sectors as diverse as textile manufacturing, trucking, software, or mining, and for employees ranging from customer service and tradespeople to technologists and professionals such as engineers.

There is little agreement, however, on how such continuous learning should be funded. Governments and employers have traditionally carried a large part of training costs. However, the numbers of adult learners needing continuous upgrading of knowledge are rising. The future scope of workplace learning needs may require new approaches to financing. Engineering professional associations, for example, recognize this factor and point to the responsibility of the individual to self-finance continuous learning. However, some observers believe that funds can be found from existing sources, and that traditional training systems must be reengineered to respond to the need (Association of Community Colleges of Canada [ACCC], 1993, p. Cxvii).

Overall, annual expenditures for formal training are estimated at Cdn $8.6 billion, comprising of $3.8 billion by the federal government, $3.6 billion by employers, and $1.2 billion by the provincial governments ("Learning for work," 1993). Often, more than one source of funds is used to finance a given training opportunity. At present, governments typically concentrate their financial support on training of disadvantaged groups, who may be undereducated, unemployed, or in need of job-entry skills or reskilling, and on initiatives targetted toward training employees in small and medium-sized enterprises. Other workplace-related training is the responsibility of employers.

According to many studies, the need for continuous workplace training exists. However, financing formulas are yet to be found to allow large-scale implementation of solutions. Therefore, while technologies and open and distance learning can make enormous contributions to satisfying growing workplace training needs, systemic solutions will have be found, and funding issues will need to be resolved (ACCC, 1993, p. Cxix).

Distance Education and Open Learning in the Workplace

This section will describe the technologies, and open and distance learning approaches, used in workplace training. It draws on three surveys of corporate training expenditures and policies conducted by the Conference Board of Canada, and on examples of workplace training applications reported by the *Training Technology Monitor.*[3]

Expenditures on Technology and Distance Learning

The 1991 Conference Board survey indicates that Canadian companies may allocate as much as five percent of their training expenditures to technologies and further, that this percentage may double every two years. Assuming that all funding sources described in the previous section invest a similar percentage in technology support, annual expenditures could be as high as $180 to $430 million, and growing.

Technologies Used in the Delivery of Training

The same survey shows that slightly more than 10 percent of companies interviewed use one or a combination of the following: CD-ROM, videos, audio- and videoconferences, computer-aided instruction, and distance learning. This figure is expected to double within two years (Conference Board, 1991, p. 19).

In its 1993 survey, the Conference Board finds that 36 percent of the respondents use distance learning in the delivery of their training[4] (p. 16). The survey also finds that larger organizations are more likely than smaller companies to use such technologies. The former are likely to be geographically more dispersed and to have sufficient capital acquisition budgets to mount the programs.

We suspect that a major push for the growth in the use of training technologies, and of open and distance learning, has come from the expansion of corporate computer systems, which were installed initially for operational applications. This increase in the installed base is also generating interest in electronic performance support systems (EPSS), which enhance computer-based work with four major functions, one of which is training. Under the training function, EPSS can:

• be the librarian to help find answers quickly;

• be the advisor, giving guidance and expert advice;

• be the instructor, providing on-demand training; and

• be the "dofer," doing routine work and letting the employee concentrate on more important tasks.

A current dilemma is that trainers are not very familiar with EPSS development tools, and that training functions are either not always built into EPSS, or have only limited input from trainers ("Technology in adult basic education," 1993).

Applications of Computer Software to the Training System

Data on current or planned applications show that course design and delivery are only two of the applications envisaged for computers in workplace training. Administration, evaluation, and planning functions may depend on computer software more heavily than delivery. Course registration, course catalogues, and skills inventions are anticipated to be the most extensive uses of computer software in training. The percentages of companies that reported they expected to use software for these purposes were 43%, 34%, and 32%, respectively. Over the two-year projections covered by the survey, computer use was expected to grow for course delivery from 11% to 21%, for needs assessment from 6%

to 38%, and for course design from 0 to 21% (Conference Board, 1991, p. 19).

Five Illustrations from Practice

1. IBM Manufacturing
(Don Mills, Ontario)

IBM Manufacturing's Desktop University addresses both corporate training goals and employees' professional development goals, and combines both in-house and college training benefits. IBM needed to transfer more technical work to production employees, necessitating retraining and the creation of a new manufacturing career path. It chose to offer 25 courses at its in-house learning centre through classroom instruction, using off-the-shelf videotapes, videodiscs and CD-ROM courseware as resource materials. Forty percent of the training is self-paced, so that it is easily accessible to employees working on three different shifts. Two regional community colleges support the initiative, providing advanced courses, instructor support, tutorials, and counselling. Employees enrolled in the program register at the colleges and receive official transcripts from those institutions.

IBM's Desktop University illustrates the use of the installed infrastructure for job-specific training and for some generic professional development. With Desktop University, IBM employees use their desk computer to download courses of their choice and study at their convenience ("IBM manufacturing and colleges form partnership," 1993).

2. Prudential Insurance and Financial Services
(New Jersey)

Prudential Insurance and Financial Services recently implemented the Prudential Learning System (PLS), which again illustrates an in-house application of open and distance learning. PLS combines print learning modules, videos and computer-based training with computer-based learning tests. The last are sent for analysis to a remote host computer. With PLS, feedback to the learner can be immediate: positive results are reinforced, and areas that need additional review are identified. Since the hardware platform is portable, learners can use these modules at their place of work or at home. Courseware consists of new, off-the-shelf or existing materials for preemployment candidates and sales representatives. It covers candidate orientation and a range of skills that representatives need ("Insurance companies install a training infrastructure," 1994).

3. Irving Forestry Products (St. John, New Brunswick)

Irving Forestry Products Division uses open and distance learning techniques and technologies to provide job-specific training as well as broader professional development opportunities. It does so through in-house and public sector course offerings. The company employs interactive videodisc, CD-ROM, and other computer-based training tools for a range of training activities. Employees may get access to TéléÉducation NB TeleEducation courses directly from the corporate premises, through a network site situated within the plant (Holmes, 1994).

4. SkillPlan/Open Learning Agency (British Columbia)

SkillPlan (British Columbia Construction Skills Improvement Council) and the Open Learning Agency (OLA) of British Columbia have combined forces to provide learning opportunities for adult tradespeople whose work schedules are heavily seasonal. Jointly, they have developed and offered customized computer-based training programs for construction workers at OLA's workplace training centre. The goal is to upgrade basic skills of workers, many of whom are technically skilled journeymen and apprentices. Access to a traditional semester-based learning system is difficult for this highly mobile workforce, and individualized learning is therefore considered important ("Technology in adult basic education," 1993).

5. The Training Group
(Edmonton, Alberta)

The Training Group provides a number of examples of applications of electronic performance support systems (EPSS), most of which have been undertaken with energy and petrochemical companies. Using EPSS, workers can get access to the "library side" of the system on the job: for example, conduct an on-line search for information on products, ISO 9000 or safety procedures. These same data files can also be obtained from the "learning side" for individualized training. One petrochemical company is using the EPSS at 23 sites internationally ("Technology in adult basic education," 1993).

Analysis

The trend and survey data identified in the preceding sections lead to reflections on their implications for workplace training as we know it. They have implications for the learning system, for the organization of learning, for the jobs of trainers, and for financing and budgeting. These issues are reviewed in the following sections.

Implications for the Workplace Learning System

Learning systems that deliver workplace learning will change. Future systems will include the following features:

• Continued growth of open and distance learning technologies, leading to use of new kinds of facilities, such as desktop computers.

• Increasingly "intelligent" applications of technologies, such as EPSS. EPSS present special challenges to the training community. Some fear that they may lead to a general deskilling of the workforce.

• Changed modes of operation of training services as we now know them. Limited hours of operation, fixed entry and exit times, access to learning based on formal prior learning, and budgeting based on learner contact-hours may become things of the past.

• Increased use of computer and multimedia technologies in learning centres in the workplace.

• Increased use of learning centres as common or shared facilities. As a result, a broad spectrum of adult learners will be able to access learning opportunities, especially employees from small and medium-sized enterprises and self-employed individuals. These shared facilities will operate very differently from most of today's learning centres.

A scan of current effective learning centres illustrates the types of facilities and services such centres may offer.

• Multimedia terminals, PCs and networked PCs (local area networks or LANs). The ratio between hardware and number of learners will depend on the learning activity.

• External video and telephone connections and computer communications modems, for audio-, video-, or computer conferencing, and access to learning and technical databases.

• Student management software that will allow students access to their learning files through a personal identification number.

• Personal learning "profiles" that will identify previous mastery of subjects and skills, serving as the basis for a personal learning path.

• Television or cable service.

• Library services for courseware and other books.

• Separate areas for individual and group work.

• Tutors at a ratio from 1:20 to 1:80 learners, depending on the type of learning activity.

• Operating and maintenance staff.

• Operating, staffing, and scheduling procedures that allow learners to use the facilities when convenient for them.

Implications for the Organization of Workplace Learning

On one side, we see a model of workplace learning that brings learning much closer to line and business functions. For example, the Conference Board reports that over 40 percent of companies are moving away from seeing training as an expense (1993, p. 13). They use some form of transfer pricing to ensure that line departments are aware of the real costs of training, and to make decisions more strategic. Also, in-house training products are being marketed externally, and technology-based products are especially suitable here. On the other side, evidence suggests that corporate training departments see workplace training as more than a way of serving corporate goals. As was evident in the examples, some companies help employees to establish and pursue individual and personal development goals. Some observers feel this shift in the functions and roles of training divisions will increase technology-based and self-directed learning. Others see the shift as a likely result of it (Conference Board, 1992, p. 6).

Practical implications of this shift in function can be seen in the Conference Board findings that 45 percent of training staff work at the operating divisions level, compared to 30 percent a few years ago. Evidence suggests that operating and training divisions are beginning to work together in the following areas:

• defining training content and delivery methods;

• delivering training; and

• evaluating training.

Observers expect that closer co-operation between the departments will result in more emphasis on the evaluation of impact or results. They further expect that impact evaluation will give a major boost to workplace training—and will also ensure that training meets business needs. Conference Board survey results show that impact evaluation has remained relatively stable at five percent of reporting companies, but that trainers expect an impact evaluation to be used in future by as many as 70 percent of the companies.

Implications for Learners, Trainers, and Supervisors

Emerging models of open and distance learning and their use of technologies will put new demands on learners as well as on trainers and supervisors.

Many adult learners will be new to defining or taking responsibility for their own continuing learning. Adults enjoy using technology-based training. They often prefer the flexibility and privacy of such models compared to traditional modes of delivery. However, the same flexibility will most benefit those who can learn independently. The necessary skills, including certain motivational and psychological attitudes, will have to be learned by many. Tutorial support from trainers, colleagues, or external sources will be essential to help learners achieve this end.

However, tutoring and other open and distance learning skills are rarely the strength of today's trainers. Most come from a background that emphasizes the development and delivery of learning materials. Alternatively, they may come from line jobs, where knowledge of content is their strength. Trainers have rarely been exposed to tutoring, counselling by telephone or e-mail, or management of learner files through computer analysis—skills essential for effective support of technology-based learning systems. Other roles required of trainers in this new arena may include proficiency in the use of distance learning techniques, in working as part of a materials development team, or in assisting employees to define personal development plans.

Supervisors and peer groups will also have important responsibilities in open and distance learning systems at the workplace. Many tasks such as tutoring, scheduling, testing, or logging learner progress will move to line departments and to peers and supervisors. Larger companies may be able to move some of these tasks—for example, scheduling—to computer support networks, thus putting less of this burden on supervisors and peers.

Few formal opportunities exist to acquire these "new" skills. However, where firms (and educational systems) have introduced training technologies in a systematic fashion, staff typically learn the necessary skills through experience and, over time, become supportive of the change.

Implications for Financing and Budgeting

Present financing and budgeting approaches to training are often disincentives to the adoption of open and distance learning and to the use of training technologies. Five factors seem critical.

• Training is normally purchased—or reimbursed internally— on the basis of hours of training provided. Evidence of this approach to financing can be found in government programs as well as in private firms. Since technology-based training often requires less time to produce the same level of mastery, the training department or training provider may not generate as much revenue as with conventional methods.

• It is almost impossible to quantify independent learning under existing budget formulas.

• Training budgets typically operate on an annual cycle, which makes economic justification over several years difficult. The economic behaviour of training technologies, however, is characterized by high front-end costs, but lower per-learner costs with frequent use. In one company, for example, the break-even point between the classroom and a sophisticated multimedia training package was around 2000 learners. The company forecasted that this number would be reached in about two years, and that a total of 4000 learners would need to be trained with the package over five years. Thus, the outlay of significant funds at the front end helped to reduce the trainee costs over time.

• General financial constraints in governments and in many industry sectors do not make the prospect of new funds for workplace training a very promising one. It can be expected that the necessary funds will have to come from reallocations of existing funds, or from new funding sources and new business opportunities.

• Data on usage, cost, and pricing for the new generation of learning technologies are limited. Few economic assessments have been undertaken. For example, the economic behaviour of learning packages that use computer conferencing for peer tutoring, or that allow learners access to databases to suit their personal learning needs, is different from the economic behaviour of the use of stand-alone technologies, such as books, CD-i, and videos. Usage and related costs of these types of learning are still open ended. Heavy usage by learners of communications links—to gain access to tutors and databases, for example—may prove costly for a training department.

Where to Go from Here

The move toward open and distance learning will not remain an option for trainers to choose or to reject. It will become a reality as a result of pressure from learners themselves. Thus, the universe of learning is in the process of change. Technology-based tools are gaining increasing importance in the process, or possibly are a cause of it.

Further, the provision of adult and workplace learning is becoming competitive. New players, such as venture capital firms, commercial training firms, and telephone companies are entering areas that were once the domain of the public sector or of in-house training departments. They enter it as financiers and as suppliers of courses or infrastructure. It will take the combined efforts of the traditional and the new players to bring about the kind of learning systems that working adults will need in the future. It is evident that new operating rules will be necessary to bring the players together.

What to Do about the Hardware Infrastructure

In terms of the hardware infrastructure, training applications will filter into many operational corporate training applications with expert systems or EPPS training software. In addition, shared learning centres may be a cost-effective basis to provide a learning system for the majority of adults who work in small and medium-sized firms— that is, in firms that do not have the economies of scale to justify the in-house investment. These learning centres can operate out of a school, another public facility, a commercial site, or a company facility (for larger firms).

However, the funds required to establish sufficient numbers of learning centres go well beyond the capabilities of public funding—and often beyond the capability of an individual corporate training department. The financing, establishment, and operation of learner centres could become a new business opportunity for private companies— in co-operation with, or on behalf of, public sector interests.

Steps that will accelerate the establishment of learning centres include:

• Implementation of policies that will make it attractive for private interests to invest in learning centres. For example, partnerships should be encouraged in which the public sector defines and accredits the learning and the private sector invests in, and operates, learning centres for a fee.

• Purchase of technology-based training services from such centres by large companies or governments. Already a number of companies are main clients of the few currently operating commercial centres. Where learner numbers warrant, the learning centre operator may set up the hardware infrastructure directly at the customer's premises. This will free customers from the need to purchase, operate, maintain, and upgrade the equipment themselves.

What to Do about Materials and Learning Resources

Present practices in design and development of learning materials need to be analyzed and reengineered to suit the future.

The following recommendations could ensure the production and availability of quality and affordable materials:

• Trainers, teachers, and instructors need to become proficient in software applications such as EPSS. Their absence from teams that develop such operational support applications leaves the design of instructional and tutorial functions of EPSS, for example, without appropriate pedagogical input.

• Planned courses in large companies and in the public education sector could be assessed to see whether they might be developed for delivery by alternative delivery systems. This will open courses to learners in small and medium-sized enterprises, or self-employed people, who otherwise might not be served at all.

• Each new training module in larger firms, or governments, should be reviewed from the same perspective. These large users should finance the development of such units, use them in-house, and recoup investments through rentals or sales. Such an approach would further widen the pool of available materials.

• Materials development should be contracted more consistently to commercial producers. This should occur in close co-operation with content experts, teachers, or trainers from the public and private sectors. The advantages of such arrangements would be that commercial producers will end up with the production volume to warrant investments in high-end production hardware and software. They also will have the flow of work to engage sufficient numbers of qualified full-time staff to develop multimedia materials in a cost-effective manner. Most importantly, they have an obvious interest in marketing successful products that will pay royalties to the initial investors, thereby offering a new source of funds.

• Change purchasing rules for training from the time-based to a mastery-based premise.

Conclusions

Technology-based open and distance learning is making rapid inroads into workplace learning. Barriers stem less from pedagogical or technical matters than from issues related to funding and to the absence of appropriate models on which to base the reengineering process.

Endnotes

1. According to the Canadian Bankers' Association, trainee wages accounted for 26 percent of total training expenditures by the major Canadian banks in 1992.

2. Some observers expect that demands from the workplace market will, for example, push colleges to become increasingly active users of technologies when they provide workplace training (personal discussions by Stahmer with participants in a Delphi study forecasting the use of training technologies in the college system).

3. The *Training Technology Monitor* is a subscription-based newsletter, published eight times per year in Toronto since 1993. It reports on matters related to the development and application of technologies in workplace training.

4. The definition of distance learning used in the 1993 survey encompasses a number of the categories used in the earlier surveys. The Conference Board states (p. 15), "Distance learning refers to teaching and learning situations in which the instructor and learner(s) are geographically separated and rely on electronic devices and print materials for instructional delivery."

References

Advisory Council on Adjustment. (1989). *Adjusting to win.* Ottawa: Industry, Science & Technology Canada.

Association of Community Colleges of Canada. (1993). *Human resource study of the Canadian community colleges and institutes sector (report and appendices).* Ottawa: Author.

Conference Board of Canada. (1991). *Training and development 1990: Expenditures and policies.* Ottawa: Author.

Conference Board of Canada. (1992). *Training and development 1991: Expenditures and policies.* Ottawa: Author.

Conference Board of Canada. (1994). *Training and Development 1993: Policies, practices and expenditures.* Ottawa: Author.

Holmes, D. (1994). Personal communications. Irving's Training & Development Division.

IBM manufacturing and colleges form partnership. (1993). *Training Technology Monitor, 1*(1), 1–3.

Insurance companies install a training infrastructure. (1994). *Training Technology Monitor, 2*(8), 1–3.

Is PSS the future? (1993). *Training Technology Monitor, 1*(2), 1–2.

Learning for work. (1993, August 7). *Globe and Mail.*

Moses, J. (1991). *Speaking notes on Canadian labour market trends.* Ottawa: Employment & Immigration Canada, Labour Market Outlook & Structural Analysis Division.

Social Planning Council of Metropolitan Toronto. (1989). *Target on training: Meeting workers' needs in a changing economy.* Toronto: Author.

Technology in adult basic education. (1993). *Training Technology Monitor, 1*(2), 6.

CHAPTER 4

Distance Education and the Transformation of Elementary/Secondary Education

NORMAN C. MCKINNON

This chapter is about educational change and convergence. It focusses on a profound metamorphosis in public education, and a convergence that is bringing the classroom and distance learning together. It argues that distance education needs to play a major role in the reform of the public school system as elementary and secondary schools strive to improve the quality of the learning experiences they provide.

The spotlight is primarily on Canadian education, but the information and analysis are not unique to Canada. Similar issues and changes are occurring in other industrial countries that are striving, as Canada is, to be successful competitors in the global economy.

The key issues include the crisis in elementary and secondary education caused by lack of public confidence; the second-class image that distance education has had to overcome within the school system; the impact of technology on distance education; and the convergence of classroom and distance learning. Three case studies demonstrate the nature of this convergence.

Distance education in the form of networked learning communities is suggested as a solution to the dilemma schools face in preparing students for the 21st century. In this chapter, the terms public education and elementary/secondary education are used interchangeably.

Issues

The Crisis in Elementary and Secondary Education

Canada's publicly funded schools are in crisis. Both elementary and secondary levels of education are facing their greatest challenge since they were created less than two hundred years ago. Without exception, the system in each of the ten provinces and two territories is experiencing a metamorphosis of profound proportions.

Everywhere, school administrators and their staffs are confronted by a multitude of pressures affecting how schools are managed and operated. Shrinking resources, changing expectations, demographic shifts, curriculum changes, innovations in technology, and the changing profile of learners and their needs are but a few of the pressures they deal with. Compounding the pressures is a growing number of critics from the media and parent groups who are demanding significant changes in how their children are educated.

Canadian journalist Andrew Nikiforuk (1993) is an outspoken critic of North America's public school systems. He wrote:

As we approach the end of the century, it's time to acknowledge that public education ... is a betrayal of our traditions, our communities, and our children. What began as an attempt to make an aristocratic education available to ordinary people has become a self-serving monopoly that promotes idiocy. (p. 18)

Harsh criticism indeed, but Nikiforuk is not alone. Parent groups from across the country are demanding changes in the system as never before. Parent activist groups, calling for a return to basics, are organizing themselves to bring about major changes in their children's education. The names of their organizations shout their main concern: in Ontario, the Quality Education Network; in Alberta, Albertans for Quality Education; and in Nova Scotia, PARENT (Parents Against Reduction in Education Quality Network Together). The pivotal word for all these groups is quality. Their concern is lack of quality and consistency in the education their children receive.

In 1993, a national survey by the Angus Reid Group Inc. asked Canadians if they thought public schools are providing a better or worse education than they were 25 years ago. Forty-six percent responded "worse," 30% said "better," 17% replied "the same," and 7% were "unsure." The fact that 46% judged the system "worse" suggests that the activist parents have public support in condemning the system.

In addition to domestic condemnation, internationally the view is similarly negative. For example, the 1994 *World Competitiveness Report,* which compared the abilities of 23 industrial countries to compete worldwide for jobs, trade, and investment, rated Canada's quality of education as low. Ranked 17th overall in education and training, Canada is seen internationally as being weak in its ability to meet the needs of a competitive economy.

Not surprisingly, those who are responsible for public education are anxious to quell the criticism. As a result, the school is being reinvented, partly in response to a demanding public and partly to meet the need to develop graduates who can compete in a global economy. Consequently, educators and politicians are working toward quality in education by developing standards that they hope will be clear and unambiguous.

For example, in 1993, Ontario launched province-wide tests for all Grade 9 students, and established a Royal Commission on Learning to investigate and recommend sweeping reforms. In the same year, Alberta announced plans to reduce the number of school boards to bring greater efficiency to its overall system. Meanwhile, in response to the 1992 Commission on Excellence in Education, New Brunswick implemented a comprehensive back-to-basics curriculum. The Premier of Newfoundland and Labrador announced in 1994 that denominational schools would be abolished in favour of non-denominational schools, with the objective of making the system better educationally and economically.

Meanwhile, parents, in concert with teachers in some provinces, are working to design the first charter schools in Canada. Simply stated, the basic concept of a charter school is to have it run by parents and teachers according to a common educational vision. While public funding would continue, and government standards would need to be met, these new schools would be free to choose how to meet the standards. To keep the government charter—and the funding—the school would need to meet a high level of quality as specified in the standards. If the school did not produce quality graduates, the school would lose its charter.

It is clear that educators need to rethink every aspect of public education. Budget cuts mean that the range of services offered continues to narrow. As schools retrench to focus on fewer services and core activities, students with special needs will be the losers. Greater attention needs to be placed on alternative delivery techniques, major curriculum revisions, more learner-focussed methodologies, and creative applications of technology to achieve the goals of quality learning.

One of many options that is attracting increased attention when educators begin thinking about doing things differently is distance education. Many of the challenges facing public education—learning to use alternative delivery systems, changing methodologies to be more learner focussed, and employing creative applications of technology—can be greatly facilitated by distance education. The current trend is one of convergence between classroom public education and distance education in public schools.

The Image of Distance Education in Public Education

Distance education is not a new concept to schools. However, it has taken many years for it to be accepted as more than a second-class alternative to classroom education. Since the 1920s, public schools in most provinces have used distance education in the form of correspondence courses to meet specific needs (McKinnon, 1986). Initially, correspondence courses were used for students who were unable to attend school because of illness, distance from school, extended family travel outside the province, or diplomatic and missionary postings of families to other countries. Increasingly during the past 20 years, however, educational systems have been using correspondence courses in schools for independent study. In many cases, courses have been needed to resolve scheduling conflicts and to provide courses not available in schools, especially in small schools that lack the teaching expertise required, or that have insufficient numbers of students to justify offering a course. As a result, distance education has grown in use, gained in stature, and been accepted by many schools as an alternative to the traditional classroom.

The extent to which distance education is used by schools varies from province to province. Two examples that illustrate the range of possibilities come from Ontario and Alberta. In Ontario, for example, 11 612 of the 91 149 enrolments in distance education in 1993–94 were full-time students in secondary school (McArdle, 1994). The remainder were largely adult students studying independently outside a traditional school environment. Conversely, in Alberta, the majority of the annual distance education enrolments of 40 508 (Council of Ministers of Education Canada [CMEC], 1994) involved school-age students doing their studies in schools. Suffice to note that distance education has been widely used in a variety of ways for many years by public schools across the country. That use is bound to increase as multimedia technology brings to students new and exciting opportunities for alternative forms of learning.

In the 1986–87 school year, there were 199 280 enrolments in elementary/secondary school-level correspondence courses across Canada (McKinnon, 1989, p. 180). Full-time students usually enrolled in correspondence courses through their schools. Adults enrolled as individuals directly with a provincially funded correspondence school, and studied independently in their homes, or in institutions if hospitalized or incarcerated. Today, there are 225 321 enrolled (CMEC, 1995, p. 12). A comparison of the statistics shows that between 1986–87 and 1993–94, enrolments increased by approximately 26 000. These statistics demonstrate a 13 percent increase in enrolments over a period of eight years.

In reality, however, the increase is larger because the statistics pertain to correspondence courses only, and not to courses that use other technologies. For example, approximately 100 secondary schools are equipped to use the Contact North distance education network in Northern Ontario. The schools using the network have access to audioconferencing and audiographics to deliver their courses. From April 1994 to June 1994, schools participated in 730 audioconferences and delivered 22 secondary school courses over the network (Contact North, 1994). Similarly in Newfoundland and Labrador, audioconferencing, audiographics, and videotapes are used to deliver distance education courses to 63 small schools through the Telemedicine Centre at Memorial University. In Alberta, the Big Sky Distance Education Consortium, involving 12 school jurisdictions, was formed in 1990 to provide distance education courses to their schools. In the 1993–94 school year, 799 students from 25 schools generated 1293 course enrolments. The schools used courses developed by the Alberta Distance Learning Centre. Audioconferencing, facsimile machines, and computerized test banks supplemented the print-based courses (CMEC, 1995, pp. 23–24). If the enrolments from these and other projects across the country that use technologies other than correspondence courses were counted, the 1994 statistic would be considerably higher than the 225 321 enrolments that have been reported.

While the statistics show an overall growth in enrolments, there appears to be a trend toward increased use of distance education techniques and methodologies in schools. Case studies supporting this statement will be presented later in this chapter. In the meantime, the hype surrounding the "information highway" and Internet in particular has made schools more aware of the numerous possibilities for access to resources worldwide, and of the ease with which education can occur beyond the four walls of a school. As a result, the first provinces to connect some of their schools to the Internet include British Columbia, Ontario, New Brunswick, and Newfoundland.

The Impact of Technology

Since the 1970s and the success of the Open University in the United Kingdom, distance education has experienced many changes. One important reason for these changes is technology. The design of print-based distance education courses has been, and continues to be, transformed by technology. The delivery system no longer entails postal and courier services delivering correspondence courses to students. E-mail, audiographics, audioconferencing, computer conferencing, videoconferencing, and the facsimile machine provide electronic connections that facilitate two-way interactivity and speed up feedback to students. CD-ROM, CD-i, the Internet, and the information highway present opportunities and challenges to distance educators to design and develop courses that can effectively use the power and potential of these technologies.

The increasing convergence of distance education and the public education system is due in large part to technology. The following case studies from the provinces of British Columbia, Manitoba, and the state of New York illustrate three different ways that distance learning is converging with the classroom.

Three Illustrations from Practice

The Convergence of Distance Education and the Classroom

1. New Directions in Distance Education (British Columbia)

Collaboration between the British Columbia Ministry of Education (MOE) and the Open Learning Agency (OLA) led to the launch of a unique distance education pilot project in the 1993–94 school year. The project focussed on students enrolled in senior secondary correspondence courses. A major strategy involved the adaptation of existing correspondence courses to technology-based delivery systems. Providing opportunities for frequent contact between students and teachers was a crucial design feature. The pilot intended to demonstrate that, through the integration of existing courses with technology, the courses would be accessible to more people, and be more cost effective.

In addition to increased accessibility and cost effectiveness, two other expected outcomes are worth noting. MOE and OLA wanted to improve completion rates over traditional correspondence rates by using mediating technologies, and to assess the training needs of teachers and site co-ordinators in order to support them in the next phase of the project. To achieve these objectives, the project adapted four senior high school correspondence courses and selected nine small schools to participate. A comprehensive evaluation process was developed to measure results of the pilot. The technology delivery systems included various combinations of audioconferencing, audiographics, television broadcasts, videotapes, and computer-mediated communication. The combination of technologies that were used depended on the particular course being delivered. Key participants in the process were the course teachers and the site facilitators in the schools.

The teachers interacted with the students via computer conferencing, audioconferencing, audiographics, and one-to-one telephone tutoring. Located in each school was a site facilitator to help students develop a study plan and solve study problems. Computer-mediated communications supported the students by providing rapid feedback on assignments, and by facilitating interactivity for counselling or to clarify abstract concepts.

The success of the pilot in meeting its goals is evident by the decision to continue and expand the project. For the 1994–95 school year, the number of sites is being increased from nine to 13, and the number of courses offered will grow from four to nine. A short-term goal for the project is to allow secondary school students to graduate with Academic or Applied Science credentials in 1996. It appears from the results of the pilot project that the desired, long-term goal of the New Directions in Distance Education project, as described by Porter and Manly (1994), will be successful. They wrote:

The desired outcome of the project is to provide a flexible and ... effective means of delivering and resourcing educational programs which will suit learner needs and be sensitive to time, distance and location. (p. 48)

2. The Evergreen School Division Project (Manitoba)

Faced with declining enrolments, school closures, the threat of merging all high schools into one super school, the possibility of lengthening school bus trips, and the increasing danger of losing community identity, Manitoba's Evergreen School Division turned to distance education for a solution. Modelled after experiences in North Dakota and Minnesota, Evergreen used videoconferencing made possible by fibre optic cable laid by Manitoba Telephone. As a result, the School Division was able to launch one of Canada's first efforts to deliver several high school courses through two-way videoconferencing via fibre optic cable.

In September 1993, Evergreen School District joined forces with a neighbouring division to deliver seven courses to four area high schools. Schools with the subject matter expertise shared courses with other schools needing the courses. For example, in one school, Grade 12 calculus was shared with two other small schools where the demand was not sufficient to justify hiring a teacher. By linking the three via videoconferencing, it was possible to create a class of 30 students: 14 students at the originating school, and nine and seven, respectively, at the other two schools. Without the two-way interactive video, half the class would not have taken advanced calculus unless they chose to do so by a correspondence course.

The organizers found that with two-way video delivery, fewer discipline problems developed and fewer drop-outs occurred than in the traditional classroom. School officials noted that the classes worked best for older, more motivated students who possessed the necessary skills to function independently without a teacher present. Unlike British Columbia's New Directions in Distance Education project, Evergreen did not use site facilitators to support students at the remote sites. British Columbia found that the site facilitators played a crucial role in assisting students to become successful learners.

Technology-based projects like the Evergreen model are not inexpensive. Manitoba Telephone levied an up-front charge of $60 000. In addition, the school division paid the telephone company a one-time charge of $40 000 per classroom and a fixed monthly line fee of $5000. The good news is that once the up-front costs have been paid, unlimited repeated use of videoconferencing will cost the same monthly line fee. Over time and repeated use, the model will become cost effective.

3. City University of New York Project (New York)

Researchers at City University of New York (CUNY) found that at-risk students can benefit socially and educationally from telecommunications-based education. The three-year study involved a group of sixth-grade students in New York City public schools who were selected at random from a pool of students categorized as potential drop-outs. A control group was created from the same pool of students. Many students were functionally illiterate; all were from poor inner city homes. Provided with computers and information systems at home and at school, the students experienced a new type of electronic learning that linked the students at home with students in school. Throughout the process, the CUNY researchers provided training and support to both students and teachers.

The initial goals of the project were to motivate students to remain in school and to empower them, as well as to train teachers how to integrate telecommunications technology into their classrooms. The project demonstrated the power of the technology in encouraging collaborative learning among the students and in helping teachers become facilitators in the learning process rather than "sages on the stage."

The project was more than simply an exercise in using modem-equipped PCs to link home and school. While this aspect was important, the project also demonstrates how a networked learning community can be created and implemented, and how disadvantaged children in inner city schools, their teachers, and the community can benefit socially and educationally by using telecommunications. New funds have been allocated for a seven-year study of tutoring and mentoring students over the network.

Analysis

These illustrations demonstrate the variety of ways in which technology can be organized to create a networked learning community. Each project was structured differently to suit local needs. In creating such networks, educators have a wide range of technologies from which to choose. An important skill is knowing how to select the most suitable technologies to achieve the learning objectives of a particular course. It appears that the organizers of each project had great success in choosing the most appropriate technologies for the courses they delivered.

Using Distance Education to Transform Schools

To accomplish the changes needed in Canada's educational systems requires new tools and new approaches to learning. As noted previously, there is widespread dissatisfaction with the quality of education students are receiving. To improve quality, the context for learning needs to be more in step with the environment that students will experience after leaving school, an environment increasingly dominated by technology and by global conglomerates. The magnitude of change expected of schools requires fresh thinking and new perspectives to accomplish the transformation and renewal that are necessary to produce quality graduates. Distance education is one important option that school officials need to understand and implement where appropriate, as they reinvent their schools and strive to improve the quality of the education they provide.

Distance education stimulates fresh thinking and new perspectives, and, as demonstrated by the three case studies on convergence, is capable of playing a major role in transforming how courses are organized and delivered. Schools need the expertise of the distance education community to take advantage of the opportunities to use the technology-based network learning that is becoming more available through local area networks (LANs), wide area networks (WANs), the Internet, and other networks. Schools will need help to deal with the new issues that distance education will bring to the school environment.

At its best, distance education equalizes access to educational opportunities, crosses social boundaries, reaches minorities, offers hope to high-risk learners, creates a second chance for drop-outs, and builds learner self-esteem. At its worst, it maintains the status quo and frustrates teachers and learners. In both cases, it uses techniques and technologies that are not found in the typical classroom, but are part of the environment students enter after formal school comes to an end. However, if designed and implemented effectively, distance education has the considerable power to reach large numbers of people and to develop the survival skills students will need when they finish school.

By making a major commitment to distance education, schools will be faced with a series of issues. How they deal with these issues will determine the success of their distance education programs and the resultant quality of learning. A key element will be how administrators, teachers, and students are oriented in distance learning techniques and methods. Curriculum design, the teacher's role, and the student's role change dramatically from what occurs in a traditional classroom. These changes are basic to success in distance education and need to be understood and implemented systematically. If they are, the impact of adapting to distance education could be profound for many school systems.

Issues that need to be dealt with include organizational changes, the design and development of learning materials, copyright procedures, teacher training, student orientation, student support systems, media selection, funding, and accountability. The degree to which these issues are addressed will affect the quality of education delivered. It is not the intent of this chapter to discuss these issues. Suffice to identify them for the purpose of awareness, and to comment briefly on two of them: teacher training and student orientation. Appropriate teacher training and student orientation are fundamental activities in preparing schools for a distance education project. The quality of the learning depends in part on the skill of the teacher and the student's ability to deal effectively with being geographically distant from the teacher.

Teacher Training

The need for teachers to be comfortable with the technology is essential. The challenge is to retrain teachers to use the power of the technology and to change their roles from "sages on the stage" to "guides on the side." Teachers need to understand facilitating skills and recognize the potential of technology to present curricula in new and more exciting formats than are used in the classroom. Television and computers are expressions of the culture of today's students; consequently, students often find media motivational. For that reason, teachers need to learn how to maximize the use of media.

A poor use of media occurs when they are added to a course but the teacher continues to teach as usual. To be effective, the teacher needs to rethink how the use of technology changes the presentation of curricula, and the nature of interactivity between the teacher and the student. One of distance education's greatest attributes is its ability to connect teachers and students, under certain conditions, through mediating technologies such as fax machines, voice mail, e-mail, or computer conferencing in order to deal with course concerns or counselling issues. The New Directions in Distance Education Project in British Columbia illustrates how important it is for teachers and students to have access to, and be able to use, the mediating technologies. The improved completion rates recorded for the project are attributed in part to the interactivity that students and teachers experienced through technology.

Training teachers, and orienting students, can be accomplished in a variety of ways. These include workshops, seminars, and demonstrations. Another less obvious, but effective way, is to involve participants with technology in personal interest activities searching for answers to questions or issues. In the process, some fundamental skills in network communication are developed. For example, the Educational Network of Ontario (ENO) is a valuable tool to introduce teachers to, and to train them in, distance education communication techniques. For students, a national program called SchoolNet provides opportunities to get involved in special projects using the Internet, and in the process, learn how to use e-mail, conduct database searches, and download files.

ENO provides an electronic link between teachers and other education officials across the province of Ontario to enable them to discuss curricula and other issues. Started in 1993 with funding from the provincial government, approximately 8000 of the 135 000 teachers in the province have signed on to the computer network. Growth continues at the rate of approximately 500 persons each week during the school year. Originally created as a communications vehicle for teachers, it has quickly evolved to include school administrators, school trustees, and others of the public who are interested in educational issues. Teachers have declared the network to be a convenient and effective system for professional development, especially during times of diminishing resources and continuing reductions in funds to attend conferences.

The network is an interesting example of how teachers are using distance education delivery techniques such as e-mail and computer conferencing to discuss issues and to learn the skills of electronic communication via computer and modem. The next step for many teachers is to adapt these skills to a teaching environment and to deliver a course over a network.

Jurisdictions that involve teachers in networking activities, beginning usually as information sharing and issue-oriented discussions, end up providing professional development in computer literacy and moderating skills that are critical in distance education. It is too early to tell whether this will affect the quality of education these teachers provide, or influence how they teach. Nevertheless, ENO has the potential of being an important way to assist the reluctant or hesitant teacher, or to help those teachers suffering from technophobia, to become more comfortable with technology. Once greater familiarity with telecommunications is established, the challenge of using technology to deliver a course will be less threatening. While the original rationale for ENO was to provide an electronic forum for teachers to discuss issues, its real worth may be in its value as a tool for training teachers in distance education communications techniques, and in demonstrating the power of telecommunications to disseminate ideas.

Student Orientation
The orientation of students needs to focus on how to use technology to enhance their communication skills, how to be self-directed, independent learners, how to enjoy the autonomy technology gives them to reach beyond the classroom, and how to take more responsibility for what they learn.

In one example of student involvement with computer networks, SchoolNet has an ambitious plan to link Canada's 16 500 schools to the global information highway in the next five years. Introduced in 1993 with the modest goal of involving 300 schools in its first year, 3000 schools had signed up before the end of the school year. The popularity is not surprising. The program allows schools to tap into education-oriented programs available worldwide on the Internet. SchoolNet became possible because of a co-operative venture among the federal and provincial governments, ministries and departments of education, and business and industry. Funds in the amount of $1.6 million have been committed for the first five years of the project.

Canada is one of the first countries to make a comprehensive effort to link all its schools to the Internet. While a commendable initiative, Internet material is mostly foreign-produced and has, as yet, little Canadian content. SchoolNet, however, will likely change this as participating schools begin to share curricula with each other. Pilot projects are being designed by SchoolNet staff to use audiographics on the Internet to deliver distance education courses. SchoolNet is a unique way to orient students to e-mail, file transfers, and database searches. It has the potential to orient students to locate resources beyond what is available to them locally, and to develop skills in navigating computer networks to enhance their research skills and their depth of knowledge.

The Educational Network of Ontario and SchoolNet are unique applications of technology. They serve as useful examples of how to get teachers and students involved and comfortable with telecommunications—fundamental developments that are essential to success in launching a quality distance education program. ENO, SchoolNet and other networks are part of an evolving infrastructure that will enable schools to develop basic distance education skills and to deliver courses. In the transformation of elementary and secondary schools, it is no longer a question of whether or not to use distance education methods and delivery techniques, but how and when to use them.

Conclusions

For most students, learning through technology, with their teacher not present in the room, is a new experience. As British Columbia's New Directions in Distance Education Project described, such students need support and direction to enable them to make the transition to self-directed learning. They need frequent and timely feedback, and tools to help them monitor their progress. Access to their teacher through the mediating technologies is critical to many students, especially when first introduced to learning via a distance education network. With proper support and training, the most unlikely successes are possible, as illustrated by the CUNY project with disadvantaged inner city children in New York City.

Distance education facilitates exemplary practices in learning. Students have different learning styles and learn best when they are actively involved in their learning. If designed properly, distance education allows for active engagement and hands-on experiences through the technology on-line. By using technology creatively, individual preferred ways of learning can be addressed in ways not possible in a traditional classroom.

For example, using SchoolNet or the Internet, students encounter an unstructured environment with information available on every conceivable topic. Students can identify a number of questions and then search the Internet to find answers. This type of distance learning is highly learner directed and suits the independent learner. It also provides opportunities for students to become more self-directed and to develop independent learning skills.

Compare the Internet experience, the case studies on convergence, and the traditional print-based distance education with its highly structured design. In whatever form distance education is presented, the walls of the traditional school no longer exist, and the learner is no longer dependent on the teacher for knowledge. Helping students to learn on their own and to communicate with technology will enable them to join the workforce and be ready for the training and retraining they will require during their careers.

Education is a sensitive issue. Many parents feel that schools are not properly preparing their children for the 21st century. Radical changes in what and how children are taught are being demanded. A practical solution to this dilemma can be found in distance education: not traditional distance education in the form of correspondence courses, but the new distance education, designed as networked learning communities.

Education that is flexible, effective, responsive to learner needs, and sensitive to time, distance, and location—these characteristics are the important basic ingredients that distance education can offer schools interested in changing and improving their quality of education. By implementing distance education where appropriate, school officials will be challenged to move beyond preoccupation with the past, and become focussed on reinventing schools appropriate to a changing world. By doing so, they will provide the quality education their students will need for the 21st century.

References

Contact North. (1994). *First quarterly report: April to June, 1994.* Thunder Bay: Northwest Regional Coordinating Centre.

Council of Ministers of Education, Canada (CMEC). (1995). *Distance education and open learning project*. Toronto: Author.

McArdle, V. (1994, September). Ontario Ministry of Education and Training. Telephone interview.

McKinnon, N. (1986). Public elementary and secondary schools. In I. Mugridge & D. Kaufman (Eds.), *Distance education in Canada* (pp. 194–203). London: Croom Helm.

McKinnon, N. (1989). Being responsive to the adult distance learner: A secondary school example. In R. Sweet (Ed.), *Post-secondary distance education in Canada: Policies, practices and priorities* (pp. 180–184). Athabasca, AB: Athabasca University/Canadian Society for Studies in Education.

Nikiforuk, A. (1993). *School's out*. Toronto: MacFarlane Walter & Ross.

Porter, D., & Manly, J. (1994). New directions in distance learning. In *Distance! Quelle distance? Conference abstracts* (p. 48). Vancouver: Canadian Association for Distance Education.

CHAPTER 5

Appropriating Learning Technologies: Aboriginal Learners, Needs, and Practices[1]

BARBARA J. SPRONK

As I write this in late August, 1994, Canada's Aboriginal peoples[2] are making the headlines. The chiefs of the 633 bands across Canada who constitute the Assembly of First Nations (AFN) have just reelected lawyer Ovide Mercredi as their national chief, by a narrow margin. Mercredi faces a divided, debt-burdened assembly that has been increasingly sidelined as self-government talks with the federal government have broken down into regional discussions. Mercredi is pushing to expand the AFN's membership, now mainly the 300 000 Indians on reserves, to give better representation to urban Indians, women, and elders, but survival of the AFN will have to take first place on his agenda.

In northern Manitoba, an Aboriginal community of 1700 is being evacuated to a community 200 kilometres to the south, because their water supply—from a major northern river—has become so contaminated with their own sewage that, in the words of the Province's Chief Medical Officer, it can kill. Nine people have already contracted hepatitis.

On a happier note, on the same date as Mercredi's reelection a headline in the same newspaper announced the opening of a shopping centre on a large reserve about an hour's drive south-east of Edmonton. This is the first initiative of its kind in Alberta, built and operated by band members, as a way of providing employment and economic development for those living on the reserve.

These news items make a useful backdrop to the issues discussed in this chapter, exemplifying as they do some of the big issues that confront Canada's Aboriginal peoples—and with them, all Canadians—as we work to find ways of realizing within Canada's political and economic structures the First Nations' rights as enshrined in the Canadian Constitution. Educational institutions and agencies are an important part of this work. Of the slightly more than one million individuals in the 1991 census who identified with their Aboriginal ancestry, only seven percent of that population are over the age of 55, in marked contrast to 20 percent in that age group for Canada's total population of 27 million. On the other hand, 38 percent of the Aboriginal population is under the age of 15, compared with 21 percent of the population in general. The post-secondary sector plays a significant role here, given the need to produce Aboriginal teachers for the growing number of band-operated schools, as well as the Aboriginal lawyers, social workers, administrators, business people, nurses, doctors, technicians, and academics that are required to shape policy and manage the many aspects of Aboriginal life that are coming under Aboriginal peoples' own control.

Given the predominantly rural location of Aboriginal people,[3] colleges, institutes, and universities are employing distance education methods and approaches in a variety of creative ways, always in collaboration with Aboriginal communities and agencies, in an effort to create and deliver programming that will meet their needs. This programming is problematic, for both the basis on which it operates and the subject matter with which it deals are contested terrain.

The aim of this chapter is threefold: (1) to outline the issues—historical, political, and cultural—that confront the contestants; (2) to bring these issues to life using case studies of distance education programs that are operating on this terrain; and (3) to draw from these issues and examples some implications of relevance not only to distance educators who work with Aboriginal peoples, but to the field of distance education as a whole.

Issues

Historical Background

Until very recently, Aboriginal peoples within Canada have been expected to enter and assimilate into the mainstream of Canadian society. This expectation has generated countless disputes between governments pursuing the assimilation of Aboriginal populations and the elimination of their rights, and Aboriginal populations intent upon preserving their identities and rights.

In the 1800s, as the fur trade gave way to agriculture and settlement in the Canadian territories,

the role of the Indian ... changed from that of a commercial partner or fighting ally to an obstacle to the expansion of husbandry. Europeans responded to the changing role of the Indian by developing an "Indian policy" that for the first time in Canadian history had a civil rather than military purpose. As this policy took shape ... it increasingly acquired an assimilationist and coercive quality. Since Indians were an obstacle, they would be removed, not by extermination but by assimilation. They would be settled in compact communities, or reserves, where they could be proselytized by missionaries and taught Euro-Canadian ways by government and church alike. Above all else, they would be taught European occupations ... so that they could support themselves in ways that would not interfere with the economic activities of the now-dominant white population. (Miller, 1987, p. 3)

Despite these concerted efforts, however, Indians did not disappear. On the contrary, sometime in the 1930s the population of status Indians[2] began increasing. Subsequently, with economic development in postwar Canada oriented more than ever to frontier, resource-rich areas that were occupied by Indians and Inuit, prospectors, entrepreneurs and governments came into direct conflict with Indian peoples, who were organizing themselves to press their claims to be allowed to control their destinies (Miller, 1987, p. 10).

Education is a major arena in which this continuing battle has been fought, and in which assimilationist policies, made flesh in the form of residential schools, have been most evident. The horrors of these schools have been comprehensively documented (e.g., Bull, 1991; Haig-Brown, 1988). As Miller points out, residential schools played an ironic role in this organizing. Destructive as they were of individuals, families, communities, and cultures, "many of the postwar Indian leaders who were to argue the case for greater Indian control of Indian policy were the products of Indian residential schools ... [having] gained their literacy and political skills in the schools designed for their assimilation." (Miller, 1987, p. 10)

Political Context

As southern society encroached increasingly on Indian lands, and as the costs of separate, residential schooling escalated owing to Indian population growth, the federal government began to argue that the best way to educate Indian children was in public provincial schools (Miller, 1987, p. 9). By the late 1960s, about two-thirds of Aboriginal children were being schooled in other than residential settings (Oddson & Ross, 1991, p. 6).

In 1969, the federal government, encouraged perhaps by the relative success of the integration of Indian children in provincial schools—at least insofar as costs had declined and the "problem" of Indian education had been rendered less visible—proposed in a White Paper on Indian policy to extend the transfer of all educational services to the provinces, with no special status for Indians. Indian response was loud and clear. In a policy paper on education (National Indian Brotherhood, 1972), Canada's status Indians declared that education was a treaty right, not a privilege, and should be funded by the federal government at all levels in perpetuity, with funds allotted to tribal councils, who would operate schools themselves or contract with public schools, where there would be provision for an Indian voice and vote in the operation of these schools. Further, Indian Education Centres were to be created and run by Indian people for Indian people, to provide skilled, highly trained, and responsible leadership at the local level (Yuzdepski, 1983).

This policy paper set the context for subsequent educational programming, for both children and adults. Increasingly, bands and tribal councils have been setting up their own schools and education centres, governed by members of the communities they serve and administered wherever possible by Aboriginal people.

Other staffing, however, especially the teaching faculty, continues to be drawn largely from the non-Aboriginal population. Although Aboriginal graduates from degree-level programs are growing in number, there are as yet nowhere near sufficient numbers to meet the demand. In addition, funding continues to come largely from the federal government, negotiated on a yearly basis or on the basis of special project funding. Finally, the content and structure of the programs must also be negotiated with non-Aboriginal institutions, since there are as yet only a few Aboriginal-controlled institutions in the post-secondary sector that are in a position to offer their own credentials.

All these constraints affect how the work of educating and training gets done in these schools and centres. All these stake-holders—Aboriginal communities, non-Aboriginal institutions, funding agencies—have their own agendas and struggles, which frequently conflict. Aboriginal communities are beset by internal power struggles and factionalism, making agreement on educational issues a matter of constant negotiation, lobbying, and power brokering. For example, personal and especially family relationships tend to outweigh externally derived criteria for determining who should be chosen as registrants in a program, and this can lead to problems of low attendance and high attrition rates.

Colleges and universities likewise wage internal battles over whether to undertake such programming and, if so, how it should be structured. Discussions of these matters at faculty and academic councils tend to be peppered with such terms as "standards," "entrance requirements," "remediation," "watering down," "rigour," "catering," and "lowest common denominator." Funding agencies, too, are far from the monoliths they appear to be in policy papers; some bureaucrats are more open than others, and better at "moving the paper." However, even the friendliest and most resourceful are accountable to their superiors, and ultimately to the taxpaying public, and run up against the limits imposed by a politically sensitive bureaucracy. In the midst of the politics, the parties involved can lose sight of the core aim of these programs, which is to enable Aboriginal people to learn about the values, structures, and processes of the dominant society in ways that build on and enrich their own heritage and culture, to come to see the world "through two pairs of eyes" (McAlpine, Cross, Whiteduck, & Wolforth, 1990 p. 83).

The Cultural Core

It is not only Aboriginal learners who come to see the world through two pairs of eyes. Non-Aboriginal educators, if they are to work effectively within this interactional (as opposed to assimilationist) framework, must try to do so as well (Goulet & Spronk, 1988, p. 218). This means coming to terms with Aboriginal ways of seeing the world, and learning to shape educational activities in terms that build on these ways rather than diminish or destroy them.

What are these ways of seeing and acting? This is an enormous question, which can barely be touched on within the scope of this chapter. Complicating the task of providing even a modestly useful answer is the fact that "there is as much cultural diversity amongst [North] American Indians as there is [among the peoples of] the comparable land mass that extends from the British Isles to Mongolia" (Urion, 1984, p. 60). Indian people were and are diverse. Even within each band, tribe, and cultural group there is diversity, which Rupert Ross describes as "[a] continuum of adaptation from the Old Ways to new ways which are still in the making ... [on which] each person occupies a unique position" (Ross, 1992, p. xxiv).

Nonetheless, within this diversity there appears to be a core set of values that inform "the Old Ways," to which almost all the writers on Aboriginal education make reference in some way. Holding this core together is the high degree of respect for a person's individuality, his or her right to be independent, autonomous, and different from others (cf. Scollon & Scollon, 1981). This respect is reflected in the five rules or "ethics" for ideal conduct which Dr. Clare Brant, a Mohawk and practising psychiatrist, suggested were central to the conduct of Aboriginal life in traditional times and which to varying degrees remain important today. As set out by Rupert Ross (1992), these rules are as follows.

1. The Ethic of Non-Interference
An Aboriginal person resists interfering in any way with the rights, privileges, and activities of another person, whether by confronting people, giving unsolicited advice, or even commenting on their behaviour. This means, among other things, that parents

and elders cannot "teach" their children; instead, children must learn on their own, by watching and emulating what they see, a process that involves no explicit cajolery, praise, or punishment, or withholding of privileges or promising of rewards. It is up to the child to observe constantly and carefully, to study entirely on his or her own. It is also incumbent on children to respect their elders as repositories of experience and wisdom, and models for their own behaviour.

2. The Ethic That Anger Not Be Shown
Rather than risk damaging individuals with anger, one sacrifices one's own feelings and their expression and discharge. This restraint of anger was clearly a survival tactic in the days when survival depended on the cohesion of the family, tribe, or clan, when the indulgence of personal hostility and emotion would have threatened the viability of the group.

3. The Ethic Respecting Praise and Gratitude
The proper way to show appreciation is to ask the other person to continue with his or her contribution rather than offer vocal expressions of gratitude. One expects excellence in all activities, both of others and of oneself. This expectation makes one reluctant to attempt new endeavours unless there is a clear likelihood of success. Again, this was clearly adaptive in a context in which resources were too scarce to permit much in the way of "practice."

4. The Conservation–Withdrawal Tactic
In order to make sure one can perform a previously untried action successfully, one walks through all possible aspects of it before attempting it. In new surroundings, for example, one does not try to dominate instantly nor draw attention to oneself, but rather retreats into a position of careful observation.

5. The Notion That the Time Must Be Right
To perform excellently, one must prepare oneself emotionally and spiritually for the course chosen before acting. Saying prayers that ask for guidance and give thanks to the guiding spirits is one of the conscious steps an Aboriginal person must take to adopt the proper spiritual stance before acting.

* * *

This respect for the individual, and the expectation that respect will be shown so that growth can occur, are also reflected in other rules, in particular those that have to do with language. These rules of interaction tend to be language-specific, but a few examples will illustrate the ways in which talk reflects respect for individuality.

Instance one concerns Athabaskan speakers, whose interaction patterns contrast with those of English speakers. When conversing with strangers, Athabaskans do not talk much. This is meant to demonstrate respect for the individuality of both parties to the conversation: any conversation can be threatening because it involves some negotiation, and hence the possibility of a change in point of view. Athabaskans thus avoid conversation except when the point of view of all participants is well known, in which case Athabaskans can be very talkative. A variety of issues arise when primarily oral cultures, like those of Athabaskans, collide with the primarily essayist culture of English speakers. Writing for Athabaskans becomes a "crisis in ethnic identity," since for Athabaskans to write, they must adopt discourse patterns that are identified with English speakers. Only by identifying as an English speaker can an Athabaskan operate within the world of essayist prose, where both author and audience are fictionalized rather than actually present in the discourse[4] (Scollon & Scollon, 1981).

Instance two concerns speakers of Cree, whose tolerance for silence contrasts sharply with the *intolerance* of silence that is typical of speakers of English. For example, for speakers of Cree, social occasions are defined by co-presence—that is, simply being together—rather than by talk. Co-presence may involve talk, but the presence or absence of talk does not change the nature of what is felt to be going on. This contrasts with the patterns typical of speakers of English, for whom talking to others is a compulsory way of acknowledging their co-presence. For example, a speaker of English who attends a gathering and is not greeted by anyone—that is, talked to or with—will likely feel ignored, even unwanted, whereas a speaker of Cree will tend to regard simply being together with others as acknowledgement enough of his or her presence in, and importance to, the gathering. Another example of this difference in approaches to silence is the tendency of speakers of Cree to use silence as a way of expressing respect for others. In fact, in the presence of power, this respectful silence is virtually obligatory for Cree speakers. To use language casually in the presence of power is dangerous. Silence for speakers of Cree "is understood to be full ... and complete in itself, like the circle which is the image of harmony in the world" (Darnell, 1991, p. 92).

These are mere glimpses into the worlds of other languages and world views, but they suggest to us voluble English speakers that silences—which in our discourse evidence non-thought, sullenness, hostility, timidity, or a dozen other possibilities—may in fact be a manifestation of care, caution, reflection, and, above all, respect. It is also humbling to realize that our eagerness to leap into conversational spaces and fill silences with talk is not always the best approach to getting to know a stranger, especially someone from a markedly different linguistic and cultural background. In fact it is likely that we will, for our efforts, be labelled "rude" if we persist in always talking rather than listening. With these cautions as a backdrop, let us proceed to a consideration of a world that depends on writing and (technologically mediated) talk, namely, distance education.

Seven Illustrations from Practice

As pointed out above, since the mid-1970s Aboriginal agencies and communities in Canada have been collaborating with universities, colleges, and institutes in programming that will provide their people with the training and education they need to take control of their own destiny. As a result, these institutions have established Native Studies programs, encouraged greater participation by Aboriginal students in other on-campus programs, and also mounted Aboriginal-oriented programming off-campus, using the "field centre" model.

This model has been described as "a supportive community which develops [students'] self-confidence, nurtures the development of a cohesive group of peers and provides a vehicle for solving problems" (Lang & Scarfe, 1989, p. 105). The programs using this model share a number of features: they are fully collaborative, in most cases jointly offered by Aboriginal agencies and non-Aboriginal institutions; they are community based, bringing programs to the learners in their communities rather than requiring learners to relocate to urban centres; they incorporate Aboriginal perspectives in program and curriculum design, learning materials, pedagogical approaches, learner support, and administrative procedures; they have flexible entrance requirements, and frequently offer intensive coursework in reading, writing, and math skills, which enables adults disadvantaged by previous, inadequate schooling to work successfully at the post-secondary level; and they maintain the same rigour and standards in their exit requirements that exist in their campus-based programs, so that students who complete these community-based programs can readily move into further programs or immediately into jobs.

There is a substantial literature that describes field centre programming for Aboriginal teacher education (e.g., Archibald 1986; Bashford & Heinzerling, 1987; Lang & Scarfe, 1985; McAlpine et al., 1990; Read, 1983; Sloan, 1981; Williams & Wyatt, 1987). The model has also been applied successfully in social work (e.g., Smith & Pace, 1987) and university transfer programs[5] (e.g., Scott-Brown, 1986). In every case, learning is brought to the students by instructors who travel to the learning sites for classroom sessions. Some programs require students to come to campus occasionally for plenary seminars or laboratory work. In almost every case, however, students can complete required practicum work close to home, supervised in local worksites by professionals who work in tandem with course instructors and program directors.

What distance education programs add to this mix of instructional approaches is some form of technologically mediated communication, such as course materials designed for independent home study, audioconferenced seminars, and fax and computer communication. As is evident in the following examples, the resulting programming is as varied as its geographical locations, the populations it serves, and the educational needs that it tries to meet.

1. Arctic College
(Northwest Territories)

In the fall of 1988, following a needs assessment, the Aurora campus of Arctic College started a distance education pilot project in computer and literacy skill development. Three locations in the Inuvik Region of the Western Arctic were selected to participate in the project: the Inuvialuit community of Paulatuk, the Gwichen community of Fort McPherson, and the community of Inuvik.

The project co-ordinator visited each community location to introduce the project. Subsequently, fax machines and teleconference calls were used for communication. Each community made use of local adult educators to assist as tutors, while the project co-ordinator acted as course instructor responsible for presenting lessons and evaluating assignments.

The project was successful, enabling scattered communities of Inuvialuit, Dene, and non-Aboriginal people to link with each other and with the instructor. It is perhaps in the remote Arctic that the true value of distance education can be recognized (Stinson, 1990).

2. Athabasca University
(Alberta, Saskatchewan, and Northwest Territories)

Since 1976, Athabasca University (AU) has been delivering programming at Native Education Centres on or near reserves in two provinces and at Arctic College campuses in the Northwest Territories. The primary focus has been university transfer programs, providing up to two years of courses transferable to BA, BEd and BSW and other programs. In addition, AU offers certificate programs in administration and in health development administration; the latter was developed and is delivered jointly with the Yellowhead Tribal Council. Programs in addictions counselling, mental health, and the Cree language are in the planning stage. A degree in Native Studies will soon be available for both home study and on-site delivery.

In all these initiatives, the predominant delivery method is on-site, classroom tutoring using the course packages that have been developed for AU's independent study students, adapted to provide greater relevance in Aboriginal contexts. With a few remarkable exceptions, the independent home study mode has proven a dismal failure for Aboriginal students at AU. There has been some experimentation with other technologies; for example, teleconferenced seminars have replaced some classroom sessions in a few instances. It is on-site, classroom tutoring, however, that remains by far the most successful mode for AU's Aboriginal learners (cf. Goulet & Spronk, 1988; Oddson & Ross, 1991; Oddson et al., 1991; Spronk, 1985; Spronk & Radtke, 1987).

3. Cambrian College (Ontario)

The Native Community Care, Counselling and Development program was developed by Aboriginal community representatives, community health workers, the Union of Ontario Indians, and the Association of Iroquois and Allied Indians. It is delivered by Mohawk and Cambrian Colleges, and administered by the Anigawncigig Institute. The program is designed for individuals already working in community positions.

Instruction is campus based for 10 weeks a year, complemented with the equivalent of 800 hours of home-based study and 200 hours of fieldwork credit in supervised settings. As students work through the study materials, they are supported by regular visits of Support Service Officers and by bi-weekly teleconferences, for which students come to designated locations adjacent to their home communities. This arrangement enables students to continue as health workers at the band level while completing the program (Haughey, 1993).

4. Contact North/Contact Nord (Ontario)

In 1986, the Government of Ontario created the Contact North/Contact Nord pilot project. One of its objectives was to improve access to post-secondary and secondary education for residents of Northern Ontario, among them Francophones and Aboriginal people, utilizing communications technologies. Contact North collaborates extensively with institutions and agencies in the region (cf. Anderson & Nelson, 1989; Anderson, 1992; Croft, 1993), delivering a wide variety of programming that makes extensive use of audioconferencing and audiographics technology. For example, the Cambrian College program described above uses the network, as does the Native Resource Technician program of the Sault College of Applied Arts and Technology, which is aimed at equipping Aboriginal people to work in modern renewable-resource management organizations. Students remain in their home communities and teleconference with college faculty three days per week, spend additional one-on-one time with a work tutor, and spend two days per week gaining practical work experience with their work sponsor. Home study materials and audio-visual aids are provided by the course team (Haughey, 1993).

5. Memorial University (Newfoundland)

In 1977–78, Memorial University of Newfoundland developed a field-based two-year teacher education program in Labrador. Approximately 10 years later, a five-year BEd in Aboriginal and Northern Education degree was approved. Administered from St. John's, the programs are offered off-campus in Labrador in the communities where the students reside. Courses are offered separately to Innu and Inuit/Aboriginal-settler groups, owing to linguistic and cultural differences.

Many delivery approaches have been tried. In the beginning, instructors were flown into communities for six-week periods or two three-week periods to deliver courses. Those students who were teacher aides were freed from their duties for an hour or two at the end of each school day to take the courses. Another variation was to offer courses in a four-week block of time in a more centralized location during the first few weeks after school finished. Yet another mode that was tried was the provision of home study materials with no on-site tutor, but this was a failure. Teleconferencing has also been used a number of times, and seems to work best with experienced students, who know the instructors from other courses that have been taught on-site. Overall, a combination of these delivery methods appears to be the best approach (Sharpe, 1992).

6. Simon Fraser University
(British Columbia)

Since 1988, Simon Fraser University has collaborated with the Secwepemc Cultural Education Society in Kamloops to offer Secwepemc credit programs, which lead to a number of academic credentials, and are designed to enhance Aboriginal students' knowledge of their history, language, and culture while providing a solid foundation in the social sciences.

Courses are offered mainly on-site, in Kamloops, by visiting faculty in once-weekly sessions and by resident faculty on a continuing basis. An initial attempt to teach via distance education (home study supported by teleconferenced tutorials) was unsuccessful, and guidelines now prescribe that students will be considered for group enrolment in distance education only after they have demonstrated their ability to study effectively. Current experiments in alternating on-site visits with teleconferenced sessions are promising, however, and program personnel are confident that this enhanced distance education format will prove successful and will give students access to an increasing number of courses (Haughey, 1993).

7. University of Victoria
(British Columbia)

Since 1990, the University of Victoria has been delivering a Certificate Program in the Administration of Aboriginal Governments. Students are predominantly Aboriginal people who are employed as administrators in, or around, Aboriginal governments, and have had little previous contact with post-secondary education.

The delivery approach combines multiple day seminars on campus with home study materials for independent study off-campus and telephone tutorials. Telephone tutors assist students to understand the readings, provide non-evaluative feedback on assignments, chair audioconferences to discuss course-related matters, and provide feedback to instructors regarding students' progress. This combination enables students who are working full time and who may live great distances from the university to participate and to succeed in the program. An Advisory Council that includes prominent members of participating bands and communities plays an important role in planning, funding, marketing, and evaluating the program, and assists students with the admissions process and other matters (Langford & Seaborne, 1991).

Analysis

The foregoing examples merely sketch some of the collaborations between distance educators and Aboriginal communities and agencies across Canada. Nonetheless, even these glimpses provide some indication of the challenges, and give life to the issues outlined earlier in this chapter. These challenges include choosing appropriate delivery modes and instructional approaches; generating and regenerating curricula and course materials that acknowledge and reflect the knowledge and experience that Aboriginal learners bring to these programs; and dealing sensitively and effectively with the political issues that such collaborations raise both internally and externally.

Instruction and Delivery

Distance education programs for Aboriginal learners are sites of creative and continual experimentation with approaches to instruction and delivery. What have we learned so far about what works and what doesn't?

What clearly does not work with Aboriginal learners is the home study model. Given these learners' heritage—the centrality of oral traditions, the need for group solidarity, and the kind of "watch, prepare, then do" that ensured learning survival in earlier times, this should come as no surprise. Correspondence materials, no matter how sophisticated their design, are text- and prose-based, and involve the learner in—at best—a fictionalized relationship with a faceless and largely unknown author. Nothing in Aboriginal learners' previous experience prepares them for the kind of learning these materials demand. Even if English is their first language—and for many it is not—if they have been raised in an Aboriginal community their language patterns will still be predominantly Cree or Athabaskan or Micmac (cf. Scollon & Scollon, 1981, p. 12). Further, the comprehension of English prose demands a particular mind set, one that Scollon and Scollon (1981) have labelled "modern consciousness," for which Aboriginal learners' previous education has not prepared them. Finally, for people for whom one-to-one relationships are central to learning, the decontextualized nature of correspondence learning materials renders them alien in the extreme.

What does appear to work for Aboriginal learners is to emphasize face-to-face contact with instructors, tutors, counsellors, supervisors, mentors, or other students, and to supplement these contacts with self-study print materials. Teleconferencing also appears to have its uses, not just in terms of making course content meaningful, but also to bring students together as a group (Langford & Seaborne, 1991, p. 121). It is important to note, however, that in most situations in which audioconferencing has worked well, learners already know the instructor personally in on-site contexts. Again, this should come as no surprise, given the greater importance of co-presence rather than talk, in interactions among at least some language groups (cf. Darnell, 1991).

In any event, it appears that the approach most likely to meet both the learner's need for co-presence and group cohesion, and the institution's need to stay within budgets that are always tight, is not a single approach but a combination of several, involving face-to-face contact, technological enhancements where available and useful, and appropriately designed learning materials.

Curriculum and Course Content

Curriculum and course content in the Aboriginal settings described above are the product of collaboration, that is, of non-Aboriginal academics collaborating with Aboriginal partners in choosing courses; selecting content emphases, objectives, and approaches; recruiting and hiring the instructors in whose hands the content will ultimately be shaped; and evaluating results. Embedded in this work are three additional issues, those of (1) hiring instructors and tutors who are experienced in working with Aboriginal learners, or at the least, sensitive to the issues involved, (2) writing or adapting learning materials that work in Aboriginal contexts, and (3) devising workloads that Aboriginal learners can actually manage, given the many demands that are made on them by others in their lives.

In terms of staff recruitment, the ideal would be to hire Aboriginal instructors and tutors, people who have clearly demonstrated that they see the world with "two pairs of eyes," having been raised in Aboriginal communities but schooled in the institutions of the dominant society. Such people are still relatively rare, however, and tend to get snapped up quickly for all manner of jobs in the Aboriginal world. The best we can do for the moment is screen non-Aboriginal candidates for experience with, or at least predisposition toward, holistic and participatory educational approaches, such as dramatic techniques (cf. Foreman, 1991) and collaborative work (cf. Sawyer, 1991, for an exhaustive list of instructional adaptations for Aboriginal contexts). Another strategy, one that has worked well for the Labrador and Arctic College programs, is to use Aboriginals as resource people for the courses, in addition to the regular instructor, a practice that not only enhances the success of the course, but also boosts the self-esteem of the resource people who themselves are often students of the degree program (Sharpe, 1992, p. 84).

In terms of materials development, those who are developing programs from the ground up are in the happiest position, since they can work collaboratively with their Aboriginal partners to shape materials appropriately, with little constraining baggage. Those who must adapt existing materials have a more difficult task, even though on the face of it one might assume that most of the work is already done. Far from it. The experience at Athabasca University, for example, has been that courses that are written for "mainstream" learners seldom serve Aboriginal learners effectively. For one thing, they are written for the more-or-less independent learner, not for the interdependent learners that populate Aboriginal classrooms, and need at least to be reformatted. More often, however, they need to be completely regenerated, since the materials are inevitably culture-bound in viewpoint and strategy.

An interactional framework calls for a re-visioning of curricula and courses that compares and contrasts Aboriginal and non-Aboriginal values, practices, and viewpoints. Such re-visions will reveal the cultural assumptions that are built into any course, and require an expansion of paradigms to include "the other" as well as ourselves. Such re-visions equip learners, as one of our collaborators phrased it, "for both Wall Street and the Reserve." In the end, they could serve our non-Aboriginal learners as effectively as our Aboriginal learners, since they would expand their views of the world as well, and enable them to see "through two pairs of eyes."

Finally, the apportioning of workloads is an issue that weighs heavily on instructor and learner alike. Faced with the challenge of dealing with both Aboriginal and non-Aboriginal worlds within the confines of a single course, course authors and instructors typically expect far too much of the learner. Even more so than most learners, those in Aboriginal communities tend to be already charged with a number of burdens, some happy, some not so happy; most programs, for example, report that the typical learner is a woman in her 30s, a mother with several dependents and a demanding family and community life (cf. Spronk & Radtke, 1987). Such learners tend not to have the kind of undisturbed study space and time that instructors assume exists when they assign reading loads and exercises to be done at home. At Athabasca, the most effective approach has been to require the learner to spend an entire day at the learning centre for each course that she is taking, and to reserve part of that day for supervised and supported study and reading. Otherwise, students tend to come to class unprepared, or not to come at all, because they have not prepared.

Politics

Political complications seem to be inescapable. Few descriptions of distance education programs for Aboriginal peoples deal explicitly with this issue, but if one reads between the lines, political constraints are not hard to find. For example, Langford and Seaborne (1991, p. 122) at the close of their article make veiled reference to political constraints with their observation that, "It is not yet clear that the modern university can adapt to the pressures that such a vision [the balance between 'the two integrities'] creates." Goulet and Spronk (1988, p. 220), in their discussion of the need for course re-visioning, make more explicit reference to the kinds of constraints that arise within universities, where faculty members are reluctant to see the integrity of courses, in which they have invested a great deal of time and care, tampered with.

Political constraints also arise from funding agencies and their policies. For example, in Athabasca University's experience, Indian Affairs' 48-month student funding limit renders completion of a four-year program virtually impossible for Aboriginal registrants, given the other demands that are made on their lives. Whatever the level and source of the political constraints, the problems to which they give rise are chronic, and merit more discussion and emphasis in the distance education literature than they have received to date.

Conclusions

Distance education for Aboriginal peoples in Canada is an important element in their struggle for self-determination and development on their own terms. Distance educators across the country are collaborating with Aboriginal agencies and communities to provide opportunities for "both ways education," to use a term that comes from programming for Aboriginal teachers in Australia (Kemmis, 1988). It is somewhat ironic that if educators, including distance educators, continue to do a good job of this collaboration, they will eventually work themselves out of it, as more Aboriginal education centres and agencies become capable of setting up their own post-secondary institutions, staffed by the graduates of existing collaborative programs (cf. Barnhardt, 1991; Josephson, 1986; Wright, 1987). In the meantime, the work of Canadian distance educators holds some interesting implications for those who concern themselves with such issues as definitions of distance education, the independent learner, and the nature of the educational enterprise.

In regard to definitions, Sharpe (1992, p. 85) closes his description of the Memorial University program with the observation that "many of the elements of program delivery discussed here are perhaps generic to a wide range of education, training and other developmental activities in remote regions." This calls to mind the arguments of such distance educators as Jevons (1990), who speak of the increasing blurring of the boundaries between distance and so-called conventional education. Aboriginal people—such as those described in the news stories cited early in this chapter—who are struggling with life-and-death issues, whether of an organization or a community, do not care how we label what we do, as long as it works.

As for the "independent learner" who continues to people a fair chunk of the distance education literature—this is a notion that is being increasingly challenged, not only by distance educators who work with Aboriginal groups, but also by those who concern themselves with women's and feminist issues in the field, as well as by such writers as Tait (1990), who argue that individualizing courses to meet specific learners' needs ought not to be confused with individualism. As Tait argues, all distance educators need to understand the importance of learning in the context of family, workplace, and community, at both theoretical and methodological levels, and to act upon this understanding in course planning and delivery.

In this regard, distance educators who work collaboratively with Aboriginal learners and communities are privileged, since they are forced by their Aboriginal partners to take seriously the social, cultural, and political contexts within which the work is being done. They are also likely to be mindful of the work of other, "conventional" educators who work in this terrain, so as to learn from their example and experience. Finally, and most importantly, they are given the opportunity to learn as much as they impart, not only about the nature of teaching and learning,

but about the way the world looks through "two pairs of eyes."
By accepting this gift and working with it, they can participate in
challenging the forces and dismantling the barriers that keep
Aboriginal peoples from taking their rightful place in Canadian
society. In the words of elder Basil Johnston (1992, p. ix), "so
long as the government and the officials of this country continue
to act as if the original peoples are the only ones in need of
instruction and improvement, so long will the walls of suspicion
and distrust persist."

Endnotes

1. I wish to acknowledge my mentors and mothers, Maggie Hodgson of
the Nechi Institute, Ella Paul of the Yellowhead Tribal Council, and
Leona Makokis of Blue Quills First Nations College, in recognition of
their unending and generous supply of wisdom and patience that has
helped me to come to whatever understanding I have of the ways of
their people.

2. There is no official or universally agreed way of referring to
Canada's original peoples. I have used "Aboriginal" and "Native" interchangeably in this chapter, capitalizing "Aboriginal" in recognition of the
fact that its use usually implies its counterpart, "White," which is
always capitalized. These usages gloss over the complex composition of
the populations in Canada that identify with their Aboriginal ancestry:
"Indians" comprise both status Indians, who are defined as such in the
Indian Act of Canada, and non-status Indians, who consider themselves
Indian but who have lost their status under the act; "Inuit" refers to the
peoples of the Arctic region; "Métis" refers to people of mixed ancestry
who still identify with their Aboriginal ancestry. The term "First Nations
peoples" is coming more and more into use, in recognition of the discrete nations of people who inhabited the continent before the arrival of
the European conquerors and settlers.

3. In 1991, Coish (1991) listed 55 percent of status Indians as living
on reserves, all of which are located outside urban areas, and some of
which are very remote.

4. The transformations involved in shifting from orality to literacy raise
a number of epistemological, cognitive, social, and political issues. In
addition to Scollon and Scollon, see Ong (1982) for further discussion of

the epistemological and cognitive issues, and Battiste (1986, 1987) for case studies and further discussion of the cognitive, social, and political issues that literacy raises.

5. These are two-year programs of courses taken at colleges or other institutions and which are granted the equivalent of two years' credit by the receiving university or universities.

References

Anderson, T. (1992). Distance education delivery networks—Role in community and institutional development. In D. Wall & M. Owen (Eds.), *Distance education and sustainable community development* (pp. 87–103). Athabasca: Athabasca University & Canadian Circumpolar Institute.

Anderson, T., & Nelson, C. (1989). Collaboration in distance education: Ontario's Contact North/Contact Nord. In R. Sweet (Ed.), *Post-secondary distance education in Canada* (pp. 209–216). Athabasca: Athabasca University & Canadian Society for Studies in Education.

Archibald, J. (1986). Completing a vision: The Native Indian teacher education program at the University of British Columbia. *Canadian Journal of Native Education, 13*(1), 33–45.

Barnhardt, R. (1991). Higher education in the fourth world: Indigenous people take control. *Canadian Journal of Native Education, 18*(2), 199–231.

Bashford, L., & Heinzerling, H. (1987). Blue Quills Native Education Centre: A case study. In J. Barman, Y. Hebert, & D. McCaskill (Eds.), *Indian education in Canada. Volume 2: The challenge* (pp. 126–141). Vancouver: University of British Columbia Press.

Battiste, M. (1986). Micmac literacy and cognitive assimilation. In J. Barman, Y. Hebert & D. McCaskill (Eds.), *Indian education in Canada. Volume 1: The legacy* (pp. 23–44). Vancouver: University of British Columbia Press.

Battiste, M. (1987). Mi'kmaq linguistic integrity: A case study of Mi'kmawey school. In J. Barman, Y. Hebert, & D. McCaskill (Eds.), *Indian education in Canada. Volume 2: The challenge* (pp. 107–125). Vancouver: University of British Columbia Press.

Bull, L.R. (1991). Indian residential schooling: The native perspective. *Canadian Journal of Native Education, 18* (Supplemental Issue), 1–64.

Coish, D. (1991). *Canada's off-reserve aboriginal population: A statistical overview*. Ottawa: Department of the Secretary of State of Canada.

Croft, M. (1993). The Contact North Project: Collaborative project management in Ontario. In L. Moran & I. Mugridge (Eds.), *Collaboration in distance education: International case studies* (pp. 132–150). London and New York: Routledge.

Darnell, R. (1991). Thirty-nine postulates of Plains Cree conversation, 'power', and interaction: A culture-specific model. In W. Cowan (Ed.), *Papers of the Twenty-Second Algonquian Conference* (pp. 89–102). Ottawa: Carleton University.

Foreman, K. (1991). A dramatic approach to teacher education. *Canadian Journal of Native Education, 18*(1), 73–80.

Goulet, J., & Spronk, B. (1988). Partnership with Aboriginal peoples: Some implications for distance educators. In D. Sewart & J. Daniel (Eds.), *Developing distance education* (pp. 218–221). Oslo: International Council for Distance Education.

Haig-Brown, C. (1988). *Resistance and renewal: Surviving the Indian residential school*. Vancouver: Tillacum Library.

Haughey, M., compiler. (1993, June). *Some programs for northern and Native communities offered at a distance*. Presentation to the Royal Commission on Aboriginal Peoples.

Jevons, F. (1990). Blurring the boundaries: Parity and convergence. In D. R. Garrison & D. Shale (Eds.), *Education at a distance: From issues to practice* (pp. 135–144). Malabar, FL: Robert E. Krieger.

Johnston, B. (1992). Foreword. In R. Ross, *Dancing with a ghost: Exploring Indian reality* (pp. vii–xvi). Markham, ON: Octopus Publishing Group.

Josephson, M.I. (1986). TEFL and the case for Indian universities. *Canadian Journal of Native Education, 13*(2), 3–9.

Kemmis, S. (1988). *A study of the Batchelor College remote area teacher education program, 1976–1988*. Geelong: Deakin Institute for Studies in Education.

Lang, H., & Scarfe, D. (1985). *Stages of group support development in a teacher education program*. Regina: Faculty of Education, University of Regina.

Lang, H., & Scarfe, D. (1989). North of the 49th: Peer support in Indian/Métis teacher education programs. *Journal of Indigenous Studies, 1*(2) 9–15.

Langford, J., & Seaborne, K. (1991). Building a management program for Aboriginal administration. In A. Tait (Ed.), *The student, community and curriculum: International perspectives on open and distance learning. Conference papers.* (pp. 115–122). Cambridge, U.K.: The Open University.

McAlpine, L., Cross, E., Whiteduck, G., & Wolforth, J. (1990). Using two pairs of eyes to define an Aboriginal teacher education programme. *Canadian Journal of Native Education, 17*(2), 82–88.

Miller, J.R. (1987). The irony of residential schooling. *Canadian Journal of Native Education, 14*(2), 3–13.

National Indian Brotherhood. (1972). *Indian control of Indian education.* Policy paper presented to the Minister of Indian Affairs.

Oddson, L., & Ross, L. (1991). *Athabasca University's role in native education programs.* Athabasca: Athabasca University.

Oddson, L., Ross, L., & Spronk, B. (1991). Turning barriers into bridges: Meeting the need for Aboriginal health administrators in Western Canada. In A. Tait (Ed.), *The student, community and curriculum: International perspectives on open and distance learning. Conference papers* (pp. 161–169). Cambridge, U.K.: The Open University.

Ong, W. (1982). *Orality and literacy: The technologizing of the word.* London and New York: Methuen.

Paulet, R. (1989). Building bridges: Northern Native teacher training. In R. Sweet (Ed.), *Post-secondary distance education in Canada: Policies, practices and priorities* (pp. 23–33). Athabasca: Athabasca University and Canadian Society for Studies in Education.

Read, E. (1983). Education programs for disadvantaged adults: A case study—Project Morning Star. *Canadian Journal of Native Education, 10*(2), 19–28.

Ross, R. (1992). Dancing with a ghost: Exploring Indian reality (Chapter 3). Markham, ON: Octopus Publishing Group.

Sawyer, D. (1991). Native learning styles: Shorthand for instructional adaptations? *Canadian Journal of Native Education, 18*(1), 99–105.

Scollon, R., & Scollon, S. (1981). *Narrative, literacy and face in interethnic communication.* Norwood, NJ: ABLEX Publishing.

Scott-Brown, J. (1986). Teaching in the University Native Outreach Program at the University of Calgary. *Multicultural Education Journal, 4*(2) 4–9.

Sharpe, D. (1992). Successfully implementing a Native teacher education program through distance education in Labrador. In D. Wall & M. Owen (Eds.), *Distance education and sustainable community development* (pp. 75–85). Athabasca: Canadian Circumpolar Institute with Athabasca University Press.

Sloan, L. (1981). Morning star students: Looking back to find direction for the future. *Canadian Journal of Native Education, 8*(2), 2–10.

Smith, A., & Pace, J. (1987). Micmac Indian social work education: A model. *Canadian Journal of Native Education, 14*(1), 22–29.

Spronk, B. (1985). The face-to-face component in distance education. In P. Babin (Ed.), *Proceedings of the fifth annual conference on teaching and learning in higher education* (pp. 263–267). Ottawa: University of Ottawa.

Spronk, B., & Radtke, D. (1987). Distance education for Native women. In K. Storrie (Ed.), *Women, isolation and bonding: The ecology of gender* (pp. 113–126). Toronto: Methuen.

Stinson, W. (1990, May). *Distance education: A pilot project conducted by Arctic College for the Inuvik Region of the Northwest Territories.* Paper presented to the Annual Meeting of the Canadian Association for Distance Education. Québec City, Québec.

Tait, A. (1990, May). *Individualisation and individualism: Contradictory currents in distance education.* Unpublished paper presented to the Annual Meeting of the Canadian Association for Distance Education, Québec City, Québec.

Urion, C. (1984). Book review: Game for anything: Multi-cultural games and activities for children. *Canadian Journal of Native Education, 11*(2), 60–63.

Williams, L., & Wyatt, J. (1987). Training Indian teachers in a community setting: The Mount Currie Lil'Wat Program. In J. Barman, Y. Hebert, & D. McCaskill (Eds.), *Indian education in Canada. Volume 2: The challenge* (pp. 210–227). Vancouver: University of British Columbia Press.

Wright, B. (1987). Tribally controlled community colleges. *Canadian Journal of Native Education, 14*(3), 29–36.

Yuzdepski, I. (1983). Indian control of Indian education. *Canadian Journal of Native Education, 11*(1), 37–40.

C H A P T E R   6

Learners and Learner Services: The Key to the Future in Open Distance Learning[1]

JANE E. BRINDLEY

This chapter considers the place of learner services in the rapidly changing field of open distance learning, with a focus on the goals of institutional responsiveness and facilitating student success. It takes the position that provision of learner services is one of the key ways in which those engaged in distance teaching can demonstrate a commitment to learner-centredness in order to become more competitive and better positioned strategically to serve the pressing demand for high-quality, accessible education and training.

This chapter does not advocate a particular set of services as being most effective for all distance learners and institutions. Rather, recognizing the importance of contextual considerations, it begins with a discussion of core issues in the development and delivery of learner services. These include defining the role of learner services within the context of an institution's culture and value system, the linking of practice to research findings in developing strategies to facilitate student success, and the emerging trends that will influence future developments in learner services. Although the author draws on experience gained mainly in large single- and dual-mode post-secondary distance teaching institutions, the issues identified are generic and will likely be of equal concern to distance education practitioners in a variety of settings.

The presentation of issues is followed by a discussion of some specific practices in linking learner services to learner needs. In this section of the chapter, some basic research findings about student behaviour in distance learning are used to illustrate how research can be applied in the context of an explicit value system regarding student learning to develop a set of strategies to facilitate learner persistence and success.

The Analysis section elaborates on the implications of the changing context within which distance education practices are evolving, and discusses some of the forces that work toward and against development of more responsive systems.

Finally, the last section of this chapter underlines how learner services can play a key role in the strategic positioning of an institution or distance education service. Some specific examples of how learner services can respond to emerging trends in education are identified.

Issues

Integration of Learner Services into the Institutional Culture

The development of comprehensive learner services in distance education is a fairly recent endeavour. Most early distance education schemes were concerned more with access and availability of learning opportunities than with the individual experience of the learner. Consequently, distance education has been typified by high enrolments and high rates of attrition (Keegan, 1983). Student support services for distance learners were first developed as a defensive response to the high percentage of "casualties" produced by the mass education model that once characterized distance education.

Early forms of student support were usually course-content based. The tutor became the human interface between the learner and the course package. Instructional support helped to personalize and humanize an essentially industrial model of education, the main feature of which was the mass production of instructional materials that could be efficiently disseminated to large numbers of students. As open and distance learning systems became a more common way for people to gain access to formal education, concern about learner success grew, along with interest in how it might be promoted.

In Canada, the concern about lack of student persistence was manifested in the development of a wide variety of student support services in distance teaching institutions. These services, described by McInnis-Rankin and Brindley (1986), include orientation and information, admissions and other registry services, advising and counselling, instructional support (tutoring/teaching), and student advocacy. McInnis-Rankin and Brindley discussed the rationale for student support as largely being a method for helping students to cope with the special demands of distance education, and in particular, to help those students who enter distance education with less than adequate skills or preparation.

While these goals for student services are legitimate and necessary, they do not speak to the core values and beliefs that might drive an institution to interact with learners in a particular way. The danger in this is that learner services are simply student retention strategies which have been tacked onto distance education programs in response to concern about high attrition rates, and as such, they can easily be removed in times of fiscal restraint or as priorities within an institution change. In Canada, and elsewhere, when institutions have looked for cost savings, the first and deepest cuts have often been made to learner services (Paul, 1988). All too often, it appears that services such as tutoring, advising, and counselling are not seen as an integral part of the core business in open distance institutions.

In the last 10 years, there has been growing concern with the inadequacy and inappropriateness of the industrial model of distance education (Evans and Nation, 1989; Sewart, 1993; Sweet, 1993; Tait, 1988; Tait, in press). Sweet (1993), in a comprehensive synthesis of literature, discusses the centrality of student support services in making distance learning more responsive to changing environments, and the strong trend toward developmental and constructivist approaches in learning and teaching. Sweet's analysis thoughtfully considers the evidence for a changing view of the learner as more instrumental and active in the learning process, and makes a strong case for changes in the development and delivery of instruction and other learner services to accommodate a constructivist view of learning. However, in this assertion lies a great challenge to distance education institutions to reconsider how they do business.

In most single- and dual-mode distance learning institutions that I have visited or with which I have worked, development of course materials and technology often take precedence over learner support systems in resource allocation. Thompson (1990), in discussing the results of a study indicating that distance learners would like more interaction with instructional staff, notes that, "Many institutions which offer correspondence courses invest substantial resources in the development of the course materials" (p. 63). He cites Moore (1989) in noting that the United Kingdom Open University spends roughly the same amount "on preparation of course materials as on learner support." In fact, in many institutions, the balance is probably tipped more heavily toward course development, particularly where resources are scarce and there is outside pressure to open new programs or increase enrolments. However, within the industrial model of distance education, which tends to treat knowledge as a commodity to be disseminated and learner services as a supplement, this balance of resource allocation is not surprising.

The challenge for distance education services in becoming more responsive to their clientele is to assess priorities continually within the context of a set of principles that clearly articulate beliefs about learners and how the learning process can be facilitated. In the current context where continual change, high expectations, and constantly shifting demands are the norm in the educational system, such defined direction is essential.

Linking Practice to Research

Whether stated or not, underlying every model of learner services is an implicit assumption about the goals of education (sometimes articulated in the mission of an institution or service but not necessarily applied consistently) and how the particular services offered "support" these goals. However, practice is not often explicitly based on theory, and even when it is, systematic evaluation is not always carried out to test and continually refine the rationale for practice. For example, when effectiveness of the services is measured, how is "effectiveness" defined? Does it mean that enrolments have increased by 25 percent? Does it mean that more students can demonstrate mastery of course content? Does it mean that students require less interaction with the institution in their second and third courses because they know how to set up their own support system? Does it mean more graduates are successfully employed? Does it mean that more students are completing courses? The point here, if it is not already abundantly clear, is that the epistemology underlying learner services in distance education is not always well defined or systematically tested (Coldeway, 1986).

Ten years ago, one of the most discussed and researched questions in distance education was why so many students who choose to enrol in this mode of study also choose not to complete their course(s). Attrition research has been fruitful to the extent that it has provided a great deal of information about the complex interplay of factors that lead to student attrition, and certain predictable patterns of student behaviour in distance courses. However, until recently, there has been little discussion about how to use this knowledge the better to understand the learning process and to serve learners by improving the quality of their experience.

There are examples of some specific services that have been designed to respond to an identified learner need (Delehanty, 1986). However, compared with other fields in distance education—for example, instructional design—it does not appear that development of learner services has been approached in any systematic fashion, nor is there evidence of much longitudinal research to evaluate the effectiveness of services in meeting stated goals.

Presumably, learner services are designed and offered to encourage students to persist in their studies, but to what end? What kind of learners is open distance learning trying to produce, and what implications does this have for the types of learner services offered? While it is encouraging that there is now a growing literature base that recognizes the need to reflect more critically on the teaching and learning process in distance education (Evans & Nation, 1989; 1992), most of this writing focusses on the design of learning materials, the use of technologies, and the tutoring or instructional function. Not a great deal of research attention has been given to other types of interactions with learners, such as the provision of information, orientation, advising, counselling, provision of library and administrative services, and the role that these interactions might play in a developmental or constructive model of learning.

The Changing Environment

As has been stated, learner services in distance education were first developed in response to criticism about high attrition rates within an essentially industrial model of education. To a certain extent, the development of tutoring, counselling, library, and other support systems formed part of the defensive stance against accusations that distance open learning is a second-class educational system.

However, the environment within which learner services were first developed has drastically changed, and forces outside distance education institutions are shifting the focus away from learner success back to access and speed of production (King, 1993; Paul, 1993). Distance learning is no longer viewed as an aberration, or an educational method of last resort. In fact, the pendulum has probably now swung too far in the opposite direction. Open distance learning is increasingly seen as the answer to all that is wrong with the current educational system. While practitioners in distance education are moving away from the industrial model of mass education, which was first described by Peters (1971), to take a more learner-centred approach (Sweet, 1993), the government and the private sector often see open distance learning systems as "high tech," inexpensive, and quick methods to provide education and training. However, if there is any message that must continually be given to those who place demands on distance education institutions, it is the complexity of the work. Distance education practitioners face all the same challenges as their campus-based colleagues and more.

There is increasing pressure on those engaged in distance teaching to use new technologies to provide greater access and reduce costs of education, and yet the complexities of choosing and making use of technologies in education are appreciated by few (see Paul, 1993).

Widespread economic changes have sent underemployed and newly unemployed adults looking for opportunities for further education and/or retraining. These learners are attracted to the flexibility that open distance learning offers. However, they present a new challenge. They come with an even wider variety of backgrounds than was the case for adult students a decade ago. Many are educationally disadvantaged, and often, independent learning is entirely unfamiliar to them.

Economic changes have also resulted in reduced funding for education. Distance education institutions are usually chronically short of resources and often work with outmoded information systems, too few staff with too little training, inadequate infrastructure to support operations, and crowded buildings.

The environment is increasingly competitive. Even traditional institutions that once questioned the validity of distance education have recognized the demand for alternative modes of study and have begun to adopt distance delivery methods for some of their courses and programs. Many institutions that have specialized in distance teaching in a wide-open market suddenly find themselves in a position of scrambling to meet enrolment targets to ensure their funding base.

Hence, distance and open learning institutions find themselves under pressure to meet incredibly unrealistic expectations to serve an ever-widening set of needs with scarce resources and little infrastructure in a highly competitive environment. In this context, where finding and responding to new markets and speed of production have become key issues, it is sometimes difficult to focus on promoting learner success. However, if open distance learning is to play a key role in the training and education of society, there is a responsibility to provide more than mere access to mass-produced knowledge. This challenge relates back to the issue of institutional culture, and the importance of having a well-defined and integrated approach to learner services based on clearly articulated guiding values about learners and how the learning process is best facilitated.

Development of a Learner Service Model—An Illustration

A model of learner services that is theory-based and firmly rooted in a clearly articulated set of values facilitates planning and resource allocation, and it acknowledges the importance placed on responsiveness to learners within the institution. It also provides a framework within which to evaluate current services and consider new ones. Of course, the development of a service model does not take place in a vacuum. There are many factors other than an institutional value system and a theoretical rationale that contribute to the choice of a particular range of services and delivery methods within a given institution.

Learner services should take into consideration the unique and changing needs of the students being served and the institutional context, and should be revised as appropriate to accommodate changes in student population, the institution, and the environment. Only in this way can an institution be truly responsive to its clientele. For example, the need to initiate new academic programs may require temporary reallocation of resources from service areas to an academic department. Lack of trained staff may temporarily constrain an institution's ability to offer certain services. Serving corporate clients may entail providing services at the workplace. However, having an articulated conceptual model that starts from the institutional value system and a strong theory base (e.g., why students persist or drop out; what contributes to independent learning and student empowerment) will provide some stability in priority setting and accommodating needed changes in a planned way.

The remainder of this section illustrates how values and research findings can be brought together to develop a service model based upon a testable epistemology. Values and beliefs determine how research findings are interpreted in order to reach conclusions about student needs, and in turn, how hypotheses are developed regarding required services.

The values and principles upon which the rationale for learner services presented in this chapter are based are presented below. They represent a constructivist and learner-centred approach to education. Although it is argued herein that this approach facilitates institutional responsiveness to its clientele, it is recognized that the model presented may not be appropriate for all contexts. For this reason, it is important to make explicit the specific values on which it is based.

• Education is a continuous, lifelong process.

• Most people can succeed in education, given the opportunity and the support to do so.

• The goal of formal learning systems is to assist individuals to become both independent and collaborative learners who can increasingly take responsibility for what they learn and how they learn.

• The teaching-learning process is interactive, not one-way, and facilitates change and self-action.

• Accessibility means going beyond merely providing opportunities.

Inherent in the commitment to open access is the following:

• an openness to different ways of learning and teaching to suit different needs and situations, and

• a responsibility to provide services for learners that give them the best opportunity for success.

The brevity of this chapter precludes a more comprehensive consideration of the rich variety of research findings regarding learners in distance education. The following are some basic conclusions about distance education student characteristics and behaviours that have been confirmed by a variety of studies and which are directly relevant to the development of learner services.

• Students' personal situations alone cannot account for attrition. Persisters experience just as potentially disruptive life events (a death in the family, a job change, an illness, a geographical move) as those who drop out. A decision to drop out usually involves a complex interplay of factors, one of which is support received from the institution (Brindley, 1987; Sweet, 1986).

• Students are individuals who come to their studies with a variety of personal characteristics that contribute to their behaviour in courses and to some extent determine their support needs. These include their abilities, learning styles, gender, culture, academic preparedness, personal support systems, and expectations (Coldeway, 1986; Powell, Conway, & Ross, 1990).

• Some students complete a course no matter what the circumstances (no support, administrative mistakes, long
delays), and some students drop out no matter what the circumstances (good support services, well-designed courses,
fast turnaround times). There is probably not much an institution can do to change these behaviours. The majority of
students fall between these two extremes, and it is for this
group that support services may make a difference (Powell,
Conway, & Ross, 1990).

• Students often enter distance education programs because
they perceive them to be an easier way to get credentials.
Many are shocked at the difficulty of studying independently.
This is probably related to the way in which the unique features of distance education—accessibility, flexibility, and
independence for the learner—are emphasized in promotion
and marketing, to the exclusion of the harsher realities.
(Brindley, 1987; Pandey in Scriven, Lundin, & Ryan, 1992).

• When students drop out, they usually do so early on, either
never starting or doing very little in their course before disap-
pearing (Coldeway & Spencer, 1980; Holmberg, 1989;
Rekkedal, 1982; Shale, 1982).

• Students who complete a first assignment are much more
likely to complete the whole course, and students who complete one course successfully are much more likely to be successful in a subsequent course (Coldeway, 1986).

• Students often enter distance learning programs, particularly if there is an open admissions policy, with inadequate levels of preparedness. They not only have insufficient knowledge of and a lack of skills to cope with the special rigours
and requirements of independent study, but they have also
not assessed their own needs, educational goals, academic
preparedness, learning style, or personal support systems
(Powell, Conway, & Ross, 1990).

• Students begin their studies with expectations that relate to
their past experiences—if they have had negative experiences

with education in the past (and many of them have), they expect the same from this experience. Powell, Conway, and Ross (1990) concluded that expectations based on past experience of education were more important than past level of education achieved.

• When students drop out of a distance education course or program, they usually blame themselves rather than the institution or circumstances. Unlike their campus-based counterparts, they usually have no one with whom to check their perceptions (Paul, 1986).

• Distance students are often isolated, not necessarily geographically, but as individual learners. Often they know no other students, and their friends, family, and employers may not be very understanding or sympathetic about the challenges they face with their studies. This is particularly the case for women (Kirkup & von Prummer, 1990).

Within the context of the values statements presented earlier, conclusions that can been drawn about learner needs from these research findings might assume that the general goals of learner services are as follows: (1) development of independent learners; (2) student empowerment; (3) personalization of the learning system; (4) democratization of the system; (5) early engagement of students and facilitation of connectedness.

These goals can be expanded upon, taking into consideration what is known about student behaviour, and used to guide the development of support services for distance learners. Examples of services that can be developed to contribute to each goal are provided below. Although the term "institution" is used throughout, these can be applied in any private or public organizations using distance education.

Development of Independent Learners

Make the development of independent learners an explicit institutional goal so that it becomes part of all operations and is used as one measure of success. An independent learner is defined here as someone who takes responsibility for his or her own learning and is instrumental and active in the learning process. This is probably the most challenging initiative because it is at the heart of what an institution is about—the way in which it teaches and interacts with learners. If an institution is going to embrace this principle, it will have to build an institutional climate and culture where it is the norm to build strategies for developing independent learners into all academic programs and services. For this reason, it may require the following:

• A review of the institutional mission statement, strategic plan, and departmental operational plans to ensure that there is a consistent rationale for activities.

• A review of existing, or the development of new, models of learner services to articulate clearly the role of services (and the role of such staff as tutors, counsellors, telephone receptionists, and librarians) and how each contributes to the encouragement of independent learning. For example, library services can promote the development of library research skills, and career counselling can teach career development skills.

Student Empowerment

Empower students so that instead of quietly going away they can actively participate in their education and communicate with the institution about how to do a better job to serve them.

• Develop information and orientation programs that ensure prospective students have the information they need in order to make decisions about enrolment and course choices. This process includes evaluating themselves as well as the institution. Students need access to services that enable them to gauge not only traditional academic readiness (e.g., mathematics, reading, and writing) but also their readiness as it pertains to distance study—time available for studying, availability of personal support systems, and so on.

• Set minimum service and teaching standards that define what every student can expect, and publicize these. At the

Open University in the United Kingdom, every student will soon receive a students' charter of rights upon enrolment. (See The Open University Student Charter, A Draft Proposal for Consultation [1994].) Other institutions are following the UKOU's lead.

• Build meaningfulness into course design by recognizing the relevance of students' experiences and ideas.

• Experiment with learning contracts (in which curriculum and assessment methods are negotiated with students). Empire State College provides some good models to follow.

• Emphasize the process as well as the content of learning (Thorpe, 1994).

• Facilitate activities where students can share their experiences with one another and challenge and validate each others' ideas and opinions.

Personalization of the Learning System

Personalize the system so that it does not isolate students. Independence should not translate as isolation.

• Have someone whom students can call when they have administrative difficulties or when they need information; do not make it difficult for students to make contact with the institution.

• Review policies and regulations regularly to ensure that they make sense, and be prepared to make exceptions to rules to accommodate the complicated lives of adult students. Consult with students and with staff who have regular contact with students (O'Rourke, 1993).

• Recognize the effect on student motivation of inconsistencies in service, slow turnaround times, and administrative red tape and mistakes; implement service standards that can be met at least 95 percent of the time.

• Assign a study partner to new students; publish a student directory.

• Send out introductory messages from tutors with a photograph, and/or audio- or videocassettes.

Democratization of the System

Democratize the system so that it not only encourages people of various backgrounds to participate but as much as possible provides everyone with an equal chance of success regardless of learning style, gender, academic preparedness, or other characteristics. Do not design courses and services that assume that everyone has the same needs and abilities.

• Help students to assess their needs. Self-assessment materials for learning styles, level of study skills, writing, mathematics, and reading have been developed for use with distance learners. (Athabasca University has some good sample materials.)

• Offer opportunities for students to inform themselves, make better decisions, and improve their skills. Strive to offer (or provide access through information and referral) the same support systems and opportunities that campus-based students usually have: career, personal, and academic counselling; library services and training; prior-learning assessment; interest and ability testing; financial aid; and services for students with disabilities and other special needs. All these services are intended to help students succeed academically; context and resource levels will determine which are most necessary and viable.

• Publicize all services well so that students can gain access to them easily.

• Continually evaluate services to ensure that resources are being used where they are most needed by students.

Early Engagement and Connectedness

Engage students early on and facilitate connectedness with the institution, with other students, with their families, and with others who can support them in their studies. View the need and desire for interaction not as a deficit but rather as part of a positive and assertive approach to learning.

- Invest in services that have an impact on prospective and beginning students.

- Help prospective students to make informed decisions about their education. For example, maintain a good information and referral system so that they can find out about choices available to them.

- Ensure that students receive an orientation that informs them about the special challenges of independent learning and provides them with strategies for success.

- Ensure that students know whom to contact for help.

- Build early contact with the tutor into course design so that students speak to someone within the first two to three weeks of enrolment. Train tutors; research shows that learners' impressions of the first contact are important to their persistence (Brindley, 1987; Burge, Howard, & Ironside, 1991).

- Use a variety of methods to facilitate connectedness: newsletters, communication through technology (such as computer- and audioconferencing), self-help materials about how to start and use a study group, or how to engage the help of family. The institution cannot provide everything, but it can facilitate connectedness with other support systems, especially other students.

The intention of this section has been to give concrete illustrations of how services can be developed in a systematic and integrated way based on values and research findings. The particular value system, and other variables that determine the choice of learner services to be offered, will be determined by context. A workplace training service may make some different choices than a distance teaching university. However, if distance education practitioners wish to be responsive to their clientele, a consistent and purposeful approach to learner services will obviously be more effective than a piecemeal system that changes each year based primarily on economic considerations. In tough economic times, it is all too easy to pay less attention to the more complex aspects of the intellectual, emotional, and self-management processes in learning.

Analysis

Many factors are transforming open distance education: a better-developed research and theoretical base, technological innovations, vast economic changes on a global scale, and increased pressure for access to educational opportunities. It is encouraging that the tone of the literature of open distance learning has changed from a defensive stance to one that reflects the confidence and pride of practitioners—not just in opening access to educational opportunities, but in the quality of educational experience that is being provided. In great part, this confidence comes from better knowledge of the field. More is known about learner characteristics and behaviour, and how to promote learning, including quality in course design and production, use of technologies to facilitate interaction, and the provision of effective services.

However, it is important to note that at the same time that open distance learning is being "adopted as a mainstream method of education and training" (Tait, in press), and progress is being made toward critically analyzing practice and developing better theoretical frameworks, there are other, possibly negative forces affecting developments in open and distance learning in the public and private sectors. The factor that appears to have had the most impact on the development of learner services in open distance learning is the economic recession and the subsequent reduction in funding that every educational institution in Canada and elsewhere has had to face in the past few years.

Most educational institutions in Canada have had to make reductions in all areas of operation; however, there is concern that learner services have taken the brunt of the cost-cutting measures (Paul, 1988; Brindley & Fage, 1992). Some examples of the cuts to service made by many distance education institutions are the replacement of tenured instructional staff with less qualified contract tutors, the severe reduction or elimination of services such as counselling, the retrenchment of staff development, and reductions in funding for applied research and evaluation of practice.

Such decisions, while they may be necessary in some circumstances, appear to fly in the face of developing a more responsive learner-centred model of practice. There is a danger that in meeting the demand, particularly from governments, to reduce costs while responding to the need for access and economies of scale in educating and training the workforce, open distance learning could be turned away from its goals of developing independent, self-responsible learners and return to a more industrial model of education.

There are encouraging indications that this will not happen in any sweeping way: the shifts and developments in practice are apparent from the ways in which distance education is being conceptualized in the recent literature. There is a movement away from a descriptive approach that focusses on the similarities and differences between open distance learning and campus-based learning, to a more analytical approach that attempts to define and question the epistemologies upon which practice is based. This is partly due to the availability of a greater body of research, and the paradigm shift from an expository teaching model to a more experiential, constructivist model. With regard to learner services, this latter shift is reflected in a move from a defensive, piecemeal approach that responds to learner deficits to a more proactive and holistic approach that attends to the individual learner's experience and how it can be enhanced.

These new ways of envisioning distance education practice can provide an advantage in an environment that demands flexibility and speed of response. In particular, a flexible and responsible learner services system can play a key role in keeping an institution or program competitive. Sewart (1993) discusses the marketplace advantages of the move from viewing distance learning as an industrial endeavour to a service endeavour, and stresses the role of learner support in making this shift. However, the danger is that under pressure, old paradigms will prevail. Lentell (1994) argues, based on her experience in the U.K. Open University, that tutoring, rather than being seen as part of a learner-focussed model, can become part of an industrial production-line approach by institutions eager to "process" as many students as possible and gain the financial benefits of economy of scale:

Indeed teaching is frequently minimised to marking—since the materials are deemed to stand alone, and students to be, if not independent, striving to become independent. In this model, students need a welter of educational counselling services—educational guidance, career guidance, study skills help, exam guidance and so forth—which are offered them as generic, not course related services ... . The model of 'teaching' has radically changed. (p. 2)

The challenge for open distance learning is to find ways to become more responsive to changes, particularly changes in market demands, while staying congruent with a strong value system that places the focus on providing quality learning experiences. Using their specialized knowledge base regarding learning and learning systems, distance education institutions and agencies can become more competitive in the educational marketplace. A number of open distance learning institutions are moving from more inflexible models of print-based, packaged learning to more responsive, entrepreneurial models that provide rapid and effective response to learner needs. Learner services can play a key role in making this move.

Conclusions

Learner services are defined by context. Whether services are offered at a distance or face-to-face on a traditional campus, at a technical college or a university, for children or adults, they exist to "support the academic mission of the school" (Lyons, 1990, p. 25). However, interpreted in its broadest sense, this purpose opens the door to a wide variety of possibilities for learner services, particularly in looking at the role that services can play in helping an institution or agency to transform its academic mission in becoming more responsive to its learners and its changing environment.

Institutions that want to become more competitive in the educational marketplace must reposition themselves to be service oriented and consumer driven. In distance education, this means giving up old ways of conceptualizing practice as dissemination of knowledge. Although many institutions have worked toward the goal of higher completion rates, it is probably fair to say that most institutions engaged in distance teaching are still losing more students than they would like. For too many years, learners have complained about such problems as long delays waiting for packages, bureaucratic red tape which causes confusion and frustration, and difficulties in receiving service that might give them access to appropriate learning opportunities (Canadian Association for Distance Education, 1993).

Individual learners and other clients who choose open distance learning as a mode of study should be able to do so because it is an attractive option that offers a high-quality educational experience. Strong arguments can and have been made that the provision of the same or better services for distance students as campus-based students is unrealistic because of the cost factor. However, embedded in these arguments is an assumption that these services are "add-ons" which distance learners either do not deserve or can do without. In a model where responsiveness to learners is a central value, these are not add-ons any more than they are for campus-based students—they are central to the business of the institution.

An institution that has the ability to respond quickly and effectively to its clientele will have the edge in what has become a very competitive market. No matter how perfectly a course package is prepared, most learners are not interested in waiting a long time to receive it unless they have no alternative. Most clients expect to receive quick response to their requests and to engage in interaction with the institution that will facilitate their success. An institution with a well-developed, flexible model of learner services will be in the best position to respond to these needs.

Following are some examples of institutions and agencies using learner services to respond effectively to their changing clientele:

• Paced learning in the workplace. Learner services such as on-site registration, orientation, academic advising, and tutoring can make open distance learning a very attractive staff development option for corporate clients.

• Custom-designed services for groups. Open distance learning institutions can respond to the needs of special groups such as First Nations people by offering courses in Native-friendly environments such as the local band council office. A custom-designed, culturally sensitive service package might include on-site academic preparation assessment, orientation and study skills help, academic advising and counselling, and tutoring.

• Academic preparation assessment for new clientele. Economic restructuring has resulted in a demand for learning opportunities for a broad variety of new clientele, many of whom have been employed for many years in work areas that no longer exist. They can be helped by assessing their readiness for study and diagnosing possible learning difficulties (which may have driven them into the job market before they completed their secondary education). Open systems, because they have been serving adult clientele for many years, should be strategically positioned to serve this group.

• Use of technology to connect learners to learning resources. New technologies allow librarians to focus on developing access to materials worldwide, interpreting the information, and finding ways to navigate through the networks, rather than buying materials for their own library. Open distance learning appears to be taking advantage of these opportunities more quickly than campus-based institutions, and should be able to offer learners better access to materials. In 1993, the Canadian Library Association issued formal guidelines for the provision of distance learning services, and the distance education literature includes more articles than ever before on library services.

These are just a few examples of the ways in which institutions can provide quick and effective responses to learner needs.
The focus for most competitive businesses has shifted from products to service. For example, the Total Quality Management movement which has had a sweeping effect on business across North America represents an attempt by some companies to implement long-term fundamental change toward a customer-driven approach to business. Many institutions and agencies produce course packages, but few are poised to serve learners as well as those institutions who have already struggled for years with the complexities of open distance learning. If they can resist the pressure to return to an industrial model of operation, and continue to work toward the goal of developing independent learners by offering responsive and innovative learning opportunities, open distance learning institutions will be well positioned to meet the challenges of the new marketplace.

Endnotes

1.   The author wishes to thank Elizabeth Burge and Ross Paul for their thoughtful commentary on the ideas presented in this chapter.

References

Brindley, J.E. (1987). *Attrition and completion in distance education: The student's perspective.* Unpublished master's thesis, University of British Columbia, Vancouver. (ERIC Document Reproduction Service No. ED 322 887.)

Brindley, J.E., & Fage, J. (1992). Counselling in open learning: Two institutions face the future. *Open Learning, 7,* 12–19.

Burge, E.J., Howard, J.L., & Ironside, D.J. (1991). *Mediation in distance learning: An investigation of the role of tutoring.* Research report. Toronto: Ontario Institute for Studies in Education.

Canadian Association for Distance Education. (1993). *The student connection: Exploring distance education from the student's perspective* (Video). Toronto: TVOntario.

Coldeway, D.O. (1986). Learner characteristics and success. In I. Mugridge & D. Kaufman (Eds.), *Distance education in Canada* (pp. 81–93). London: Croom-Helm.

Coldeway, D., & Spencer, R. (1980). *The measurement of attrition and completion in distance learning courses.* REDEAL Technical Report No. 8. Edmonton: Athabasca University. (ERIC Document Reproduction Service No. ED 256 770.)

Delehanty, R. (1986). *Multimodal evaluation of preventive orientation programs for adults entering a distance university.* Unpublished doctoral dissertation, University of Alberta, Edmonton.

Evans, T., & Nation, D. (Eds.). (1989). *Critical reflections on distance education.* Deakin Studies in Education Series: 2. London: The Falmer Press.

Evans, T., & Nation, D. (1992). Theorising open and distance education. *Open Learning, 6*(2), 3–13.

Holmberg, B. (1989). *Theory and practice of distance education.* London: Routledge.

Keegan, D.J. (1983). On defining distance education. In D. Sewart, D. Keegan, & B. Holmberg (Eds.), *Distance education: International perspectives* (pp. 6–33). London: Croom Helm.

King, B. (1993). Open learning in Australia: Government intervention. *Open Learning, 8*(3), 13–25.

Kirkup, G., & von Prummer, C. (1990). Support and connectedness: The needs of women distance education students. *Journal of Distance Education, 5*(2), 9–31.

Lentell, H. (1994). *Why is it so hard to hear the tutor in distance education?* Paper presented at Educational and Cultural Barriers to Open Distance Learning Conference, Sheffield, U.K.

Lyons, J.W. (1990). Examining the validity of basic assumptions and beliefs. In M.J. Barr, M.L. Upcraft, & Associates (Eds.), *New futures for student affairs* (pp. 22–40). San Francisco: Jossey-Bass.

McInnis-Rankin, E., & Brindley, J.E. (1986). In I. Mugridge & D. Kaufman (Eds.), *Distance education in Canada* (pp. 60–80). London: Croom-Helm.

O'Rourke, J. (1993). Quality in the eye of the beholder? Strategies for self-assessment of quality in distance education. In A. Tait (Ed.), *Proceedings of the International Conference on Quality Assurance in Open and Distance Learning: European and International Perspectives* (pp. 215–224). Cambridge, U.K.: Open University.

Paul, R.H. (1986). Access to failure? The challenge of open education at Athabasca University. *Catalyst, XVI*(2), 18–22.

Paul, R.H. (1988). If student services are so important, then why are we cutting them back? In D. Sewart & J. Daniel (Eds.), *Developing distance education* (pp. 50–56). Proceedings of the 14th World Conference at Oslo, Norway. Oslo: International Council for Distance Education.

Paul, R.H. (1993). Government intervention in open learning: A Canadian perspective in response to Bruce King. *Open Learning, 8*(3), 57–58.

Peters, O. (1971). Theoretical aspects of correspondence instruction. In O. MacKenzie & E.L. Christensen (Eds.), *The changing world of correspondence study* (pp. 223–228) University Park: Pennsylvania State University Press.

Peters, O. (1983). Distance teaching and industrial production: A comparative interpretation in outline. In D. Sewart, D. Keegan, & B. Holmberg (Eds.), *Distance education: International perspectives* (pp. 95–113). London: Croom Helm.

Powell, R., Conway, C., & Ross, L. (1990). Effects of learner characteristics on student success. *Journal of Distance Education, 5*(1), 5–19.

Rekkedal, T. (1982) The drop-out problem and what to do about it. In J. Daniel, M. Stroud, & J. Thompson (Eds.), *Learning at a distance: A world perspective* (pp. 118–122). Edmonton: Athabasca University.

Sewart, D. (1993). Student support systems in distance education. In B. Scriven, R. Lundin, & Y. Ryan (Eds.), *Distance education for the 21st century* (pp. 120–129). Proceedings of the 16th World Conference at Nonthaburi, Thailand. Brisbane: International Council for Distance Education and Queensland University of Technology.

Scriven, B., Lundin, R., & Ryan, Y. (Eds.).(1993). *Distance education for the 21st century.* Proceedings of the 16th World Conference at Nonthaburi, Thailand. Brisbane: International Council for Distance Education and Queensland University of Technology.

Shale, D. (1982). Attrition: A case study. In J. Daniel, M. Stroud, & J. Thompson (Eds.), *Learning at a distance: A world perspective* (pp. 113–117). Edmonton: Athabasca University.

Sweet, R. (1986). Student dropout in distance education: An application of Tinto's model. *Distance Education, 7*(2), 201–213.

Sweet, R. (Ed.). (1993). Perspectives on distance education—Student support services: Toward more responsive systems. *Report of a Symposium on Student Support Services in Distance Education, Delhi.* Vancouver: The Commonwealth of Learning.

Tait, A. (1988). Democracy in distance education and the role of tutorial and counselling services. *Journal of Distance Education, 3*(1), 95–99.

Tait, A. (in press). The end of innocence: Critical approaches to open and distance learning. *Open Learning.*

The Open University Student Charter. (1994). A Draft Proposal for Consultation, The United Kingdom Open University, Milton Keynes.

Thompson, G. (1990). How can correspondence-based distance education be improved? A survey of attitudes of students who are not well disposed toward correspondence study. *Journal of Distance Education, 5*(1), 53–65.

Thorpe, M. (1994). Modelling the learning process: A UKOU undergraduate course in adult studies at a distance. In R. Coreau, J. Dawson, & B. Signaty (Eds.), *Proceedings of the 13th Annual Conference of the Canadian Association for the Study of Adult Education* (pp. 412–417). Vancouver: Simon Fraser University.

CHAPTER 7

Virtual Realities or Fantasies? Technology and the Future of Distance Education

Ross H. Paul

There is growing criticism of our universities and colleges: pressures for universal higher education mount, while fiscal realities require more accountability and fewer dollars invested in public education. Tremendous strides in communications technologies have combined with the pressures for accountability to put technology in the forefront of the educational debate. This chapter starts with the thesis that long-term practitioners of distance education should have much to offer to this debate as distinctions between conventional and distance education are blurred. However, evidence suggests that university distance education as a field has not progressed substantively over the past 15 years in the application of new technologies to education.

Further analysis of the nature of technology, and especially its institutionalization into formal organizations, suggests that the matter is far more complex than is often portrayed. Based on this analysis, some suggestions are made as to the most likely profitable paths for distance education practitioners to follow over the next few years. It should be noted that, reflecting the author's experience, the context is limited to the university sector. It is not intended to suggest that this analysis is equally appropriate to schools, health organizations, or workplace training.

Issues

Criticisms of Traditional Institutions of Higher Education

We are entering a period of major change in higher education around the world. Just as earlier 20th century reforms changed elementary and then secondary schooling from the domain of the elite to a democratic right for all, universal higher education is increasingly touted as an essential, in terms both idealistic (notions of equality and the right to self-fulfillment) and practical (as an economic necessity in the global society). Hence, economist David Wolfe (1990b, p. 107) wonders whether Canada has the capacity to cope with the demands that will be placed upon its educational system to deal with the competitive pressures of the current technological revolution, a question that has parallel interests for politicians and business leaders in every modern country.

Especially in the west, this democratization of higher learning is being espoused at a time when it is broadly recognized that we cannot afford current levels of investment in government services, and that these reforms will have to be achieved with fewer resources and in a climate of greater accountability to the taxpayer. However overwhelming the challenge, there is confidence, at least in some quarters, that it can be met through the development and application of one of the most tangible outcomes of increased investment in education—new technology.

New Technology as Panacea—Toward an Idealized University

The breathtaking rate of technological change in our society is increasingly confronting our traditional institutions and the ways they are organized and managed. The introduction of new technology can be both exciting and alienating. It may create or destroy jobs, and it can both enhance the quality of our lives and seriously undermine it. It poses challenges for all aspects of our society, including the ways in which we teach and learn.

The traditional university sector is demonstrating more and more interest in communication technologies and their application to teaching, learning, and administration. The challenge for the mainstream, as posed, for example, by Heterick (1994, p.1), reads as if it had been written by proponents of an open university:

The enterprising college or university must understand that its mission is not so much to teach as it is to create a culture—driven by technology—in which students, faculty and staff are continuously learning.

Given the need to cope with huge student numbers in the classroom and the capacity of modern technology to focus attention on the learner, those in conventional institutions should have much to learn from the experiences of distance education. It is not difficult to imagine conventional and distance organizations converging fairly rapidly toward what one might term an "idealized" university.

In the idealized university, lifelong learners could use various technologies to interact with the institution in their own time and place and according to their self-identified learning needs. In this perfect world of independent learners and a receptive institution, the only goal would be to maximize the learning potential of each student in the eternal quest for truth and competence.

Such an institution would render irrelevant distinctions between "conventional" and "distance" education. All education involves some distance between the learner and the materials and teachers. A student sitting in a large lecture hall may have no more personal contact with a professor than one sitting at home watching the same lecture on television. An isolated student discussing a module with a telephone tutor may have more personal contact with an instructor than does a student on a crowded university campus who can never get an appointment with his or her supervisor.

The Potential Contribution of Distance Education

To the extent that this vision is increasingly shared by the many proponents of the need for major changes in higher education, the future of distance education should be very promising indeed!

After all, the field appears to respond to many of the most prevalent current criticisms of traditional, classroom-based learning.

• Traditional institutions[1] have been criticized for focussing on teaching rather than learning, often at the expense of the latter. Distance education has always claimed more of a "learner" focus.

• Conventional universities are geared primarily to serving younger full-time students, whereas an emphasis on lifelong learning suggests an increasing interest in older, part-time learners, the primary target group for most distance-based programs.

• Conventional institutions have usually served a privileged elite, while the evidence is strong that universal access to higher education is central to a country's economic success. Distance education has done much to democratize higher education by providing access to previously underserved groups (women, workers, Aboriginals).

• Universities have traditionally been teacher-centred rather than learner-centred, with an emphasis on knowledge dissemination through one-way lectures and "chalk-and-talk" methods. Perhaps because teaching is less readily taken for granted when students are separated overtly by time and/or distance from the instructor, the emphasis in distance education programs has been more on the learner and on learning.

• Universities have been broadly criticized for sacrificing teaching in favour of research, whereas the primary focus in most distance education institutions has been on learning processes.

• Universities no longer have a monopoly on higher education, and there are strong public pressures for them to link much more effectively with businesses, government, and other agencies. Because of its relative flexibility and adaptability, distance education lends itself more readily to collaborative ventures with other institutions and agencies.

• Strong traditions of autonomy have meant that most university teaching has taken place behind closed doors with little direct accountability on the part of faculty. Conversely, distance education institutions have used course teams and open publication of course materials, which have underlined such accountabilities.

• One of the advantages of classroom teaching has supposedly been the interpersonal contact between teacher and student. This has increasingly been lost as class sizes have grown rapidly, yet there has been little adaptation to the "distance" this introduces. At least in distance education the distance is overt, perhaps necessitating more comprehensive efforts to compensate for it.

These arguments appear to have had some impact, as there is evidence in the 1990s of a new and strong interest in distance education on traditional university campuses. When the International Council for Correspondence Education changed its name to the International Council for Distance Education (ICDE) in Vancouver in 1982, distance education was the domain of a select few, including a handful of institutions in Canada. Less than 15 years later, every university in Canada is involved in some form of distance education, consortia are springing up everywhere, and there is considerable excitement about new technologies and new ways of delivering education at a distance. Almost every provincial government's ministry of education has conducted or is conducting inquiries into open learning and distance education. Indeed, some of the most zealous proponents of distance education are those who have only recently learned of its existence (and therein lies one of the central problems, explored later in this chapter).

Whatever one's beliefs about the future of distance education, there is little doubt that the university of the future must and will be much more responsive to its potential constituents than the traditional ivory tower on the hill has been. The need for change is being driven by recognition of the economic importance of universal higher education, pressures for accountability arising from the realization that taxpayers can no longer afford the educational and social services currently provided, and growing acceptance of the notion of lifelong learning, that we can no longer learn "once" during youthful student days and be well served by that formal education for the rest of our lives.

In other words, in the educational institution of the future, all learners will be lifelong learners, they will have increasing control over what they learn, and they will have access to knowledge and skill development via a wide-ranging host of technologies. Some formal learning will take place in learning centres or on campuses, and other learning will take place at home or in the workplace. The emphasis will increasingly be on learning how to learn, the ultimately desirable product being independent learners who take full responsibility for their learning needs and know how to go about fulfilling them.

All of this can be construed to suggest that experienced practitioners of distance education should be in the forefront of educational change. They have been forced to wrestle overtly with problems of learner distance that have largely been ignored in traditional classrooms (even though it can be argued that most distance between student and teacher is intrinsic rather than extrinsic). If anyone has solutions for the future, it must be the distance educators—it would seem that their time has come!

This is an interesting theoretical proposition, but does it stand up to scrutiny of the actual development of distance education over the past 15 years? We need more than interesting theories to determine to what extent distance education will be a central determinant of the university of the future. Perhaps the best indicator for the future is the extent to which distance education is currently living up to the expectations held for it by its proponents, especially in the application of new technologies to education and training.

Illustrations

How Distance Education Has Fallen Short of Expectations

Unfortunately, there is little evidence to date to suggest that university-based distance education will provide strong leadership in the adaptation of new technologies to the learning needs of the

future. The significant educational technology that established
the Open University in the United Kingdom and so many of its
imitators around the world was not characterized by innovative
use of "high tech" but through a systematic approach to learning.
While educational television was supposed to be central to the
concept of the new "University of the Air," it quickly became a
supplement to well-produced printed course materials. The significant innovation was the systematic approach to instructional
development, using teams of faculty, editors, and designers to
produce competency-based learning materials, supplemented by
various modes of academic and personal support via tutors,
counsellors, and regional centres. While there has been effective
subsequent criticism of some of the rigidities in the application of
such an approach (Harris, 1987; Evans & Nation, 1989), the
instructional design model has nevertheless been the central feature of distance education, to the point that it has become a new
orthodoxy with its own built-in resistance to change.

If there have been significant recent breakthroughs in the
application of technology to distance learning, they are not evident in the literature. A useful barometer is the regular world
congress of ICDE which has been held in 1982 (Vancouver), 1985
(Melbourne), 1988 (Oslo), 1990 (Caracas), and 1992 (Bangkok)
and its associated conference publication. If the latter is repre-
sentative of the field, there has not been much progress in the
quality and sophistication of the treatment of educational technology, at least within university distance education, over the
past decade or so.

While much is written about technology in distance education, there is little evidence of significant breakthroughs, even in
comparison to development on traditional university campuses.
For example, in the 1992 ICDE conference publication (Scriven,
Lundin, & Ryan, 1992), over one-third of all submissions (28 out
of 77 articles) are contained in the section on "Applications of
Technology." Of these, 11 concern at least a cursory evaluation of
the effectiveness of a particular technology, 10 are primarily
descriptive, four are micro case studies, two discuss the innovative use of simple technologies, and only one might be described
as experimental.

Even though almost all the authors come from North
America, Europe, or Australia, most of the technologies covered

are at the low end of any scale of sophistication, including articles on satellite television (4), audioconferencing (2), videotapes (1), television (1), and mixing two or more of these (8). In the "middle" range are writings on computer conferencing (3), electronic classrooms (2), or a mix of these (1). While there are a few articles at the high end, discussing virtual reality (1), videoconferencing (1), computer-based simulations (1), expert systems (1), and a mix of these (2), they are primarily theoretical rather than reflective of actual experience.

Perhaps most telling is that less than half of the articles can be seen to have adopted a critical perspective, with no fewer than a dozen being primarily advocacy papers for a particular technology or approach. Without a critical perspective and without more rigour in experimental design, it is difficult to see how these various micro studies will contribute to an overall conceptualization of an enhanced educational technology for distance learning.

Problems with the Idealized Approach

There is another concept of distance education, most prevalent in the United States, which runs somewhat counter to the above and bears little resemblance to the instructional design model that has dominated European and British Commonwealth literature in the field over the past 15 years.

When participating as a keynote speaker at the annual distance education conference at the University of Wisconsin at Madison several years ago, I was struck by how differently the (almost exclusively) American delegates envisioned distance education from those more influenced by the British/European traditions cited above. For the Americans, distance education was almost synonymous with new technologies and their applications to learning—using computers, interactive video, and even virtual reality. Compared to their European counterparts, they were less interested in course design or student support, and were somewhat indifferent to the linguistic debates about the relative meanings of open learning and distance education, which received considerable attention at that time in *Open Learning,* the journal of the Open University in Britain.

In fact, I focussed my closing keynote speech on my concern that most of the delegates seemed to have a naive, idealized view of educational technology, being more interested in the hardware than in the actual learning experiences it was supposed to engender. This was illustrated by my observation that, when a rather mundane interactive video session was scheduled opposite a presentation of an award-winning paper on drop-outs in distance education, the former outdrew the latter by about 50 to one!

Again, on a recent quality tour of top American universities, I was struck by the tremendous excitement and faith placed in multimedia classrooms and fancy video equipment by the schools of engineering and business at such leading institutions as University of Wisconsin and Penn State. One dean of engineering even boasted about the tremendous innovation that would result from all the opportunities his faculty had to play with technological "toys"!

The latter approach may be contrasted with the prevailing wisdom in distance education over the past 25 years, which has been that one must start with the educational problem and thence determine which technologies are most appropriate to assist students in overcoming their barriers to learning. Only in this way, it has been argued, can one ensure that the technology truly serves the needs of the learner and hence, that the investment in it is justifiable.

However, over and against this rational approach to educational decision making is the recognition that breakthroughs may often come, not from systematic planning, but from less structured, more creative approaches. Given the resources to afford it and the willingness to take the appropriate risks, providing creative people with access to new technology may well result in breakthroughs that could not otherwise be achieved. This may be particularly the case with younger teachers and students brought up with computer and video games, whose learning patterns may be quite different from those of previous generations.

In summary, the prevailing modes of university distance education over the past 25 years have been developed according to a fairly rigorous instructional systems design model, one that has served new classes of learners extremely well. However, the very rigour of these systems has created a new orthodoxy, one that may not be well suited to the demands for new breakthroughs in educational technology. Over and against this is a newer, more entrepreneurial corporate model, one more enamoured with technological hardware and software. Will this newer notion of distance education prevail? Further analysis about the nature of technology and its place in institutions dedicated to distance education is required before we can consider this question further.

Analysis

The Nature and Management of Technology in Organizations

As technology plays an increasingly important role in our lives, there is increasing recognition that it is not simply a neutral resource available for whatever purposes, good or bad, we choose for it. Indeed, those interested in the philosophy of technology, after Heidegger, Dewey, Marcuse, and others, increasingly recognize that technologies have cultures (Ihde, 1993, p. 117) and politics (Winner, cited in Ihde, 1993, p. 117), and that managing them makes new kinds of demands on our organizations.

To control technologies ... is much more like controlling a political system or a culture then [sic] controlling a simple instrument or tool ... particularly in a contemporary high technology setting. (Ihde, 1993, p. 117)

Describing new technology as "a new type of culture system that restructures the entire social world as an object of control," Feenberg (1991, p. 7) draws a parallel with the fast-food industry. Not only has the latter changed the way food is prepared and served, but it has also had serious implications for how families interact (or don't interact). Similarly, technology can have unintended consequences for those who attempt to apply it to life's problems and challenges. We have already learned this lesson through the dramatically unintended consequences of attempting to use technology to harness or improve upon nature (as with the tragedies at Chernobyl and Bhopal). There is a need to recognize that, as for nature itself, how technology is managed is a critical variable in its successful application. On a less dramatic level, many organizations, including entrepreneurial businesses and almost every educational institution, are faced with many dilemmas in their efforts to select and integrate the most appropriate and cost-effective technologies.

One dilemma faced by any institution, especially a smaller one where resources are more limited, is deciding how—and how much—to invest in new technologies. Such decisions are crucial, and yet our ability to predict which technologies will be of the "breakthrough" variety has been extremely limited. Heterick (1994, p. 1) notes that we always seem to overestimate the short-term and to underestimate the long-term potential of a given new technology (a theme to which we will return later in this chapter when discussing the experience of distance learning institutions).

Noted philosopher of technology, Don Ihde (1993, p. 116) reminds us that new technologies frequently end up having applications that were not even envisioned at the moment of their invention, the prototype telephone having originally been designed for the hearing impaired and the typewriter for the blind.

Furthermore, today's new technology may be taken for granted tomorrow. When they first appeared, the telephone, television, bank machines, and faxes were fascinating gadgets; all are now taken for granted in most societies. On the other hand, whatever happened to eight-track stereos, Telidon, or teaching machines, each of which generated just as much excitement at its outset? There are lessons therein both for those who downplay the future importance of technology and for those who are almost religious in their zeal for new inventions.

Selecting the appropriate technology is not the only challenge. Unfortunate experiences have strongly underlined technology's non-neutrality when efforts have been made to apply it within formal organizations. For example, David Wolfe (1990a, p. 63) has written extensively about the impact of technological innovation on organizational structures and processes, noting that the organization's ability to adapt to the new technology is its greatest determinant of success.

New technologies often do not live up to the expectations held for them because they have not been effectively integrated into the organization. Top management may be isolated from customers and from the shop floor, and may tend to support organizational forms that reinforce individual fear of failure rather than accept failure as part of the innovative process. Managers tend to prefer order, productivity, and control, while innovation is frequently the product of more random, unpredictable, and even chaotic circumstances.

Wolfe (1990a, pp. 69-72) blames outdated management attitudes for problems of transmission of technology and knowledge in Canada and then goes on to look at common features of effective innovation and entrepreneurship. Successful companies ensure that their product technologies are in a high state of development and then avoid direct competition by focussing on areas of comparative advantage and developing their own market niche. He concludes that, in order to succeed, research and development activities must be integrated effectively into the strategic management of the firm.

Integration does not mean top-down control, however, for significant change is usually achieved, not through systematic, formal analyses, but rather through less stable and even chaotic organizations that place a premium on innovation and change. The seminal work here is that of Thomas Kuhn (1962) who, in examining the history of science, argued that significant breakthroughs were usually the products of whole new ways of looking at things (paradigm shifts) rather than a cumulative buildup of knowledge. It would follow that top-down formal bureaucracies that emphasize predictability and control may be less conducive to major innovation than are less structured organizational forms.

Perry and Sandholtz (1988, p. 11) provide the useful metaphors of the symphony orchestra and the jazz combo in their analysis of the relationship between organizational climate and the achievement of true innovation. In their analogy, the orchestra is hierarchical, with the conductor in control and everyone else having to perform his or her role according to rigidly defined requirements. This is an appropriate model for performance but a very poor one for composition.

Good jazz, on the other hand, needs a much more flexible organization, one characterized by open design and a liberating organizational form. The same technical competence of the musicians is required, but they are given more freedom to improvise and to create within the confines of an overall structure, more like the academic model prevailing in universities.

While most formal enterprises are organized more like the orchestra, Perry and Sandholtz (1988, p. 18) offer the "chaotic" organizational structure at Star Electronics as a successful example of the application of the academic model to an industry where innovation is at a premium. They also describe many negative side effects that render the high turnover in managers at Star understandable (Perry & Sandholtz, 1988, p. 24). This combination of successful entrepreneurship and managerial difficulties is a very common reflection of the challenges of managing in a "high tech" environment.

The fundamental need of technical systems is to control variances quickly and as near to their point of origin as possible. People in an organization need autonomy and discretion, as well as opportunities for ongoing learning, social support, recognition, and the opportunities to make a meaningful contribution. In order to satisfy all of the above needs effectively, a high degree of self-regulation and participation must be built into the day-to-day operation of the organization. (Wolfe, 1990a, p. 82)

What Wolfe is describing sounds very much like a conventional university, a point not missed by Charles Handy (1989, p. 113), who believes that the demands of the knowledge society will require more and more private sector organizations to be organized like universities. In this new age, the search for truth (or, in business parlance, quality) is as essential to private enterprise as it is to the academic sector, and the challenge is to find new ways to manage effectively employees who are increasingly specialized professionals.

Some companies have created new structures that establish and support the sort of academic freedom enjoyed on university campuses. Perry and Sandholtz (1988) and Wolfe (1990a) agree that the creation of a dedicated new venture unit is an excellent way to overcome resistance to change within a formal organization. This can be an effective response to fundamental contradictions within institutions between managerial needs for control and employee needs for autonomy in the knowledge society.

The trend to an increasingly well-educated workforce has been well documented. Quoting Statistics Canada projections, Harry Strain,[2] a senior federal deputy minister, told a recent meeting of the Association of Universities and Colleges of Canada (AUCC) that half the new jobs in Canada over the next 10 years will require at least 17 years of full-time study (a university degree plus specialized training). To be effective in this context, managers must recognize the real worth of the tacit knowledge of workers and ensure that they have the autonomy and support to apply it to their work problems. The strong current corporate interest in chaos theory and Total Quality Management programs may be evidence of growing recognition of the value of providing more autonomy to self-directed work groups more traditionally associated with universities than with large business enterprises.

It is not only management that has difficulty coping with rapid and often discontinuous technological change, for worker alienation has been well documented as well.

One of the most consistent themes that emerges repeatedly in the body of labour process studies is the fact that workers experience technological change as something that happens to them in the workplace rather than as a process that they are integrally involved in developing and controlling. (Wolfe, 1990b, p. 90)

While many employees will be empowered in the new organization, others will be increasingly alienated, given Wolfe's (1990b, p. 94) observation that technology produces jobs at both ends of the knowledge spectrum. This is supported by Strain, who went on in his AUCC presentation to suggest that a full one-third of future jobs would be "McJobs"—those requiring relatively little formal schooling. Given that increased technology leads at the same time to deskilling (such as for the routinization of data entry) and to higher skill levels (for problem solving), it is the primary force in the trend toward a bifurcation of job requirements between the highly sophisticated and the mundane. This reinforces the central assertion of this chapter that adaptive management styles and organizational forms are a prerequisite response to rapid changes in the application of technology in our institutions.

What conclusions for universities can be drawn from this brief analysis of the integration of new technologies into other organizations?

• Technology is not a neutral tool but a value-laden culture that must be both understood and taken into account in any attempt to apply it to change in an organization. Hence, changing the way we teach or expect students to learn will require us to change our universities in ways that we often do not anticipate.

• While there can be little doubt of the long-term impact of technological change on our universities, we need to be wary of uncritical investment in any particular technology as the latest panacea for the shortcomings of our educational system.

• Management and faculty attitudes toward technology are fundamental to its effective adaptation into a university.

• Successful users of new technologies are those who define their own narrow niche and become the best in that area. This suggests that individual universities should be selective in their choice of areas for technological innovation.

• Paradigm shifts are more apt to be achieved outside, rather than within, formal organizational structures. However, institutions (such as universities) that grant their professionals significant autonomy are more conducive to major change than are more tightly managed organizations.

• A total, continuous growth improvement approach to management may encourage employees to be innovative but less constrained. Dedicated research units might be more effective in achieving significant breakthroughs in the long term.

Two contrasting viewpoints have been presented in this analysis. On the one hand, effective application of new technologies requires careful planning and full integration into the organization if it is to be successful. On the other hand, the very structures that make this possible are not particularly conducive to the technological breakthroughs imagined by dreamers. What does all this mean for universities in general and for distance education in particular?

Conclusions

We might conclude from this analysis that, at least in theory, universities are well suited to adapt to change and to integrate new technologies. While some might use history to suggest that the most significant developments in applying technology to education will likely originate outside the formal educational system, universities offer the best organizational models for innovation within that system. Ironically, conventional universities may be better suited than the more systematized and regulated distance teaching institutions to realize important breakthroughs in the application of new technologies to education. High-status institutions with semi-autonomous research centres and strong corporate support may be in the best position to foster the sorts of breakthroughs that the formal education sector needs if it is to continue to function as a central component of a modern democracy into the 21st century.

Nevertheless, ironies abound here. Academic freedom and the latitude given to highly specialized professionals in universities should produce innovation and technological breakthroughs, but this is so often undermined by the innate conservatism of faculty and their resistance to change, even if such can be justified in terms of the university's role as the preserver of culture and resistor to superficial new trends. Indeed, Alcorn (1986, p. 32) has noted that homeostatic tendencies are essential to our ability to withstand the rapidity of technological change in the modern world.

Even if the mainstream university model is appropriate, recent pressures for public accountability and fiscal responsibility that challenge professional autonomy may be breaking down the very research and development model that is being espoused! Nevertheless, these same pressures have led some to see distance education as an appropriate response, as a new panacea to all the ills of conventional educational systems.

In theory, formally established distance education institutions, like open universities, should be ideally suited to live up to these expectations. There are implicit dangers, however, in their very organization, especially to the extent that the prevailing industrial model for course development and delivery has become a new orthodoxy in some of our leading open universities. Innovation in such institutions may best be achieved, then, through the establishment of side units, pilot projects that promote research and experimentation in distance learning. In dual-mode institutions, the distance education unit itself may well serve as the pilot project for the mainstream campus.

Another possibility is that all education will become "distance learning," following the United States Distance Learning Association's notion as contained on the cover of its most recent promotional pamphlet. The pamphlet defines distance education as "the delivery of education or training through electronically mediated instruction including satellite, video, audiographic computer, multimedia technology, and other forms of independent study." This scenario is most probable in wealthier educational systems, where the sheer volume of investment in technological "toys" is almost bound to yield some creativity and innovation. While the price of failure and wasted resources may be high, this approach may also produce major breakthroughs in the application of technology to education.

A third, more ironic outcome of such strong recent interest is that distance education may disappear as a specific field, merging with the mainstream, or, as Pacey (1993, p. 443) has suggested, by being "leapfrogged" by the latter. In such scenarios, while the new focus will be on learning, the techniques of distance education will be absorbed into the total package of delivery strategies.

Over and above the successful application of new technologies to learning, there is another critical role for distance education institutions that can ensure the lessons of the past 25 years are not lost in the technological excitement. Most distance education practitioners know first-hand the problems their students face in attempting to overcome the barriers to learning in their everyday lives. The field of distance education can ensure that euphoria over new technologies and their potential for education is tempered by a critical approach, one based on research on learners, the skill sets they need, and the barriers they need to overcome.

Ultimately, it should not matter where the breakthroughs come from or whether a discrete field of distance education persists. Distance education has already demonstrated that open learning and its associated values work, that higher education can and must be democratized, and that a high percentage of the population can succeed in university-level studies. Technological hardware and software can contribute much to education and perhaps even revolutionize it, but the most important issues relate back to the individual, to his or her learning needs and personal commitment.

While the technologies may be new, the ideas need not be. In all of my formal education, the most stimulating educational experience I had was in the Post-Graduate Certificate in Education program at the University of London in England in 1964. Every Friday morning, I attended lectures given by such stimulating thinkers as Richard Peters (philosophy) and Basil Bernstein (sociology). These were supplemented by small seminars that mixed students from many disciplines and from many cultures. We thus had the benefit both of exposure to new and sparkling ideas and then an immediate opportunity to test our interpretation of them in interaction with fellow students. This atmosphere could be simulated today with such combinations as videotaped lectures and videoconferencing, television and computer conferencing, or even via virtual reality, but the fundamental approach to learning would not be different.

The challenge, then, is an old one. It is not so much about which new technology works best but which models are best suited to the various needs of diverse learners. Perhaps the biggest problem with educational technology is our preoccupation with it. This might be the final irony in our analysis. As Landauer (1988, p. 23) has observed, in an increasingly technological society, "daily living, and education as its reflection, will eventually become less technical and more social in its goals and content." To the extent that we can thus more readily take technology for granted, then education itself will be expected to be concerned less with the technological and scientific and more and more with social and cultural aspects of our lives.

Perhaps the ultimate contribution of distance education to the future development of learning systems, then, will be to focus attention back where it belongs—on the individual learner and his or her learning needs. If we get this right, the appropriate technological breakthroughs will almost certainly follow.

Endnotes

1. The terms "traditional" and "conventional" are used interchangeably in this chapter to refer to predominant mainstream educational practices and institutions.

2. In a speech to the Association of Colleges and Universities of Canada, Ottawa (March 9, 1994).

References

Alcorn, P.A. (1986). *Social issues in technology: A format for investigation.* Englewood Cliffs, NJ: Prentice-Hall.

Evans, T., & Nation, D. (1989). Critical reflections in distance education. In T. Evans & D. Nation (Eds.), *Critical reflections on distance education* (pp. 237–252). Lewes: The Falmer Press.

Feenberg, A. (1991). *Critical theory of technology.* New York: Oxford University Press.

Handy, C. (1989). *The age of unreason.* London: Basic Books.

Harris, D. (1987). *Openness and closure in distance education.* Lewes: The Falmer Press.

Heterick, R.C. (1994). Technological change and higher education policy. *AGB Priorities 1,* 1–12.

Ihde, D. (1993). *Philosophy of technology.* New York: Paragon House.

Kuhn, T.S. (1970). *The structure of scientific revolutions* (2nd ed.). Chicago: University of Chicago Press.

Landauer, T.K. (1988). Education in a world of omnipotent and omniscient technology. In R.S. Nickerson & P.P. Zodhiates (Eds.), *Technology in education: Looking toward 2020* (pp. 11–24). Hillsdale, NJ: Lawrence Erlbaum Associates.

Pacey, L. (1993). Strategic planning and open learning: Turkey tails and frogs. In B. Scriven, R. Lundin, & Y. Ryan (Eds.), *Distance education for the twenty-first century* (pp. 436–446). Queensland: ICDE & Queensland University of Technology.

Perry, L.T., & Sandholtz, K.W. (1988). A "liberating form" for radical product innovation. In U.E. Gattiker & L. Larwood (Eds.), *Managing technological development: Strategies and human resources issues* (pp. 9–31). Berlin: Walter de Gruyter.

Scriven, B., Lundin, R., & Ryan, Y. (Eds.).(1993). *Distance education for the twenty-first century* (pp. 182–321). Queensland: ICDE & Queensland University of Technology.

Wolfe, D. (1990a). The management of innovation. In L. Salter & D. Wolfe (Eds.), *Managing technology: Social science perspectives* (pp. 63-88). Toronto: Garamond Press.

Wolfe, D. (1990b). Innovation and the labour process. In L. Salter & D. Wolfe (Eds.), *Managing technology: Social science perspectives* (pp. 89–111). Toronto: Garamond Press.

CHAPTER 8

The Francophones of Canada: A Global Network

THÉRÈSE LAMY
PIERRE R. PELLETIER

Tes donc bien de bonne
humeur!
Yatu kukeun qui t'a fait
keukjose?
—Réjean Ducharme, *Dévadé.*

The positioning of the Francophones of North America in the
21st century and their continued development as a genuine
community depend upon a collective creativity in the use of new
information and communication technologies. In order to challenge and defeat the dispersion, isolation, and collective incoher-
ence that always threaten their cultural identity, they must
define new territories of space and time.

The Francophone community needs to define territories of
communication that are unique to its own needs, territories
where the flow of information is constant, transparent, and easily
accessible, and where the immediate, considered feedback of
changes and deep transformations is assured. The efficient and
accelerated circulation of information must be central to the
actions of all our community development.

The Francophones of Canada

In Canada, three major cultural communities have distinct
identities and coherence that are confirmed by institutional or
alternative structures both at the provincial and federal levels of
government: the English-speaking group (the majority), the
French-speaking group (a minority), and finally, the third group,
the Aboriginals. Obviously these groups, whose languages and

cultures are in subtle osmosis, are not closed entities with respect to one another. They should share a respect for their identities and a sense of history and belonging—the prerequisites for dynamic intercultural relationships. The resulting dialectics make it possible to avoid the more or less absolute misunderstandings that are always disastrous.

The French-speaking group forms a majority of about six million in the province of Québec. Across Canada, the French-speaking minority is dispersed in smaller groups. All told, it represents some 26 percent of Canada's total population. The Canadian Francophone community, although it speaks the same language, does not necessarily share a single culture. One can distinguish the cultural communities of Québec, Acadia, Ontario, Manitoba, Saskatchewan, Alberta, British Columbia, Yukon, and the Northwest Territories.

What Do We Want?

There is no doubt in our minds that we Francophones are different from the other major cultural communities. We want to live and create in French, wherever we are in this country, as members of a real, distinctive community, in a society that values the quality of life of the individual. For the Francophones of the North American continent, it is necessary to use the new culture of information and communication technologies to interact with the Francophone world. The objective of all our networking should be to maximize the global Francophone culture. Our cultural identity will then be enriched by the multiple and complex interconnections with other Francophones throughout the world.

This chapter is about the culture of information and communication technologies, and about how the Francophones of North America can develop their own global culture by using these distance education technologies.

Open and Transparent Communication

Norbert Weiner (1948) dreamed about an open and transparent culture of communication. Such a culture can only help the development of the Francophone community of North America,

especially if it is integrated with all the components of the information culture. However, the latter—and all the networking it
implies—must be understood in the socio-historic context that
allows a critical approach to the global development of our distinctive communities.

A good example of this critical contextualization would be the
creative integration in our daily lives of information and communication technologies in all types of learning situations, both formal and informal. The use of these technologies would give the
Francophone community better control of its development in different categories of activity. The Village électronique/Electronic
Village (described in Chapter 10 of this book) is a very good
example of this creative use of communication and information
technologies.

A distinct cultural community will further its growth and
development if it can integrate information and communication
technologies into its culture. In so doing, a community opens new
access to global development and to better dialogue with other
cultural communities, whether they be a majority or a minority.

The appropriation of a technique makes it possible to increase—or
maintain—the professional qualifications of the individual concerned to
ensure maximum flexibility and mobility in the job market; in certain
cases, it can even lead to the more collective objective of universal social
emancipation. (Breton & Proulx, 1989, p. 251; translated by authors)

Communication Technologies and the Francophone Community

For this dispersed population, the mastery of information technologies and the implementation of communications networks
(such as distance education networks) are not only necessities,
but ways of protecting creativity and allowing it to thrive. But
what kind of technology? Ursula Franklin defines technology in
this manner:

Technology, like democracy, includes ideas and practices; it includes
myths and various models of reality. And like democracy, technology
changes the social and individual relationships between us. It has
forced us to examine and redefine our notions of power and of accountability. (Franklin, 1990, p. 12)

Franklin sees the current world as dominated by the prescriptive technologies that control our work and our learning:

Think of a word processor. A freestanding word processor is indeed work-related technology. But link those word processors into a work station—that is into a system—and the technology becomes control-related. Now workers can be timed, assignments can be broken up, and the interaction between the operators can be monitored. Most modern technological changes involve control and thus new control-related applications have increased much faster than work-related ones. (Franklin, 1990, p. 18)

On the other hand, there are the holistic technologies, those usually associated with people who are the craftspersons of their fields. They work at their own rhythm from beginning to end. This does not mean that the craftspeople of holistic technologies cannot work together toward a common goal, "... but the way in which they work together leaves the individual worker in control of a particular process of creating or doing something" (Franklin, 1990, p. 19).

When holistic technologies are used—such as the communications technologies that are common in distance education and that should be oriented toward the personal growth of the users—control of the transformation process is in the hands of the users. Generally speaking, all tasks that require special attention to people or things, or those that necessitate immediate feedback, require holistic technology, a technology open to sharing with one another. Certainly the process of education, of personal growth and of learning, is essentially a holistic process that cannot be addressed by prescriptive mass technology.

Franklin reminds us that prescriptive technologies eliminate all types of subjective judgements that could modify the way work is accomplished. Prescriptive technologies have brought us, through the production of objects, an improvement in our way of living. However, they have also contributed to a culture of complacency:

The acculturation to compliance and conformity has, in turn, accelerated the use of prescriptive technologies in administration, government and social services. The same development has diminished resistance to the programming of people. (Franklin, 1990, p. 25)

Unfortunately, prescriptive technologies have also invaded the world of education. In many of our schools, colleges, and universities, education refers more to models of production than to the growth of people:

Not only are students tested and advanced according to a strictly specified schedule ... but the prospective university students and their parents are frequently informed that different universities produce "different products" ... . The implication is that choosing a particular university, following a particular regimen, will turn the student into a specifiable and identifiable product. (Franklin, 1990, p. 28)

These distinctions between prescriptive technologies and holistic technologies described by Franklin also remind us of the questions raised by members of the "Invisible College." In their work, Bateson, Jackson, and Birdwhistell (1981) have described the negative effects of a mechanistic model of communication and promoted the orchestral model of communication as one giving a more global vision. Communication is "a permanent social process, integrating multiple modes of behavior: speech, gestures, sight, facial expressions, proxemics" (Bateson et al., 1981, p. 24).

This concept of orchestral communication can be mediated only through a holistic technology.

Distance Education and Holistic Technologies for Francophones

Recent technological developments indicate a trend to the convergence and integration of different technologies. Global communication is becoming a daily reality. Distance education networks should therefore implement holistic technologies that focus on the growth of the individual, which is the basis of community development.

Distance education for the Francophones of North America is a valuable tool for the development of our cultural communities. Our definition of distance education includes all types of learning through a variety of media. It is open to formal and informal learning and to all dimensions of time and space.

This open definition of distance education undoubtedly covers many situations, but two conditions must be present if distance education is to be a catalyst for the global development of North American Francophones. The first condition is that distance education must happen in a multimedia context, integrating first-generation media (such as print) with the latest-generation information and communications technologies. The second condition is that distance education implies networking, not with machines, but with people.

First Condition

Distance education, new information and communications technologies, and the culture of communication: these three concepts are at the heart of the development of the Canadian *francophonie.*

Jacques Ellul (1988) and Jean Baudrillard (1972), with their inspiring work on communication, open up new avenues for weaving and networking between educational technologies and new systems of communication:

• Global digitalization of information, making possible the merging of visual and graphic data.

• Generalization of fibre optics for the transportation of information.

• Development of telecommunications networks linking together individual users.

All these elements attest to a developing global communications culture, mushrooming all over the world and facilitating, for the Francophones of Canada, the use of holistic technologies in distance education. Distance education thus becomes multiform, with universal access, open to the integration of all types of data that can be rendered completely user-friendly. Distance education then allows the Francophones of Canada to integrate these information and communications technologies into the fabric of their culture, thereby facilitating collective creativity and the social emancipation of their cultural communities.

Second Condition

Distance education can be a precious tool for the development of the Canadian *francophonie* if it is done by networking people in their own environment, whether rural or urban. For the dispersed Francophone communities of Canada, the possibility that information and communications technologies could advance their collective growth has been evident for some time.

Six Illustrations from Practice

1. Collège Mathieu of Gravelbourg (Saskatchewan)

The Collège Mathieu of Gravelbourg has been at the centre of a network that allows Francophones in small villages to have access to formal and informal education at all levels. For example, once a month, the Distance Reading Circle of the Service Fransaskois d'éducation des adultes meets by audioconferencing to discuss books they have read. A variety of linked localities have explored over the last year the theme, "The West and the Prairies," as seen by Saskatchewan Francophone authors. Assembled during one hour, the group discusses, laughs, shares their common culture, and realizes that distance education lessens the isolation and brings them together (Marchildon, 1994).

2. Le Collège de l'Acadie (Nova Scotia)

In Nova Scotia, the Acadians have established a distance community college without walls. Le Collège de l'Acadie has an administrative centre and six centres of learning linked together by videoconferencing and audiographics. This electronic college offers to the Acadian population such programs as business computer studies and general studies. Participants can complete primary school and also get a secondary school diploma in French. Nine programs are offered at a distance (REFAD, 1993, pp. 23–24).

3. La Corporation pour l'avancement de nouvelles applications des langages (CANAL) (Québec)

In Québec, CANAL is an educational TV broadcaster, composed of a partnership of universities, colleges, school boards, and the government-operated educational broadcaster Radio-Québec. It offers credit courses, learning support programs, and cultural and educational programs seven days a week, 24 hours a day. CANAL has now decided to be part of Ubi-Éducation, a partnership with private enterprise that will bring the information highway to its clientele. The partners intend to offer information services, learning services, and support services through the information highway and special converters attached to television sets. Again, the Francophone community is integrating information and communications technologies into its own network (Godbout, 1994, p. 8).

4. Four Institutions (Ontario)

In other regions of Canada, Francophones have set up similar networks. In Ontario, Franco-Ontarians have access to post-secondary education through a network of four institutions: l'Université Laurentienne à Sudbury, l'Université d'Ottawa, le Collège Glendon de l'Université York à Toronto, and Le Collège universitaire de Hearst. With videoconferencing sites in three cities, these institutions are sustaining the development of major distance educational programs for the Francophone community, including one leading to a graduate degree in speech pathology.

5. TéléÉducation NB TeleEducation (New Brunswick)

TéléÉducation NB TeleEducation (TENB) has established an open distributed network, compatible with the information highway. TENB is a bilingual network providing training, information and educational services to the population of New Brunswick. In

1993–94, TENB established close to 50 distance education sites in colleges, universities, schools, hospitals, community centres, First Nations reserves, private companies, and libraries. The network uses audioconferencing, audiographics, and computer teleconferencing, as well as videoconferencing. L'Université de Moncton, one of the partners in the network, has three videoconferencing sites that teach in French (TENB, 1994).

6. Le Réseau d'enseignement francophone à distance du Canada (REFAD)

The Francophones of Canada, as these illustrations demonstrate, have successfully created strong regional networks and set up the major buoys of a national network, using the most recent technologies. This network is Le Réseau d'enseignement francophone à distance du Canada (REFAD). REFAD has a very flexible structure, in which each participant retains its autonomy and can opt out of national activities. The national network encourages its members to use information and communications technologies in a holistic way. REFAD wants to be a link between different partners and to contribute to the extension of the regional networks throughout the land. REFAD encourages sharing of experiences, human resources, and programs. It can also lobby for its members, bringing forward Francophone projects to different levels of government.

Conclusions

Thus it appears that distance education is an excellent tool for the global development of the Canadian *francophonie* in a context where educational technologies are integrated within a communications culture. But the practice of distance education in a culture of communication technologies must be holistic and accomplished through networking. The networks should become ecotechnologic, reflecting *nos rapprochements, nos complicités au sein des collectivités francophones du pays et du monde.*

References

Bateson, G., et al. (1981). *La nouvelle communication*. Paris: Edition du Seuil.

Baudrillard, J. (1972). *Pour une critique de l'économie politique du signe*. Paris: Gallimard.

Breton, P., & Proulx, S. (1989). *L'explosion de la communication, la naissance d'une nouvelle idéologie*. Paris–Montréal: Boréal.

Ducheme, R. (1990). *Dévadé*. Paris: Gallimard (p. 67).

Ellul, J. (1988). *Le bluff technologique*. Paris: Hachette.

Franklin, U.(1990). *The real world of technology*. Concord: House of Anansi Press.

Godbout, S. (1994). Le canal de télé-enseignement devient diffuseur partenaire d'Ubi-Éducation. *Connexion, 5*(3), 8.

Marchildon, M. (1994). Franchir les distances avec un roman. *Connexion, 5*(3), 1–6.

REFAD. (1993). *Répertoire de l'enseignement à distance en français*. Montréal: Author.

TéléÉducation NB TeleEducation. (1994). *Annual Report*. Fredericton: Author.

Weiner, N. (1948). *Cybernetics or control and communications in the animal and the machine*. Paris: Herman.

CHAPTER 9

A Collective Approach to Distance Education

Denise V. Paquette-Frenette
Daniel L. Larocque

In Canada, the rapid growth of distance education in the past 20 years has been mostly due to the creation in the 1970s of many institutions, such as Athabasca University or Télé-Université, to serve large populations. Mass education has thus been linked for some time with distance education. Learning packages in distance education have therefore been designed for large numbers, resulting in economies of scale.

However, this approach may not always be appropriate. What about smaller populations for whom economies of scale are not possible? What about small groups of learners with very specialized needs? It is not enough to rely on strategies developed for large-scale organizations. Rather, learning design and delivery must be adapted to meet the specific needs of learners in smaller population groups, especially when linguistic and cultural differences come into play. For such learners, there is a need for new approaches in distance education to overcome the limitations of established models.

Much past writing on distance education, in both English and French, has been about individualization and independent self-study (Abrioux, 1985; Henri, 1985; Henri & Kaye, 1985; Kaye & Landry, 1985; Holmberg, 1977, 1981). An individualized approach may, however, be contrary to the values of certain groups of learners. The distance education model described in this chapter has been developed in order to answer the needs of:

- a relatively small population distributed in many communities over a large territory;

• learners who are defined by their deep links to their community, who identify with a group, and who learn best when learning situations flow from these social and cultural connections; and

• a minority group with few resources and with limited control over access to education.

The collective approach attempts to answer the particular needs of such learners by linking context to distance education design, delivery, and organizational structure.[1] Rather than tackle distance education activities in a piecemeal manner, leaving decisions to individual institutions or organizations, it proposes that all aspects of these activities be viewed as a whole and be undertaken as a common project by several stakeholders. Further, the collective approach has at its core the common characteristics and priorities of a community or collectivity. It derives its coherence from the collaborative efforts of members of this community. Because of its emphasis on interaction and collaboration, the model is more than a model catering to small populations, even though it works for them as well. The approach is called a "collective" model rather than a "small populations" model precisely because of the qualitative difference between catering to small populations and moulding them together into system-wide alliances. The common goal or vision of a community constitutes the added element.

This chapter describes the issues raised by the needs of learners in minority populations who are defined by their common networks. Some of these issues are familiar to distance educators, while others call for special attention to cultural aspects. Following a description of the context in which the collective approach was designed, a case study of the application of the collective approach to a minority population is presented. The major points addressed are a definition of the approach, the teaching models and technological configurations flowing from the definition, and a description of local and system-wide organizational structure. The analysis reviews the issues from the perspective of learners' needs or preferences and from that of organizational networking, by pointing out some of the advantages of a collective approach and some of the problems that need to be addressed.

Issues

In Chapter 2 of this book, Pacey and Penney point out that over the last decade "we have witnessed changes throughout the world that none of us anticipated or ever believed could occur." In this type of environment, which others have termed "turbulent" (Emery & Trist, 1972; Gray, 1989; Gray & Wood, 1991; Heimer, 1985; Pasquero, 1991), industrial and uniform approaches to distance education may not be effective. Distance educators must devise new design, delivery, and management models that are better suited to such a "changing landscape" (see Pacey & Penney, Chapter 2).

While acknowledging the difficulty of planning in sometimes chaotic circumstances, Pacey and Penney offer a solution, that of adapting strategic planning to reflect context. In Chapter 1, Haughey discusses the importance of "our place in the world," in her reflections on the meanings of distance as a social and cultural construct evolving around people's perceptions and needs. Thus, to be most successful in reaching its learners in a changing, turbulent world, distance education must be derived from the context of the community it wishes to serve.

The collective approach offers a model of design, delivery, and management that seeks to reflect the particular context of a community. Seven aspects of this central issue of context need to be addressed. Five are identified as pertaining to the socio-political dimension: demography, equity of access, rationalization, choice of technology, and ownership of technology. Two others are more culture-specific: a preference for learning through group interaction and a propensity for networking.

While all these issues may be relevant to other situations, the socio-political issues are more generally applicable than the culture-specific dimensions. However, from the perspective of this chapter, the two dimensions are closely connected, since it is difficult to talk about the importance of context in general without referring to a particular situation.

The Context

The Franco-Ontarian community, about five hundred thousand strong, is dispersed over a large territory of more than one million square kilometres. It is distributed mostly in small groups in a large number of communities. Comprising about five percent of the province of Ontario's population, Franco-Ontarians maintain their language and culture through a network of institutions and associations based mostly on voluntary community activity.

They have partial access to educational opportunities and limited control over course offerings in their own language.[2] Some educational institutions cater exclusively to people who speak French as a mother tongue (two community colleges[3] and approximately 55 secondary and 300 elementary schools); others are bilingual, offering some courses, programs and services to a French-speaking minority (four community colleges, four universities, and approximately 50 secondary schools).

During the past few years, distance education for Franco-Ontarians has evolved considerably. From its beginnings 40 years ago in the French-language division of the Department of Education's correspondence sector,[4] it has increased in its courses, programs and services. For example, until 1990, three bilingual community colleges offered fewer than a dozen courses at a distance to French-language speakers, and it was impossible to complete a program at a distance. By 1994, more than 100 courses were offered, as well as six complete college-level programs in seven colleges. University and secondary-level activities have also increased substantially. Much of this increase may be attributed to the application of a collective approach to the development of distance education courses and programs.

The Franco-Ontarian population ascribes a particular meaning to the term "community." In this chapter, we will use this term to mean the collectivity (as defined by Breton, 1984, p. 5): that is, the large group made up of Franco-Ontarians who define themselves from the point of view of "belonging" to this wider community. As a result of their strong cultural affinity, Francophones from one part of the province might feel much closer to French-speaking people from a completely different section of the province than to English-speaking neighbours in the same town (see Lamy & Pelletier, Chapter 8 of this book).

Socio-Political Elements

Demography is an important issue. When small numbers of learners are spread across a large area, only one or two individuals in a single town or village might be interested in a program, especially at the post-secondary level. In the past, it has been impossible to meet the needs of such learners. Because of the small numbers of potential students in each municipality, courses conducted in French have consistently been cancelled or have simply not been offered. Low population levels do not allow traditional economies of scale, obtained from the production of large quantities of materials. It is essential, therefore, to seek economies on a smaller scale while ensuring access. The organizational model based on bringing together individuals with similar needs has allowed the creation of a virtual classroom of 15, 20 or more learners through the use of interactive technology.

A second issue, equity of access, is linked to the demographic situation of particular groups. For example, owing to historical and geographical factors, the Franco-Ontarian population has not participated as actively in post-secondary education as have other cultural and linguistic groups (Churchill & Frenette, 1985). Yet, more and more Ontarians (both French- and English-speaking) recognize the importance of education and training for the social and economic development of their communities and of the province. In the last few years, this recognition has taken the form of shared control of some learning institutions and service providers in the field of education. With only five percent of the province's population, the minority has often had a lesser voice in decisions about needs, priorities, and the means to answer them. Decisions have not always reflected the preoccupations of the Francophone population. To ensure equity of access, a distance education model should allow each linguistic group to make the final decisions on how to implement its priorities. If recipients of educational activities are empowered to create services that respond to their needs, participation rates will increase.

The present climate of rationalization is a third important element of the context. Educational systems everywhere are being asked to offer a wider range of services to more people while avoiding duplication and making more efficient use of existing resources. Franco-Ontarians are not excluded from this climate of rationalization. The need for increased efficiency requires administrative and structural solutions on a system-wide basis.

A fourth issue related to the collective approach is that of technology—a critical element in the development of distance education. The choice of technologies must be determined by what is most appropriate, not only to the content of courses but also to the ways in which target groups prefer to learn. These preferences may be linked to traditions, such as the strong oral tradition among Franco-Ontarians, or to socio-economic factors, such as a relatively low literacy level, or even to demographic factors, such as dispersion of small numbers.

Beyond the choice of technology, there is a fifth issue, that of ownership of technological installations (who buys and maintains the equipment? who rents the site?) and, more specifically, of their use (who makes decisions pertaining to schedules?).

Cultural Dimensions

Two issues addressed by this collective approach to distance education are closely related to the cultural characteristics of the Franco-Ontarian community. These dimensions are the Franco-Ontarians' preference for learning through group interaction and a propensity for networking.

Interactive group learning, not individualized self-study, is essential to people who identify strongly with a specific community. The centrifugal forces that bind them together are critical to their learning. Franco-Ontarians generally favour learning in small groups in direct interaction with an instructor and with other learners. In a feasibility study conducted among Franco-Ontarians by the Addiction Research Foundation for a certificate in drug-abuse intervention, 80 percent of the respondents indicated that they wanted to be in a group at least part of the time (Larocque, 1992). A research project conducted for the Ontario Prevention Clearinghouse arrived at the same conclusion (Larocque, 1994). The majority of respondents indicated that they wanted to learn in a group context, even though they expected to receive individual reading materials. In another study, Marchand discovered that French-speaking learners in Ontario and Saskatchewan showed a marked preference for being linked in learning activities (Marchand, 1994, p. 164).[5]

Another distinguishing characteristic of a strong minority cultural community is the importance of networking, among both individuals and institutions (Breton, 1983, 1984; Cardinal, Lapointe, & Thériault, 1990). Because of their common difference from the rest of the population, members of a minority feel a strong need to be in touch with one another. Because of their sense of collective identity, they "become tied together in a cohesive interpersonal network" (Breton, 1964). Their small numbers also facilitate the creation of both human and technological networks. Both formal and informal networks have been a key to cultural survival and to social development, since a community is constituted by an interorganizational system (Breton, 1984, p. 6). Franco-Ontarians exhibit this minority group behaviour, and the strength of their networks is the basis for the Franco-Ontarian collaborative model of distance education.

Thus, this collective model for distance education design, delivery, and organization deals with issues very familiar to distance education in general, such as rationalization, costs, technology choice, learners' needs, and management issues such as ownership and use of equipment. However, it also raises issues of a different order, such as the overriding importance of the cultural context.

Case Study

A Collective Approach for Franco-Ontarians

The model described in this section has evolved over the past five years in the context of existing structural elements and the community's characteristics and needs. It has been developed and partially implemented by the FORMA-DISTANCE program of the Ontario Ministry of Education and Training, in a concerted effort to stimulate the development of distance education for the Franco-Ontarian community.

A definition, in a nutshell

The model is based on three major principles: it is *collective*, *interactive*, and *decentralized*.

The model is termed collective since the development of distance education is directed toward a common goal, that of the good of the Franco-Ontarian community. This basic value underlies all efforts. The model's sphere of action is provincial. Its objective is to help elaborate a common policy concerning distance education within a large number of institutions and associations (colleges, universities, school boards, non-profit organizations) and to develop a means of collaboration among them.

The approach is based on consolidating existing activities in distance education into a loose network, on providing ample opportunities for system-wide collaboration at various levels, and on making design and delivery choices that will best enhance learners' collective needs. It is thus concerned as much with learning design as with delivery and with overall management of distance education among Franco-Ontarians.

The principle of collectivity holds that learners' needs are considered in the collective rather than in the individual sense. It is this definition of learners as a group with identifiable characteristics that distinguishes the model from much of the distance education literature on learners' needs.[6]

The model is founded on the premise that for members of the Franco-Ontarian community, learning in a group situation is preferable to learning individually.[7] Real-time interaction, facilitated by the use of flexible, accessible, and interconnected technologies, is thus a second important component of the model.

The third component, decentralization, is based on local and regional responsibility for distance education activities, partnerships among equals as opposed to hierarchical management, and the use and networking of existing resources rather than the creation of new, centralized superstructures.

These three basic principles are illustrated in four areas: teaching–learning approaches, technology choices and configurations, local co-ordination and management, and provincial co-ordination.

Teaching–learning approaches

Since the model is based on interaction, the favoured teaching models resemble the extended classroom approach for learning in groups. Learners who are part of a "cohesive interpersonal network" are uncomfortable studying on an individual basis from modular material (Breton, 1964). Socializing, or being with others, is an important condition for learning. This is particularly true for learners who may feel culturally isolated in their locality and who need to communicate with other members of the minority in other provincial locations.

Thus, "collective pedagogy" calls for a grouping of learners through audioconferences or videoconferences for several hours a week, rather than studying individually. The role of the instructor is to provide both content and support in a group setting. Even though learners may telephone an instructor for individual tutoring, the basis of the teaching approach is group-centred. Similarly, computer conferences are favoured over individual exchanges through electronic mail or via computer-assisted learning programs.

The advantages of learning at a distance through interaction with peers and an instructor have been described by several authors (Garrison, 1989; Harasim, 1987, 1990; Henri, 1994; Shale, 1988). When peer learning is emphasized, the teaching source is shared among all participants and is decentralized. Thus, the collective approach to teaching and learning is one that is already familiar to adult educators.

Since cultural minorities, such as Franco-Ontarians, form groups rapidly, design techniques developed for computer conferencing (Davie, 1989; Harasim, 1987), for videoconferencing (Lochte, 1993), and for audioconferencing (Robertson, 1986; George, 1990) could all be used to advantage in order to capitalize on this characteristic. Some design techniques used to promote collaborative learning might also be applied (Henri, 1994).[8] For example, group projects can link learners who are dispersed in various localities or who are together in on-site study groups.

Technology choices and configurations

These collective values and teaching models depend upon technologies that (1) are easiest to use and that build on acquired competencies (2) are most interactive in real time, (3) are the least expensive to operate, install, buy, and maintain, (4) are easiest to connect in networks for group work, and (5) are easiest to connect with existing installations (at the local, regional, provincial, and national levels).

The telephone, electronically linked to other technologies, is considered the technology of choice because it is accessible, multidirectional, familiar, easy to use, and relatively inexpensive.

Figure 9.1
Equipment in a typical learning site.

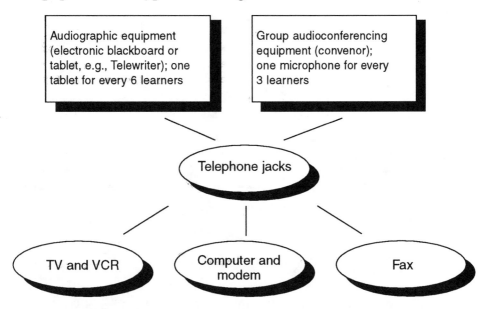

In a teaching site, the same equipment is used, with the addition of a head-set, a scanner, and a video camera to create more interesting teaching materials. For a learner at home or in the workplace, equipment needs are simpler: a head-set, a fax, a computer, and a modem.

This technology can be enriched by audiographics, computer conferencing, fax transmissions, VCRs and television monitors, according to learners' and teachers' needs and to course content. The advent of inexpensive and easily accessible videoconferencing equipment also allows interconnection and may soon become the preferred medium.

In most audioconferencing systems in Canada (e.g., Contact North/Contact Nord in Ontario or TéléÉducation NB TeleEducation in New Brunswick), equipment in learning and teaching sites is linked through a large central bridge containing a hundred lines or more. However, the technical configurations typical of the collective approach rely on the networking of several small bridges, sometimes containing as few as six lines. The bridges connect sites where a few learners (usually between two and 10) can gather around the equipment shown in Figure 9.1. The teaching site can have the same equipment but also head-

Figure 9.2
Technical configuration in a centralized network.

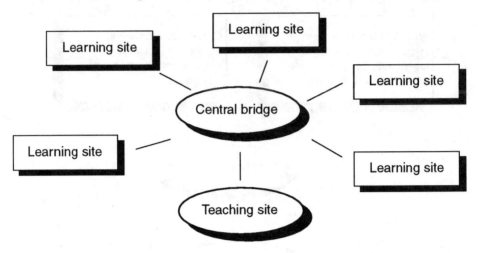

phones for the teacher, video cameras, and scanners, to permit the teacher to use enriched teaching materials if appropriate. A learner who is too far from a site can participate from home or the workplace, although without access to audiographics.

Teaching and learning sites can be temporary or permanent. They can be found in post-secondary educational institutions, or in local meeting places such as cultural centres or schools. These venues often constitute the centre of Francophone social and cultural life in communities, particularly those with a small French-language population.

Connecting sites through small local bridges allows learners to be networked inexpensively. Because of their small numbers, it is often impractical to set up expensive large bridges. Often, different localities can be linked without incurring long-distance costs through use of minibridges. These can be located in any host institution that makes its lines available at night, when most distance courses take place. If necessary, two or more minibridges can be linked together. This configuration of linking minibridges nevertheless depends on access to one or more large central bridges. If numbers are small enough, the three-way

Figure 9.3
Technical configuration in a decentralized network based on the collective approach.

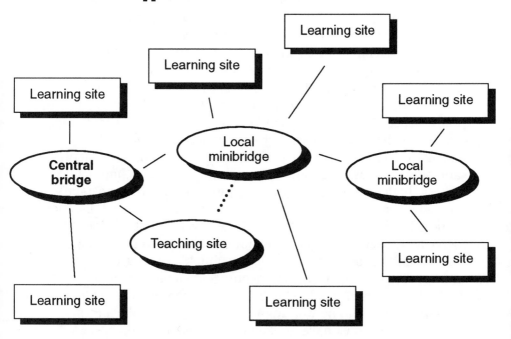

Three-way calling options may replace some local bridges. The dotted line indicates that a teaching site could be linked either to the central bridge or to a local minibridge.

calling feature available through most North American telephone companies can replace the use of a minibridge, thereby further reducing costs.

By favouring the connection of a large number of local or regional minibridges to one or more central bridges, the model thus applies the principle of interaction by linking locations. It builds on what is available and prefers networking to establishing parallel and competing installations.

Figures 9.2 and 9.3 illustrate the difference in technical configurations for a centralized approach and for the collective approach.

Local co-ordination and management

A third illustration of the basic principles of the collective approach is a local organizational structure. At least three organizational options are possible, based on the locus of control over distance education activities, sites, and equipment: (1) exclusive community control in a local district education council, (2) exclusive institutional control, and (3) shared control in a consortium. Control is defined as the power to determine which groups have priority of access to equipment and to sites, to make scheduling decisions, and other prerogatives of ownership.

In the first option, local distance education councils have exclusive community control of distance education, equipment, and sites. Access sites can be in community centres, municipal offices, high schools, non-profit organizations such as hospitals or social service agencies, or even private spaces. A local distance education council would stimulate the development of projects, serve as broker between the community and learning establishments, and bring educational decision making closer to target groups. These councils could encourage regional partnerships in order to increase inter-level collaboration, as well as provincial and interprovincial networking. Even though several aspects of the collective model have already been applied among Franco-Ontarians, this structure of local distance education councils has not yet been established.

In the second option, an institution manages a site or a network for its own programs, but allows other groups to use it if there is extra capacity. For example, the University of Ottawa's sites and equipment are available during off-hours to other institutions or to associations who request access (see Thomas & McDonell, Chapter 10 of this book). The RUISSO network, which links 14 secondary schools in central Ontario, has a policy of open access to its equipment, its sites, and to its 14-line bridge, written into its mission statement.

In a third option, responsibility for distance education might rest with separate institutions, community groups, or professional associations, which would then combine their resources to administer distance education along a consortium model. Emphasis would be on joint development, consensus building, and collaboration. Partners would seek a variety of funding sources, and the forms of sharing would depend on situations.

The difference between this option and the first is that in the first, there would be no institutional partners, only members of the community. As in the first option, there is not yet an example of this form of local structure.

Whatever option of local management is chosen, it is critical to provide other services to ensure learner success. Local councils, institutions, or consortia must provide technical assistance, administrative support, and tutoring to individual learners or to groups. Sometimes one person can carry out all the above functions, especially in small communities.

Provincial co-ordination

In some instances, a province-wide focus is critical to the growth of distance education for a minority distributed across a province. A voluntary planning council, functioning as an "adhocracy," can provide such a co-ordinating structure. Over the past five years, the FORMA-DISTANCE program has co-ordinated such a council. This Strategic Planning Council has been responsible for interinstitutional educational planning, co-ordination of course registrations, promotion, development and management of access sites, professional development for teachers and administrators, training learners, and advising government on needs assessment and evaluation.

Figure 9.4 (p. 170) outlines the structure of the present Council. The Council is made up of senior French-speaking representatives of: (1) colleges (five), universities (four), and school board consortia (three) that offer distance education programs; (2) provincial community groups, such as the Association canadienne-française de l'Ontario and Direction-Jeunesse, representing young adults; (3) distance education service providers, such as Contact North/Contact Nord and TVOntario, Ontario's educational programming network; and (4) government ministries and agencies with a mandate to serve Franco-Ontarian educational needs.

Representatives do not necessarily hold equivalent positions of authority within their own organization. Mixing people of different areas of expertise and interest, ideally in a relationship of equality, has advantages, but it also presents the challenge of ensuring mutual respect among members who do not hold the same rank.

Figure 9.4
Structure of the provincial Strategic Planning Council.

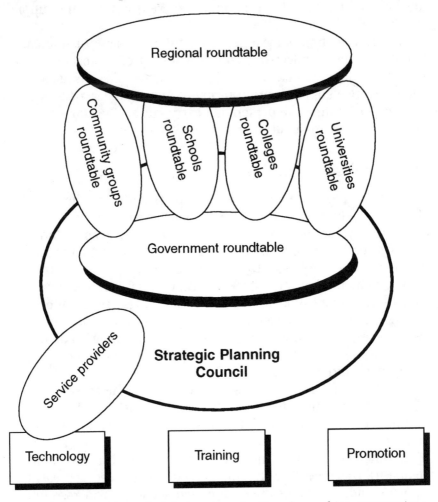

The Council is composed of the most senior French-speaking representatives of the various groups:
• Colleges, universities, and school board consortia that offer distance education programs
• Provincial community groups, such as umbrella groups or youth associations
• Distance education service providers (Contact North/Contact Nord, TVOntario, La Chaîne française)
• Government ministries with a mandate to serve Franco-Ontarian educational needs.

This Council meets twice a year to exchange information on distance education activities, to determine overall priorities for the Franco-Ontarian community, and to co-ordinate allocation of sites.

The Council sponsors various roundtables,[9] which meet more often in order to implement its decisions.

• A roundtable for each educational level (college, university, elementary/secondary) plans common province-wide distance education programs and writes joint funding applications.

• A second roundtable represents other stakeholders in distance education.

• Roundtables on specific themes (training, technology, marketing and promotion) exchange information and undertake joint action.

• Regional roundtables combine representatives of all levels to address geographical areas needing special action.

Any of these working groups can add members from other constituencies for their meetings.

The Council contracts and supervises a secretariat which in turn organizes professional development activities, provides research, prepares meetings of the Council and its roundtables, and generally serves as a catalyst.

This collective approach encourages local autonomy and responsibility while offering provincial co-ordination. Local sites respond to local needs and strengths, while working with others toward a common provincial vision which combines all educational levels. Each institution or area contributes according to its means and its interest in the common development of the Franco-Ontarian community.

Analysis

To date, the collective approach has met with success in the Franco-Ontarian community, since it has developed in response to this unique situation. However, other communities with similar contexts could benefit from the lessons learned. In this section we discuss the advantages and disadvantages of the collective approach, revisit the issues mentioned earlier, and briefly describe how other communities might benefit. The section is divided into two parts: the first looks at the model from the learners' point of view, and the second from the organizational perspective.

From the Learners' Point of View

According to Schermerhorn (cited in Gray, 1985, p. 921), cultural norms are a powerful, if not essential, source of incentives for collaboration. For people such as Franco-Ontarians, who define themselves primarily as members of a group rather than as individuals, collaboration is part of their cultural norm, of their ways of being and acting. For such populations, networking is a common sociological trait. Thus, learning activities emphasize direct communication between student and teacher as well as among students; discussion groups; and on-site or field research grounded in the collective community. Connections are made between learners in various areas through distance learning technologies, because of the natural affinity of a strong cultural group. Geographic and demographic isolation are reduced because of a much stronger force, that of the virtual network created by a common characteristic: namely, these learners are different from the larger community—the majority—that surrounds them and are similar to other learners in far-flung places.

Since the collective model has evolved from a particular context, it is especially well adapted to the demographic characteristics of minority French-language populations in Canada outside Québec. However, other communities, such as women[10] or Aboriginal people (see Spronk, Chapter 5 of this book), may also identify with the centrifugal forces related to belonging to this type of virtual community. Franco-Ontarians are currently involved in projects to share learning materials and real-time courses with other French-speaking minorities in New Brunswick, Nova Scotia, Manitoba, Saskatchewan, and British Columbia.[11] It seems that similar socio-political and cultural contexts among French-speaking minorities in Canada have given rise to similar ways of learning. These include the learners' preference for learning within a group, in real-time interaction with a teacher and peers (Larocque, 1992, 1994; Marchand, 1994).

As noted earlier, Franco-Ontarian learners are frequently separated by large distances and often live in small communities. For this reason, the following additional services, beyond real-time teaching, are central to the success of a collective, group-based approach to distance education[12]:

• Technical trouble-shooting (in person at first, then perhaps through a toll-free line) will help teachers and learners to use educational media. This should be intensive both when new technology is being introduced and when a new cohort of learners begins a distance education course.

• Administrative support, especially for students who have been away from institutional learning. Examples include advice on interacting with a registrar's office, knowing how to use library resources, understanding course calendars or admission requirements.

• Support in how to learn at a distance (time management, reading and writing skills, research methods).

• Local facilitation for learner groups, for example, active and personal student recruitment, encouragement of learning partnerships, publicity at community functions.
• Program planning at a local level and encouragement of inter-level collaboration and partnerships.

Many options are available for providing these learner support services. In the past, Franco-Ontarians have responded positively when a local facilitator was hired. This person, working at least part-time (much like Contact North/Contact Nord community site co-ordinators), can perform all five functions, acting as an intermediary (or even an advocate) between the learner and the learning establishment (Anderson & Nelson, 1990). It would appear to be better to integrate functions on a local basis rather than provide specialized services from a distant central point.

From the Organizational Point of View

Breton (1984) notes that certain socio-cultural conditions, such as minority status combined with geographic dispersion, entail a need for collective choices concerning the development of a community. The organizational aspect of the collective approach attempts to deal with the administrative consequences of a minority's geographical distribution, that is, the need for management of small numbers, for respect of local autonomy, and for rationalization on a provincial level.

Thus, an emphasis on interaction and collaboration must be present in the organization of learning activities and services. The Strategic Planning Council and its roundtables handle joint planning, training, management, and promotion on a provincial level. Learning institutions, government, and the community share the responsibilities inherent in offering education and training at a distance. They pool dispersed resources to create economies of scale. While providing a wider gamut of services such as information dissemination and marketing, registration, courses and programs, and learner support, each participating stakeholder gains access to a larger number of students. Learners benefit as well, since without collaboration among providers, they would not have access to services in each village, town, or city.

Partners in the venture may be varied. They include elementary and secondary school consortia or co-operatives, colleges, universities, community organizations, the private sector, government ministries and agencies, and service providers such as educational television or computer networks such as the Village électronique francophone.

While the collective approach allows for a more efficient use of resources, and thus achieves rationalization, the situation is not without problems. For one, the sharing of power must be negotiated. Every participant must eventually have an equal voice.

The political economy of any domain, the fact that some stakeholders have greater control over the decision process than others, cannot be ignored. ... For solving problems with widespread impact, mechanisms may be needed to disperse the relative power among several stakeholders. There is considerable evidence to suggest that effective collaboration cannot take place unless key stakeholders possess roughly equal capability to influence [the identification of problems and the decisions regarding solutions]. (Gray 1985: 926; see also Nathan & Mitroff, 1991; Day & Day, 1977; Pasquero, 1991; Sarason & Lorentz, 1979)

Fortunately, the "distribution of power among stakeholders is closely linked to the degree of perceived interdependence among them" (Gray 1983, p. 927). When more powerful stakeholders recognize the benefits gained from collaboration, they are more likely to share control over decision making. Furthermore, the use of neutral players, not associated with any of the partners, can also offset inequalities and ensure that all partners have an equal place at the table. Some of these conditions for success have been met in the past, such as the hiring of FORMA-DISTANCE's small part-time secretariat on contract for the first five years.

In addition, successful functioning of the Council requires that partners demonstrate their willingness to collaborate and their flexibility in managing agreements, and that governments develop inter-ministerial agreements and appropriate policies to support provincial and local initiatives. Several members of the Council have collaborated on projects and developed consortia, aided by government policies such as the FORMA-DISTANCE funding mechanism.

Members of the Franco-Ontarian community have a highly developed sense of interdependence, as evidenced by the many alliances between socio-political and educational groups and their strong networking. The reference to a common community aids in overcoming the worst effects of power imbalances among partners.

While providing many advantages, collaboration among learning establishments may also present a challenge to learners. There may be confusion about where to obtain information, where to register, which course equivalencies are available, which institution offers a specific course, who offers learning support, etc. At this time, partners in the collaborative approach highlighted in this chapter are putting system-wide services and communications programs in place to minimize the potential for confusion. For example, inter-level French-language course calendars, in addition to institutional calendars, have been prepared. Universities have signed an agreement for inter-institutional equivalencies and credit recognition for French-language courses and programs. Community colleges are working on a provincial secretariat which will operate a single, province-wide, toll-free line for information and registration.

The number of players and the structural complexity of a decentralized approach can create challenges for funding. More specifically, cost-sharing formulas need to be established. Through Ontario's collective approach, school boards are jointly funding co-operatives, which operate interconnectable sites or which pool school services throughout a region. Programs in early childhood education as well as in drug prevention and treatment were jointly funded and developed by five colleges. Universities agreed on the financing of three inter-campus video-conferencing sites. While it is true that the collective approach raises questions, a centralized approach with a great number of institutions, each trying to offer services to the same small population, may also present problems, albeit of a different order.

Choosing the appropriate technologies—another important aspect of the collective approach—assumes added significance when placed in a wider context of shared planning and management. Technologies must be chosen, adapted, or even created (see Thomas & McDonell, Chapter 10 of this book) to best suit the course content and the learners' preference for group learning. In this way, a community of learners can "appropriate" its technology (see Spronk, Chapter 5). In a system-wide perspective, technologies must also be evaluated in terms of portability (can they be easily moved?), accessibility (do they fit rural and urban infrastructures?), compatibility (are they compatible with technologies from other companies?) and interconnectability (can they interface with other kinds of technologies?).

Sharing sites and equipment has many advantages among different users. For one, initial capital costs are reduced. Not only can the cost of hardware be shared, but other operational costs may be divided among partners, whether these be long-distance, software development, or human resources costs. For example, sharing lines in an existing building, such as a social service agency, avoids installation costs until use of the lines increases and warrants purchase of dedicated lines and bridges. An institution hosting a minibridge can use the lines during the day for its own meetings and in-house training sessions. Furthermore, the local installation will allow better access for community discussion groups or for association meetings.

The technical configuration proposed in Figure 9.3 (p. 167) has other advantages. Besides helping learners identify with their own regional group, minibridges sometimes reduce long-distance costs, especially in regions far from a central bridge. The use of minibridges set up at strategic points reduces demand on large bridges, especially at peak times, and thus ensures access to lines for minority groups or for other constituencies that might not otherwise have priority.

Admittedly, reliance on local autonomy can also present problems. While empowering each small community, this structure can be ineffective if local distance education councils are not sufficiently dynamic or if the players change. Gradual implementation of such a structure by, for example, establishing pilot projects to develop working models, can partially offset this problem. Fortunately, the collective approach allows for such flexibility. As a continually evolving model based on concepts of change, adaptation, and responsiveness, it encourages stakeholders to find ways that will best answer the situation at hand.

Conclusions

In this chapter, we argued that developing distance education from the context of a particular community of learners is both possible and desirable. We demonstrated that by moulding the services from the needs and the "ways of doing" of a community, by choosing teaching models related to learners' preferences, and by providing learning support and access to appropriate technology, courses and programs could increase substantially. Furthermore, we demonstrated that these increases could occur within an adapted economy of scale that permits efficient use of human and physical resources, thus responding to the present climate of rationalization.

The example used was that of the collective approach developed by and for the Franco-Ontarian community. The approach responded to seven main factors related to that particular community: the demographics of a small population distributed over a large territory; equity of access; rationalization; choice and ownership of technologies; response to learners who strongly identify with their virtual cultural community and who prefer group learning over other delivery modes; and capitalization on the tradition of informal and formal networking.

What about results? Between 1990 and 1994, the Franco-Ontarian community has (1) set up an audiographic network (RUISSO) to add to those of Contact North/Contact Nord and the University of Ottawa, (2) developed increasing expertise in the use of technologies for teaching, (3) purchased several minibridges, (4) created a videoconferencing network between four universities called the Réseau franco-ontarien d'enseignement à distance, (5) introduced over 400 teachers/professors and administrators to distance education, and (6) more than doubled course offerings at various levels.

Future challenges include increasing the number of access sites, improving the infrastructure for distance education, and integrating concepts of distance education in workplace training and in community groups, professional associations, and new post-secondary institutions. In other words, the challenge will be to maintain the infrastructure of existing inter-institutional networks during a period of rapid growth.

It will be especially interesting to chart the progress of two new community colleges offering courses mainly at a distance and developed specifically for French-language minorities; the Collège de l'Acadie in Nova Scotia, and the Collège des Grands Lacs serving central and southwestern Ontario. These colleges have both chosen the teaching models and technology outlined in this chapter to serve small dispersed populations.

What have we learned? Firstly, there is a need to build from within the community. Distance educators must respond to learners and their learning preferences, organize both human and technical infrastructures based on what is already in place, and envision all future possibilities and challenges from the perspective of the community. Since the community is at the heart of the approach, it must be empowered to make decisions, to plan and to implement services. Once empowered, the community will know how best to respond to its needs.

There is also the recognition that many challenges can be dealt with only through collaboration. In order to build a Franco-Ontarian "space" or "our place in distance education," each partner had to accept his or her essential part in the design and implementation of a common network. Furthermore, the community reminded distance educators that any attempt at providing courses, programs, or services that do not tie into existing networks has little chance of success. By the same token, those endeavours that take advantage of natural linkages between members of the community stand a much better chance of having large enrolments. Fourthly, a large-scale industrial model working with traditional economies of scale may be inappropriate for some groups of learners. Both demographics and learner preferences may require new, smaller economies of scale based on a holistic approach and on collective values.

Finally, there is the overarching importance of a dynamic approach. In this age of socio-ecological turbulence, it is imperative to develop a model that is designed to adapt continuously to change. This recognition explains the use of system-wide co-ordination with open membership and the variety of ad hoc roundtables mandated to resolve emerging problems on a system-wide basis.

The collective approach may seem complex and, in some ways, it is. After all, it brings together stakeholders from all three levels of educational institutions (universities, colleges, elementary and secondary schools), community groups and associations, the private sector, and government. However, working as separate entities, competing for funds, trying to answer the gamut of needs of the same, highly dispersed population can also be complex. Whereas the latter seeks individual solutions (often bound to come up short because of the system-wide nature of the problems), the former is based on collective action for system-wide solutions.

A collective approach will enable the Franco-Ontarian community, as well as other communities facing similar issues, to deal with the challenges of the 21st century. Having appropriated and developed its own human and technical infrastructure, the collective model is well adapted to forces of global change precisely because it is well grounded locally and in a cultural context.

Endnotes

1. The authors wish to acknowledge the considerable contribution of Noël Thomas to the development of their approach. However, the

present chapter contains new elements with which he may not agree. The authors take full responsibility for the text, including the added or different features.

The approach described in this chapter has been partially implemented over the past five years through the FORMA-DISTANCE program of the Ontario Ministry of Education and Training. The case study presents features of this implementation through June 1994. Other aspects of the model are presented as possibilities of future directions.

2. In 1986, the Ontario Legislature passed Bill 8 granting access to French-language services in government agencies and ministries in designated areas with an important minority. More specifically, Bill 75 (1986) provided for partial control of French-speaking rate payers over elementary and post-secondary schools. "In terms of educational services, however, the procedures adopted were permissive in nature, not obligatory. The result is that, 25 years after the enabling legislation, French-language minority education in Ontario has a certain hodgepodge appearance" (Frenette, Quazi, & Girard, 1993, p. 1). At the time of writing, there were several cases before the courts requesting respect of the law in these matters.

3. In July 1993, the Ontario government announced the creation of two more French-language community colleges that will begin operations in the fall of 1995. The four bilingual community colleges which now exist will no longer offer courses in French after that date.

4. This sector of the Ontario Ministry of Education and Training is now called the Independent Learning Centre. The French-language division is called Le Centre d'études indépendantes.

5. Other authors and researchers, of course, have also stressed the importance of group interaction for learning: Shale (1988); Robinson, Saferton, & Griffin (1988); and Hunt (1991).

6. For example, most psychological approaches, such as the application of cognitive psychology to learning in distance education as proposed by Deschênes (1989), refer to learners treated as individuals and abstracted from their context.

7. This fundamental preference in learning does not exclude independent self-study, however.

8. According to Henri (1994), there is a clear difference between learning in a group and co-operative or collaborative learning, the first being much less structured than the last two. In a group, learners discuss, exchange ideas, and help each other learn, but for co-operative or collaborative learning to take place, activities must be structured in such a way that group members interact interdependently.

9. The expression "roundtables" is used here to translate *tables ron-des*, usually translated into English as "workgroups." (Pasquero introduced the word in 1991 in the *Journal of Applied Behavioral Science*.) The image conjured up by this word, that of equals sitting around a circular table, is closer to the spirit of collaboration inherent in the collective approach and its overall organization.

10. The literature on women in distance education and on women as "relational learners" seems to point to their need to be linked to others when learning. For women also, then, group technologies such as audioconferencing or computer conferences would appear to be well adapted (Paquette-Frenette, 1994).

11. In 1994, French-language high schools in five provinces participated in a joint journalism course offered via audiographics. The University of Ottawa has given courses in Saskatchewan, Alberta, and New Brunswick via audioconferencing and the electronic blackboard. Colleges in Ontario are planning exchanges with colleges in New Brunswick, Nova Scotia, and Saskatchewan.

12. Brindley argues that all learners, from minority groups or otherwise, need various forms of pedagogical and administrative support. This chapter does not claim to cover all distance learners. However, the need for support services by Franco-Ontarians has been effectively demonstrated in the first five years of the implementation of the collective approach.

References

Abrioux, D. (1985). Les formules d'encadrement. In F. Henri & A. Kaye (Eds.), *Le Savoir à domicile. Pédagogie et problématique de la formation à distance* (pp. 179–203). Québec: Télé-Université/Presses de l'Université du Québec.

Anderson, T., & Nelson, C. (1989). Collaboration in distance education: Ontario's Contact North/Contact Nord. In R. Sweet (Ed.), *Postsecondary distance education in Canada: Policies, practices and priorities* (pp. 209–216). Athabasca: Athabasca University/Canadian Society for Studies in Education.

Breton, R. (1964). Institutional completeness of ethnic communities and the personal relations of immigrants. *American Journal of Sociology, 70*(2), 193–205.

Breton, R. (1983). La communauté ethnique, communauté politique. *Sociologie et Sociétés, 15*(2), 23–38.

Breton, R. (1984, November). *Les institutions et les réseaux d'organizations des communautés ethnoculturelles.* Paper presented at the first national research conference of the Fédération des francophones hors Québec, État de la recherche sur les communautés francophones hors Québec, Ottawa.

Cardinal, L., Lapointe, J., & Thériault, J.-Y. (1990, March). *Individu, société et politique. La sensibilité des années quatre-vingt au sein de la recherche relative aux communautés francophones hors Québec* (Report). Ottawa: Fédération des jeunes canadiens français/Université d'Ottawa.

Churchill, S., Frenette, N., & Quazi, S. (1985). *Éducation et besoins des Franco-Ontariens.* Toronto: Conseil de l'éducation franco-ontarienne.

Davie, L. (1989). Facilitation techniques for the on-line tutor. In R. Mason & A. Kaye (Eds.), *Mindweave: Communication, computers and distance education* (pp. 74–85). Oxford: Pergamon Press.

Day, R., & Day, J. (1977). A review of the current state of negotiated order theory: An appreciation and a critique. *The Sociological Quarterly, 18,* 126–142.

Deschênes, A.-J. (1989). Autonomie et enseignement à distance auprès des adultes. In *La formation à distance maintenant* (pp. 13–29). Sainte-Foy: Télé-Université.

Emery, F.E., & Trist, E.L. (1972). Towards a social ecology. London: Plenum Press.

Garrison, D.R. (1989). *Understanding distance education: A framework for the future.* London & New York: Routledge.

George, J. (1990). Audioconferencing—Just another small group activity. *Educational Training and Technology International, 27*(3), 244–248.

Gray, B. (1985). Conditions facilitating interorganizational collaboration. *Human Relations, 38*(10), 911–936.

Gray, B. (1989). Collaborating. San Francisco: Jossey-Bass.

Gray, B., & Wood, D. (1991). Collaborative alliances: Moving from practice to theory. *Journal of Applied Behavioral Science, 27*(1), 3–22.

Harasim, L. (1987). Teaching and learning on-line: Issues in computer-mediated graduate courses. *Canadian Journal of Educational Communication, 16*(2), 117–135.

Harasim, L. M. (1990). Online education: An environment for collaboration and intellectual amplification. In L. M. Harasim (Ed.), *Online education: Perspectives on a new environment* (pp. 39–64) New York: Praeger.

Heimer, C.A. (1985). Allocating information costs in a negotiated information order: Interorganizational constraints on decision making in Norwegian oil insurance. *Administrative Science Quarterly, 30*, 395–417.

Henri, F. (1985). La formation à distance: Définition et paradigme. In F. Henri & A. Kaye (Eds.), *Le savoir à domicile. Pédagogie et problématique de la formation à distance* (pp. 5–28). Québec: Télé-Université/Presses de l'Université du Québec.

Henri, F. (1994, January). L'apprentissage collaboratif à distance. *Bulletin FAD, 1*(4), 1–8.

Henri, F., & Kaye, A. (Eds.). (1985). *Le savoir à domicile. Pédagogie et problématique de la formation à distance.* Québec: Presses de l'Université du Québec, Télé-Université.

Henri, F., & Kaye, A. (1985). Enseignement à distance—apprentissage autonome? In F. Henri & A. Kaye (Eds.), *Le savoir à domicile. Pédagogie et problématique de la formation à distance* (pp. 99–144). Québec: Télé-Université/Presses de l'Université du Québec.

Holmberg, B. (1977). *Distance education: A survey and bibliography.* London: Kogan Page.

Holmberg, B. (1981). *Status and trends of distance education.* London: Kogan Page.

Hunt, D. E. (1991). *The renewal of personal energy.* Toronto: OISE Press.

Kaye, A. (1985). *Les enjeux organisationnels.* Québec: Télé-Université/Presses de l'Université du Québec.

Landry, F. (1985). L'imprimé: un moyen d'enseignement privilégié. In F. Henri & A. Kaye (Eds.), *Le savoir à domicile. Pédagogie et problématique de la formation à distance* (pp. 209–259). Québec: Télé-Université/Presses de l'Université du Québec.

Larocque, D.L. (1992). *Concepts fondamentaux en toxicomanie. Profil de la clientèle* (Research report). Toronto: Fondation de la recherche sur la toxicomanie (ARF).

Larocque, D.L. (1994). *Une école d'été en promotion de la santé. Étude de besoins* (Research report). Toronto: Centre ontarien d'information en prévention (COIP).

Lochte, R. (1993). *Interactive television and instruction: A guide to technology, technique, facilities design and classroom management.* Englewood Cliffs, NJ: Education Technology Publications.

Marchand, L. (1994). *Conception de l'apprentissage chez des apprenants adultes qui suivent des cours à distance.* Unpublished Ph.D. dissertation, Université de Paris VIII, Paris.

Nathan, M.L., & Mitroff, I.I. (1991). The use of negotiated order theory as a tool for the analysis and development of an interorganizational field. *Journal of Applied Behavioral Science, 27*(1), 163–180.

Paquette-Frenette, D. (1994, May). *Les femmes et les technologies interactives de groupe—des stratégies pour combler les distances.* Paper presented at the 10th annual conference of the Canadian Association for Distance Education, Vancouver.

Pasquero, J. (1991). Supraorganizational collaboration: The Canadian environmental experiment. *Journal of Applied Behavioral Science, 27*(1), 38–64.

Robertson, W. (1986). Use of audio teleconferencing. In I. Mugridge & D. Kaufman (Eds.), *Distance education in Canada* (pp. 283–295). London: Croom Helm.

Robinson, J., Saberton, S., & Griffin, V. (1988). *Learning partnerships.* Toronto: OISE Press.

Sarason, S.B., & Lorentz, E. (1979). *The challenge of the resource exchange network.* San Francisco: Jossey-Bass.

Shale, D. (1988). Towards a new concept of distance education. *American Journal of Distance Education, 2*(3), 25–35.

Thomas, N. A., Paquette-Frenette, D., & Larocque, D. (1993). Pour l'Ontario français: L'approche collective en formation à distance. In *Selected Readings from the presentations at the 8th Annual Conference of The Canadian Association for Distance Education/Lectures choisies parmi les communications prononcées au 8e Congrès annuel de l'Association canadienne de l'éducation à distance.* Vancouver: The Commonwealth of Learning, 155–177.

The Role(s) of Technology in Minority Group Distance Learning

NOËL A. THOMAS
DONALD J. MCDONELL

This chapter addresses some of the roles and issues in using technologies to provide distance education services to minority groups. While the chapter is illustrated with the dilemmas faced by Francophones in Ontario and the solutions provided by video- and computer conferencing, the issues raised probably apply to many other minority groups in Canada and in the world and to many other technologies. A few definitions are in order to focus the chapter.

For purposes of this chapter, a *minority group* is defined as a section of society whose identity is determined by cultural properties not shared by all members of the society and whose needs are not necessarily served when the needs of the society as a whole are being served. Demographically, "La minorité francophone" in Ontario (less than five percent of the population) and in Canada (less than 25 percent of the population) can be described as both "a few people in many places" and "many people in a few places." Thus, there are areas that have sufficient population levels to draw many, if not most, traditional educational services (e.g., Francophones in the province of Québec or in Northern and Eastern Ontario), and there are areas where educational services are severely curtailed because of the absence of a critical mass of students (e.g., Francophones in Western Canada).

Technology can be defined as the application of the knowledge of a practical or industrial art or the knowledge of how to do things. Technology, in its generic meaning, encompasses all media including the pencil and paper, which were the first technologies used for distance learning. In this chapter, we focus on technology that depends on digitization, that numerical computer language which has had an impact on society no less radical than the appearance of language itself. We further focus on the communications aspect of the educational endeavour, which bridges the distance in distance education. By combining different media through the process of digitization, we end up with audioconferencing, audiographic conferencing, computer conferencing, and videoconferencing. These combinations of media are often referred to as interactive multimedia or multi-mode technologies.

The technologies of video- and computer conferencing illustrated in this section are often complementary to each other and may or may not co-exist within the same learning group, the same program, or the same course. Videoconferencing reaches small groups of learners in a few areas in a synchronous mode—people are "live on-line" in different locations at the same time. Telematics (which includes e-mail, computer conferencing, database access, and file transfers) reaches individual learners in many areas in an asynchronous mode—that is, people connect from different places *and* at different times. As in all technologies, neither is fundamentally better. The challenge remains to select the best technology to meet the objectives of the learner and of the teacher.

In many ways, Francophones have had to "invent" their own technologies or make considerable modifications to existing ones. We introduce a number of issues related to serving small distance education markets and suggest conditions for success in introducing new technologies to minority group learners.

Issues

Size of Markets and Cost Effectiveness

By definition, minority markets are too small to be self-sustaining for traditional learning and often too small to warrant the use of industrial processes and economies of scale inherent to, for example, delivery by correspondence. While distance education can reach out to increase the size of the cohort, there are costs associated with all outreach strategies. It generally remains more expensive to serve a few students in many locations compared to the cost of serving many students in a few locations. Luckily, doing both together can average costs so that larger groups can subsidize the provision of services to smaller groups.

Belonging to a Group

Minority group members often feel isolated because they do not have easy access to their group of reference. Thus, technologies that reinforce the relationships between members of a group and strengthen the group experience also strengthen the sense of belonging to a community of shared interests. Being able to engage in a public dialogue with other students and to compare ideas with, and be challenged by, other group members is a worthwhile educational process and, equally importantly, a worthwhile sociological process.

Perception of the Quality of Distance Education

Minority groups throughout the world must battle constantly in order to receive the same level of educational services as is offered to the majority. Even though education is seen as a fundamental right, minority groups are often concerned that "new delivery methods" is a synonym for saving dollars and not providing the same level of service as offered to the majority. (Even the majority often thinks that distance education is second-class or cheap education.)

Indeed, quality education is seen, rightly or wrongly, as coming from the face-to-face encounter between learner and teacher in the traditional classroom setting. The fear of being short-changed, as both a Francophone *and* as a distance learner, can be accentuated by the introduction of new technology that will modify the learning experience. Thus, new technology must not only provide the best in service but, more importantly, must be perceived by learners and teachers as doing just that. While not a full counterweight to traditional resistance to distance education, the possibility of learning via new technologies can be seen as modern and leading-edge and compensates for what might otherwise be perceived as an unfair burden on a minority group.

Distance Education and Distance Management

While not well documented in the literature, the distance management aspect of distance education is important to the provision of services. Some distance education processes and technologies can be borrowed for distance management (e.g., telephone and computer conferencing), but they often have to be enhanced considerably to create efficient and effective management of a distance education project. For example, there is a need to book multipurpose rooms, to transfer picture files for audiographics ahead of time, and to provide group calendars and many workgroup services for collaborators, site administrators, registrars, library personnel, and others associated with the successful delivery of the course or program.

Technological Adaptations and Innovations

Not all equipment can be taken off the shelf and used to serve minority groups. Both hardware and software have to handle languages other than English, usually by interconnecting equipment not originally designed to work together, be it computers or video terminals.

While there is some movement toward respecting international characters, most equipment still cannot handle accented characters, either locally (on the screen) or through telephone lines. In some instances, accented characters are accepted if sent and received from a similar platform but will not display properly if sent, for example, from an IBM-compatible machine to be displayed on a Macintosh. Some systems will work if connected to other equipment supplied by the same manufacturer, but will not support accented characters when connected to other equipment. Some providers of transmission services (X.25 packet switching, Internet, etc.) may not provide support for accented characters unless changes, occasionally quite significant, are made to the protocols being used. At least half of the widely used communications software packages drop accented characters from any string being sent. In summary, the International Standards Organization (ISO) "Latin #1" norm (for accented characters) is not yet widely or reliably respected by all components of many distance education or communications services.

There is a natural tendency for equipment suppliers to adapt screen displays and command structures from English. Because French text is roughly 20 percent longer than the corresponding English, it is often necessary to compromise clarity in order to fit basic commands, instructions, or "help tools" on one screen. This problem is compounded by the fact that technical terminology in English often does not translate crisply into French. For example, "upload–download" is translated by "téléchargement en aval–téléchargement en amont," creating two screen problems: length and the lack of suitable abbreviation. Similarly, there is no easy way to write the French equivalent of the often-used "PgUp–PgDn" keys.

Existing software is not always engineered with bi- or multilingual capacity. Unless the initial design included the capacity to support more than one language, it is nearly impossible to reverse-engineer software to add a second language. Even though it is easier simply to translate unilingual English software to unilingual French, the market is usually not large enough to warrant the effort and the costs.

While the road to multilingual software development is paved with good intentions, the reality is that much commitment is required to bring to market simultaneous versions of software in more than one language. Over and above the costs of software development, there are costs related to translation, adaptation, and testing; to writing on-line help screens; and to producing user guides. Significant costs are incurred to co-ordinate these components whenever a change has to take place, either to correct an unforeseen problem or simply to add a new feature. The cost of managing the logistics of software development are not insignificant for one language, and costs more than double when a second language is added.

As a result, the natural tendency is to develop software in English and, a few months or years later, to produce a French version. By then, however, Francophones have started to use the English version of any new product and are reluctant to have to relearn commands in their native language or to pay the cost of upgrading all their work stations. Consequently, many Francophones operate with English versions of new software, thus completing a self-fulfilling prophecy that Francophones do not support the development of French services.

Two Case Studies

1. The Franco-Ontarian Interactive Video-conferencing Network (Ontario)

Background

The Franco-Ontarian Distance Education Network is the result of a joint effort involving the University of Ottawa, Laurentian University, York University's Glendon College, and the Collège universitaire de Hearst. Their goal is to improve access to post-secondary studies for Franco-Ontarians through the exchange of services and courses on the network. Such an exchange makes it possible to set up, jointly or in close co-operation, a variety of professional development programs relevant to the Franco-Ontarian community, to enhance the regular programs that each institution already offers partially or completely in French, and to offer a variety of basic programs on several campuses, through the exchange of live real-time courses.

The challenge of the Network was to install a technology that would make it possible to offer courses in the traditional face-to-face mode in the on-campus classrooms and simultaneously transmit them live and interactively to classrooms in other institutions or off-campus sites. This had to be done while respecting the teaching/learning environment—that is, without affecting negatively the traditional face-to-face environment, yet at the same time creating a high-quality learning experience at the remote sites. The force driving this objective is the often-heard negative perception expressed by distance education learners that their courses are not of the same quality as those offered to their counterparts on campus. History has shown minority groups that the services they receive are not always equal to those of the majority. Thus, there is a need to create a network that provides, within the conditions of possibility, an equal if not higher-quality learning experience.

Another challenge for those setting up the Network was to find a technology that would allow both professors and learners to use it without unduly modifying their teaching/learning habits and without having to spend long hours learning to teach on it.

The amount of time required for teacher training is minimal: the technology is so simple to install and operate that anyone can walk into the room and be at ease offering a course within a few hours.

As mentioned earlier, one of the limiting factors when running a network for minority groups is the number of students at each centre for each course offered. By offering courses live from one classroom to another the cost usually associated with course design and development is greatly reduced. The material used by the professor can simply be duplicated and forwarded to the other centres, where it is made available during class. There are those who would claim that this is not sufficient for a *distance education* course, which requires special preparation of course materials to meet the requirements of distance education students.

Two points must be noted in discussing this criticism. The first is that the statement implies a fundamental difference between the on-campus students and the distance education students. This may have been the case at one time when all on-campus students were fresh from high school, and distance education students were all working adults. Today, this distinction is not as valid. More and more adults are showing up on campus as full-time students, while more and more young learners are working and studying part time. The second point is that quality on-campus teaching should fulfill all the requirements of good teaching under any conditions and therefore need not be modified perceptibly for an interactive multimedia network that puts at the disposal of the professors more teaching aids than are available in the traditional classroom.

The Network is operated by two committees: an Academic Planning Committee, and an Educational Technology Committee which reports to the former. Both committees comprise members from all the institutions exchanging courses on the Network.

The technology

Although the Network is frequently referred to as an interactive television network, it is in fact an interactive multimedia network. The heart of the system is a computer-based interactive television codec (coder/decoder) with an operating tablet displaying a set of

simple icons used to control all integrated media. In a point-to-
point setting, learners at either end have full control over all the
cameras in both classrooms. A computer card was installed in
the codec to run the a large rear-screen projection board that
displays all free-hand writing and can also be used to present
computer-generated graphics, computer conferencing, videotapes,
and images from the electronic overhead projector. The projector
can be used to present print material as well as three-dimension-
al objects. A facsimile machine running inband is available at all
times to exchange print material. A full duplex sound system
with a microphone in front of each student allows for good interactive teaching with student participation from all centres. At the
centre of the Network is a videoconferencing bridge that can be
used to offer several courses to various sites simultaneously. It
can be operated through a modem from any institution on the
network in line with the philosophy that a decentralized network
empowers rather than weakens the member institutions.

In order to maintain operating costs at an acceptable level,
the Network operates at 112 kbps and requires two 56 kbps telephone lines per site. The equipment can run at a much higher
speed, but the operating costs would increase accordingly. The
lower operating costs mean that a course can be offered to a
centre when only a few students are registered. The trade-off is a
slightly diminished image quality.

The outcomes

During the Network's first year of operation, all the first-year
courses leading to the Masters Degree in speech pathology were
offered between the University of Ottawa and Laurentian
University. Masters of Education courses were also offered, and
two courses in education were offered in the multipoint configuration from the University of Ottawa to students at Laurentian
University and Glendon College in Toronto. All students taking
the courses completed them successfully, and all the professors
teaching on the Network for the first time found the equipment
much easier to operate than they had anticipated. The professors
spent from one to six hours learning to operate the equipment.
Once the course began, the students and professors were left
alone with the equipment, which was operated without difficulty.

The audio delay was the only negative point mentioned, but after only a few hours, both learners and teachers adapted.

This type of teaching/learning experience may not be the same as that in the traditional classroom, but it is not of lesser quality. The ability to adapt creatively may be the one character- istic required for successful teaching on the Network. However, it is also the mark of all good teachers.

This is a technology destined to augment radically the partici- pation of minorities in the life of their culture. Not only can such a network be used for offering courses; it can also be exploited by any group for meetings and conventions, and for providing med- ical, psychological, and social assistance to the most isolated members of the community, thus contributing to the creation of an electronic village in the language and culture of the minority.

2. The Electronic Village—A Distributed Telematics Network (Ontario)

Background

The Village électronique/Electronic Village is a computer confer- encing network available by modem from any regular telephone line, anywhere in Canada. Founded in 1989 to serve the Francophone community, it has rapidly grown as one of the few totally bilingual public access networks in Canada. The Electronic Village now operates a network of 14 interconnected hubs serving over 10 000 registered users in both French and English (August 1994). The system has been redesigned to serve an expected 200 000+ users by 1997. Services offered are private e-mail, conferencing, database access, and Internet gateways.

The technology

In terms of hardware, the network runs on 14 Pentium comput- ers located in various communities in Ontario. These are inter- connected and linked to the Internet with dedicated 56 kbps lines. Callers have access to the closest hub through a total of 112 regular phone lines serviced by 14 400 bps modems or through public dial packet-switching.

The operating system is Unix to allow for multi-user/multi-function operations. All international standards are respected to allow for easy connection to other networks and institutions. Thus, access to all services of the Village can be gained from anywhere in the world, and any teaching institution can provide computer-mediated courses without having to run its own computer conferencing system.

Since there was no multilingual conferencing software available, organizers initially tried to adapt existing Anglophone packages to a Francophone environment. This proved to be a futile, frustrating, and expensive strategy. All efforts have since been invested in developing a brand-new multilingual communications system based on an open systems philosophy and respecting all international standards for the transmission of accented characters. Once accented characters leave the Village, where they are processed and stored under the Latin #1 ISO standard, they face a number of transmission barriers. Packet-switching protocols had to be modified and user-end software often has to be replaced for a clean flow-through of the extended ASCII set.

While e-mail and database searching are fully Internet functional and are often available to all users, the main component of the Village software, which is of special importance for distance learners, is asynchronous conferencing. This allows for any type of group work and the creation of a community of interests, both important ingredients in providing educational services to minorities. The conferencing module has been designed specifically with distance education in mind—the professor simply creates a private conference and adds those students whom he or she wants registered. The professor can check attendance at any time to verify, for each student, the date of the last visit and the number of unread messages. There is also a binary file transfer area for each conference, and users and professors can upload and download course material and assignments as needed. Any student can also create private sub-conferences: for example, to collaborate on an assignment or to engage in group discussion.

Outcomes

After five years of experimenting with various software, hardware, and support solutions to meet the needs of Francophones in

Canada, and after a small number of courses were offered and a large number of discussion groups were held, several generic outcomes can be noted.

Computer-mediated courses are not everyone's preferred choice. Yet they are increasing in popularity as more powerful, more reliable, and cheaper equipment is available for homes, even those in remote areas. Computer conferencing also allows "time shifting" of teaching/learning, just as the VCR allows people to view previously taped television programs at their convenience. (An important difference is that television is a one-to-many medium, compared to computer conferencing, which is a many-to-many medium.) This is important for adult learners, who often have to juggle shift work and family life with their decisions to continue their formal and informal education.

The increase in volume of traffic and the duration of connections for distance education purposes increased the cost for telephone connections. Because the Francophone population is often distributed in small and remote communities and often calls in on long-distance lines (paid for by the teaching institution), the provision of off-line reading and writing capacity was seen as the solution to reduce line charges to the central or regional hubs. Once again, attempts at integrating existing software packages proved costly and frustrating, as they were not designed to work together or to work with accented characters. The sponsoring organization is now developing its own Macintosh and Windows version of an off-line reader/editor to be seamlessly integrated with the Electronic Village and to allow the development of new features not presently possible with off-the-shelf packages.

Users are not static in the way they consume services. As they become more experienced and sophisticated and as they read about the promised land of the information highway, they demand more and more new services and speed. The integration of fax and voice technology with computer technology, the creation of a multisession environment, and increased speed are the requirements of the immediate future.

Analysis

Conditions for Success in Introducing New Technologies to Minorities

Assuming that the decision has been made to offer services to minority groups (not an easy decision in the best of circumstances), experience indicates that a commitment to a number of guiding principles augments the chances of successfully delivering technology-based services to any group—especially to minority groups. These principles cover engineering, human, and political issues.

Multilingual Design
Even though such design costs more money, is more complex, takes longer, and is more difficult to manage, both the management and the development team have to be committed to this principle so that every element of input, transmission, output, and feedback can operate in more than one language with accented characters. Luckily, the international market for multilingual systems is increasing rapidly, and these will probably become the norm.

Humanization
Because most learning, including distance education learning, is a person-to-person process that uses technology merely as a conduit, the person–machine interface must be as natural, transparent, jargon-free, and user-friendly as possible. It is better to use warm words like "village" rather than "xNet" or even "Internet," attach users' real names to any letter sent on their account code, welcome people by name when they logon, and thank them personally for visiting when they logoff.

Socialization or Group Belonging
Because members of minority groups are often alone in the process of learning, it is important that they have a sense of community or at least of belonging to a group with similar interests. Creating "classroom" and "lounge" environments for both structured and unstructured discussions is crucial to reduce the drop-out rate, a critical issue in distance learning.

Politicization or Empowerment

Students on campus have many avenues to express themselves, to participate in working groups and think tanks, and to influence the process of their learning experience. An equivalent capacity has to be built in to new modes of delivery so that consumers can not only provide their input but receive feedback from peers and managers and have a genuine sense of participating in making the educational system better.

Collective Responsibility or Ownership

With empowerment comes responsibility, and with collective empowerment comes collective responsibility. Learners and consumers of technology must assume responsibility for the present delivery and future direction of the service, for the promotion of present courses and for suggesting future courses, for the recruitment of new users/learners, etc. Managers of distance education must create an environment and design technical and management systems that make it easy for consumers to participate in service delivery.

Animation and Moderation

Any system of delivery needs a champion to act as promoter, innovator, and energizer. For the distance student who "sees" the providing institution through the filters of various technologies, there has to be one or many energetic leaders to moderate conferences, answer computer or voice mail messages, launch new ideas, challenge old ways of thinking, etc. While this is often done by professors as a matter of course, not all have the time, the energy, or the personality to act as a "one-person institution." Volunteers or tutors may help, but managers have to ascertain that the required level of energy is injected in the learning group process.

User Support

People need to be able to call for help, and different levels of help are needed depending on literacy levels of users. Some people do not know that modems have to be connected to telephone lines; some people do not know where the escape key is on their keyboard or that they need communications software, while others are "power users" who want to use the information highway through a satellite connection or handle multisessions on a single modem connection. The proper level of support is required to keep all, newcomers and experienced users alike, motivated and interested. Support needs to be provided when users need it— that is, at 10:00 p.m. on Sunday evening "because the essay needs to be uploaded for tomorrow morning's deadline"! Much support is of the "hand-holding" type and much time needs to be spent dealing with affective issues of resistance to and fear of technology.

Full Services

In setting up a network, all the services required by the students must be made available. All administrative and counselling services, as well as professors' office hours, can be handled via computers and telephone lines. A toll-free line for office hours works very well. Providing complete library services remains an obstacle to be overcome. Many of the services are already available via computer, telephone lines, and facsimile machines. The libraries will supply books and photocopies of articles on very short notice, but this is still not sufficient for higher-level research projects that cannot be removed from the library. The solution is coming in the form of mass storage of all library materials in a digitized form. This is a scenario that is slowly developing, but it will be some time before it becomes a reality for every distance education learner. In the meantime, creative thinking and much good will are required to make the service available in an acceptable form.

Conclusions

If technology is defined as the application of the knowledge of a practical or industrial art or the knowledge of how to do things, then, as evidenced by the preceding observations, there is more to technology than wires and black boxes. In selecting technologies in general and technologies to serve minorities in particular, there are social, political, business, and pedagogical concerns and interests.

Will distance education in general and, by extension, distance education technologies help or hinder the development of minority groups? Will the economists dictate the medium and the process and thus, the message (à la McLuhan) to minority groups, or will decisions be determined by the politics of the situation? What about pedagogical considerations—or is it andragogical considerations that should dominate the discussion and prescribe the value system that will direct deployment of services? Whose decision should this be?

And by the way, have we asked the learner yet?

Part 3
Analysis

C H A P T E R   1 1

Evaluation and Research Frontiers: What Do We Need to Know?

Judith M. Tobin

Research is integral to the development of any field—its theory, knowledge, and practice. As distance education has been developing in Canada for over 100 years, a substantial inventory of research has accumulated. This chapter will examine the current state of research as it pertains to distance education. For this purpose, the term research has been used in its broadest sense— case studies, evaluations, adoption and usage studies, and inventories, as well as quantitative and qualitative academic research. This review is not comprehensive but illustrates what is being learned and what is being asked. Following this analysis is a consideration of distance education in the 1990s and the congruence between the research and the needs of those working in the field—and ultimately, of the learners.

In her review of distance education research, Calvert (1986) stated:

Those of us committed to the ideas and practices of distance education must realize the importance of documenting, analyzing and evaluating every one of our cherished beliefs if our enterprise is to achieve its potential. ... On the educational side we are concerned with defining student populations and designing appropriate curricula with instructional design and academic quality, with the provision of student support services and with choices among communications technologies. On the administrative side, we must address the economics of distance education, the design of institutional structures and their staffing, and the marketing of programs and the relationships among institutions. (pp. 94–95)

Calvert's listing of the major areas of activity in distance education continues to be reflected in the themes found in research published since her review. Consequently, those same eight themes will be used to present the research reviewed in this chapter—defining student populations; designing appropriate curricula; student support; communications technologies; economics; institutional structures and their staff; marketing; and relationships among institutions. A ninth heading has been added to include the research on training through technological and distance education methods.

This present survey of the literature included over 120 articles published in the last three years in the *Journal of Distance Education* from the Canadian Association for Distance Education, *Open Learning* from the Open University in Britain, *The American Journal of Distance Education* from the American Council for Distance Education and Training, *Open Praxis* from the International Council for Distance Education, and *Research in Distance Education* (no longer published) from Athabasca University. These major distance education journals are the most accessible research resources in Canada. Face-to-face interviews and computer conference proceedings, major studies undertaken by government, industry and other bodies, and interviews with practitioners have supplemented the periodical literature.

One limitation of the study was that the majority of the sources were focussed on distance education. This choice was deliberate, despite agreeing with the counsel of Evans and Nation (1989) that other disciplines can greatly enhance the study of distance education. However, the assumption is made that the literature dedicated to the field is the central conduit for disseminating findings and advances in theory and practice.

The following section provides outlines and results of the studies arranged under the nine headings listed above. After this review of the research, the recent choices of topic and analysis are compared with the changes in distance education as a field and the needs of the practitioners.

Recent Research

Defining Student Populations

Included under the heading of Defining Student Populations are studies on learning; learner needs, behaviour and characteristics; and diverse learner groups.

A number of recent articles have looked at the independence of the learner and how this can be supported. Beatty and Morgan (1992) used longitudinal research to track the development of student skills in learning that lead to independence from the instructor, in terms of content and process. Confidence, competence, and control, linked to the conception of learning, emerged as learner characteristics that needed to be encouraged. Similar attributes appeared in another study, which concluded that learning styles did not significantly account for the perception of barriers between completers and non-completers of a baccalaureate degree program. Gibson and Graff (1992) found that competence, confidence, and commitment were the major differences between the two groups. These findings led to recommendations for direction and support in the early stages of distance education participation, including self-assessment, study skills, coursework, and pre-registration counselling. The assessment of prior learning within a distance context, outlined by Butterworth and Edwards (1993), could fit well into this enhancement of confidence and control.

Through an assessment of the transactions in a computer-assisted teleconference, Henri (1992) established that many of the exchanges indicated independent activity rather than group interaction. The input into the computer conference articulated the results of study and analysis that the learners had undertaken independently. The learners are now publishing the results of this activity for their colleagues. Informal interactions among students and among students and teachers/instructors were also associated with the growth of learner autonomy as demonstrated by their development of their own learning environments (Hall, Greengrass, & Metcalfe, 1993).

Baynton (1992) stressed control rather then independence. She presented the six components of distance learning transactions—student competency, teacher/tutor support, choice, flexibility, value orientation, and access to resources—as the factors that have to be negotiated between learner and instructor for the locus of control to shift from the institution to the individual.

Spronk (Chapter 5 of this book) and Paquette-Frenette and Larocque (Chapter 9) describe providing service to particular populations and how methods may differ from the accepted practice of distance education. They have asked how well equipped distance educators are to cope with the multiplicity of demands that will come from new or more numerous groups of learners. The research surveyed for this chapter has also investigated who these groups are and how they might best be served.

Women have received almost all the research attention related to learner groups. For example, in a dedicated issue of *Open Praxis* (1994), many case studies or stories were told of women learners in distance education and how they are faring. Comparisons with the situations described in Karlene Faith's 1988 publication, *Towards New Horizons for Women in Distance Education: International Perspectives,* indicate that for some, those new horizons may not be any closer (Enoch, 1994), and for others, the progress has been notable (Va'a, 1994; Taylor & Kirkup, 1994). There is always a sense of more progress to be made. For example, in Phillip's (1993) research on the opportunity that home-based study methods can give to women living in or around the capital of Papua New Guinea, she found that courage and perseverance are needed when study is located in what is often a prime locus of oppression. These women also encountered the interrelated challenges of finances and the pressure from family and society against continuing education.

Authority is also a factor for prison populations, as these learners may use education as a way of distancing themselves from the regime. Tutors are challenged by the contradictions between liberal education and closed incarceration (Worth, 1994).

This review of the literature did not find that research has paid attention to a wide spectrum of the disparate learner groups. However, at the *Distance!... Quelle Distance!* conference held in Vancouver in May 1994, there were more than a dozen sessions that looked at Aboriginals, Francophones, women, rural dwellers, and others with respect to their needs for, and experiences with, distance learning.

Designing Appropriate Curricula

Designing appropriate curricula has been defined to include all aspects of instructional design, in which the learner, content, technology, desired outcomes, and institutional or individual support are blended into an effective learning package.

Electronic interaction has become more important in instructional design as computer-based technologies have become more commonly accessible tools. To the three types of interaction suggested by Moore (1989)—learner–content, learner–instructor, and learner–learner—Hillman, Willis, and Gunawardena (1994) have added learner–interface interaction and recommended instructional design strategies so that learners can effectively participate in the electronic classroom. Reiterating the dominance of design over carrier, Davie and Inskip (1992) looked at three different instructional methods for a computer-managed communications course and found that creative designs mattered far more for active learning than any particular system.

The learning activities that distance educators have included in their written materials were analyzed by Deschênes, Bourdages, Michaud, and Lebel (1992). In looking at four courses offered in Québec, they found that there were too few activities that promoted the organization, integration, and transfer of knowledge. Most activities required the learner to find the information in the text rather than assimilate and apply the information. The authors recommended the inclusion of activities that encourage learners to manage their learning.

Citing poorly designed course development models and a dearth of strategies for effective design, Schiemann, Teare, and McLaren (1992) recommend that distance educators use the basic instructional design practices drawn from theory-based general education research. Wolcott (1993) studied how teachers of adults using interactive telecommunications plan their teaching, and discovered a heavy reliance on content and the syllabus.

These articles imply a closer link to classroom practice than most distance educators might expect. The literature surveyed for this chapter did not contain many studies that tied together our concern with the learners who use the technologies and the instructional design principles that are the basis for designing appropriate curricula.

Student Support

Student support comprises all the elements of a particular course, program, and/or institution that support learners in their efforts to learn at a distance.

In his review of the literature on the directions for change in distance education institutions and the implications for student support services, Sweet (1993) presented numerous points of change—some of which were brought forward in the above section on learner and curricular design. A new point advanced by Sweet is that, as institutions move from the industrial model of distance education to the post-industrial model (or what has been called post-Fordism), the concern should be for the way that students interact with the subject and come to understand the ideas studied. The concept of the "learner" becomes that of a person who engages with the ideas and makes personal sense of the knowledge. Hence, interaction becomes integral to the instruction. Sweet advances the hypothesis that to achieve this convergence of interaction and instruction, the roles and responsibilities of both student and academic counsellor must change.

The links between student support and success rates have been established in Tallman (1994), while high levels of satisfaction with the service provided are documented by Morgan and Morris (1994). Sewart (1993) portrayed support services as the interlink between the institution and the learner and therefore the element that most closely resembles traditional teaching. The regional and client-centred nature of support services means that they cannot be transferred from one institution to another.

Distance educators must also remember that they are not alone in providing the support that learners need. Libraries are critical (Burge, Snow, & Howard, 1988). Yet, a study of what library schools teach their students about distance education support was disappointing. The topic was minimally represented in the curriculum and of low priority for deans and directors of library schools (Kascus, 1994).

In Chapter 6 of this volume, Brindley asks what kind of learners we are trying to produce and analyzes the implications that our answer has for the learner support systems we put in place. Although our understanding of these systems and the needs of learners is improving, the research showed little evidence that institutions have developed clearly articulated beliefs about learners and their roles in facilitating this learning. The need for this vision is evident in the study by Brindley and Fage (1992) that contrasted the student support services that are available at the Open University in the United Kingdom and those at Athabasca University in Canada. The latter lacks the necessary vision and so has dismantled many of its previous student support offerings, while the former clearly recognizes their necessity and so has retained and expanded the services it delivers to its varied learners. Student support services are expensive. Research with students, as cited above and in Sweet (1993), indicates that their success is closely tied to the provision of these services. The research has provided the evidence; it is up to the institutions to determine their commitment.

Communications Technologies

Communications technologies are defined as any technology that is or can be used for the sharing of information and communication, for learning, student support, or administrative purposes.

Learner satisfaction and outcomes were the themes of the research that focussed on technologies. Computer-assisted coaching (Hotte, 1993), computer communications compared with audioconferencing and audiographics (Tuckley, 1993), satellite-delivered courses for secondary school students (Martin & Rainey, 1993), and combinations of computer conferencing and computer-based instruction (Lauzon, 1992) have all been tested and reported. These studies indicate that the technologies were effective for learning and that their continued use would have implications for instructors, students, institutions, and the practice of distance education.

The claim that the use of video-based material makes "no significant difference," whether via broadcast, ITFS (Instructional Television Fixed Services), satellite, or video, was reiterated, with the conclusion that no matter how the material is produced or delivered, and whether it is "low tech" or "high tech," students still learn effectively (Russell, 1992).

Chacón (1992) looked at computers as tools for teaching and for linking in distance education. He concluded that it is not the technology but its relationship to the users and to the other media used that is significant; that low-end technology does not impede the learning process; and that, in short, there is no best technology. He posed three questions for the choice of computers in distance learning that could be extended to the application of any technology: Is it possible to serve all students in the desired population? To what learning purposes is the computer to be applied? Is the computer really better than any other less expensive medium for the intended purpose?

Paul (Chapter 7 of this book) criticizes the research that has been done on technologies as mostly evaluation and descriptions of "low tech" uses. His concern is that distance education bring a critical perspective to the application of technology to learning so that the learners, the skills that they need, and the barriers they must overcome are the foci. Some research has begun this process by asking the hard questions about what has to be delivered to whom, and what is the most effective way of doing so. However, the literature does demonstrate some continued fascination with the technological capacities, detached from the educational mission of distance education.

In a comprehensive review of research on educational technology, Thompson, Simonson, and Hargrave (1992) stated that:

It is curious to read the large number of recently published studies that advocate the superiority of a particular medium when research clearly indicates that no one medium is inherently better than any other. ... However, the evidence supports the position that technology-based teaching and learning is effective. ... Once it is understood that there is no superior medium, researchers and practitioners can concentrate on the important questions of instructional design and effective methodology. Understanding the learner and the process of organizing instruction are the critical issues of educational technology. (p. 68)

Economics

The definition of economics extends to studies of courses, programs, services, and institutions to determine the costs incurred for distance education.

This category from Calvert's research review in 1986 was not well represented in the current survey. There are some useful studies and papers (Curran, 1993; Bates, 1994; Mugridge, 1994) that investigate costs and funding of distance education development and delivery, but the journals consulted were almost silent on this issue. Rumble (1992) has looked at the possible cost advantage of the single-mode distance teaching universities in keeping direct student costs low and serving large markets. However, the dual-mode institutions can develop courses more cheaply, provide more varied education, and achieve economies of scale by using the materials to reduce the costs of their on-campus teaching. Rumble gives the long-term economic advantage to the dual-mode institutions.

Comparative information on the costs of developing courses among institutions is difficult to find as the costs are determined in many different manners. The importance of student services for the effective delivery of these courses adds to these costs, and to the multitude of accounting practices. Although distance education can be cost effective, the idea of developing distance education solely as a low-cost solution to educational challenges is antithetical for many distance educators. The issue of cost effectiveness has largely been looked at in isolated case studies rather than institutionally or longitudinally. Full-cost analysis studies will help distance educators to demonstrate that effective learning does not result from mass producing and disseminating low-cost material. They will also clarify the costs and benefits of such components as student support services.

Institutional Structures and Their Staff

Institutional structures are defined to include how distance education is managed and valued in institutional settings and how changes in distance education affect institutions. The definition of staff includes all those involved in the production, administration, delivery, and assessment of distance education.

The dominant theme in this research was the need for change within the institutions themselves. Henderikx (1992) used quality as the guide for this change in setting out key issues for management. The essential managerial decisions involve a clear mission statement, an elaborated marketing statement, and strategic direction toward a product that integrates materials and systems. The production process and the technology of product development must be closely tied to management as well. Ultimately, he sees co-peration on a national or even European scale as the only feasible path to quality because of the need for budgetary and human resources.

The challenge of this change was recognized by Farnes (1993) in his comparison of post-Fordism (post-industrial thinking that moves away from the factory or mass production model) and distance education. He likened third-generation distance education to post-Fordism in its capacities to offer flexible teaching and opportunities for autonomous learning (although it has yet to accomplish this on a mass scale). Any expansion will depend on organizational change, including diversity of modes of study for all students, credit transfer, and redefinition of roles within the institutions. Farnes restates Edwards's (1991) questions on whether post-Fordist education is only for a select group of workers and whether the rest will receive narrow training, except for learning the responsibilities of coping with being poor or on the periphery. Alternatively, Edwards asks, "Can we use new technology and organizational changes to increase and support autonomous learning for large numbers of people in a flexible system of mass higher and continuing education?" (p. 18).

Henri (1993) examines the proposition that distance education is transforming the educational process and democratizing learning through learners' control over their own learning. Tensions can arise between an institution's need to expand accessibility, establish credibility, and attain economic stability, and adults' desire for more control over their learning process. Technologies can facilitate the reconciliation of these forces, but an institution that operates on an industrial or Fordist model has great difficulty adapting.

An extensive international study on the impact of information and communications technologies on post-secondary education (Organization for Economic Co-operation and Development [OECD], 1994) provides overviews of distance education in each of the OECD countries. The Council of Ministers of Education, Canada (1993) has made available their contribution on the Canadian situation, including examples of initiatives in various institutions. The OECD will issue the "clarifying" papers that tackle such concerns as the future of face-to-face and distance education and of technology in post-secondary education.

The continuing separation of distance education from the mainstream of the university was a subject for research and discussion. Kirby (1993) suggested that changing our name from distance educators to educational technologists or learning specialists might help to bridge this schism. In the early days of distance education, according to Moran (1993), distance educators had to convince their colleagues that distance education was not second-rate but could be effective, high-quality, and satisfying. Some recent studies indicate that the struggle is not yet over. Black (1992) found that the controversy continues as faculty were not very familiar with, or supportive of, distance education. Faculty members' main concerns were the lack of dialogue and transactions, as well as the trade-off that they see between accessibility and quality. Faculty could accept that distance education might be used for undergraduate education, but required that the principles of distance education be congruent with their own beliefs and values about education in general.

A national study in the United States (Clark, 1993) on faculty receptivity to distance education for college credit revealed mixed reactions. Administrative staff, women, and instructors in two-year colleges were more likely to be supportive. All expressed concerns with standards, quality, and teacher rewards. Distance educators still have some work to do in convincing their colleagues.

For organizational change to become a reality, we need many more among the converted. Further international light is thrown on these issues in a study of distance education in single- and dual-mode universities, including case studies from Canada, Australia, Malaysia, India, and United States (Mugridge, 1992).

Dillon and Walsh (1992) state that research on faculty in distance education has been largely neglected, as they found only 24 directly related articles. Their search indicated that distance education faculty are well-educated, full-time veteran instructors, from a variety of fields, with positive attitudes toward distance education that become more positive with experience. Their motivation is intrinsic rather than extrinsic, and they do, in fact, alter their roles. Although the link between this alteration and the type of technology used is uncertain, faculty development programs emphasize training in technology rather than the change in roles. It is this change in roles, making learning learner driven rather than faculty driven, that lies at the foundation of distance education. The leadership that would bring this change about is not being developed.

Marketing

The definition of marketing is the positioning and selling of distance education overall and of the specific courses and programs offered by institutions.

None of the articles that were reviewed for this chapter directly tackled the question of marketing. As presented above, some of them looked at the changing perceptions of distance education within traditional institutions. However, marketing needs to be extended to our potential learners, to funders, and to the new groups who are entering distance education—predominantly industry, labour, and government. The literature has revealed a deep belief that distance education requires unique values, understandings, skills, and a conception of learners and control. The question arises of how well we are getting this message out. A more conscious approach to marketing, whether it be of our courses or of our philosophy, needs to be launched and documented.

Relationships among Institutions

Partnerships, co-operation, resource-sharing, even competition, are aspects of the definition of relationships among institutions.

The most dramatic study of changing relationships among institutions was the paper by King (1993) on the new model for distance education established in Australia. The establishment of the Open Learning Agency of Australia centralized the offering of distance education with the involvement of universities and the Australian Broadcasting Corporation. Economics was the major impetus for this new structure, but increasing learner access was also a priority. The author laid out the many challenges ahead, particularly the level of student support, the development of programs of study, the need for professional development, and the change of culture necessary in the institutions that will be supplying the content.

U.S. efforts to develop a consensus for the interstate authorization of distance higher education through telecommunications has moved ahead because of a combination of economic and learner pressures (Reilly & Gulliver, 1992). The policy issues and framework for inter-institutional program design for the state-wide delivery of degree programs through telecommunications were examined by Olcott (1992). McGreal and Simand (1992) discuss the problems that were created by the lack of centralization in an article on Contact North.

Articles about the transfer and adaptation of distance learning materials between institutions (Dhanarajan & Timmers, 1992) and the successful and unsuccessful international co-productions (Koumi, 1993) provided useful criteria on how co-operation can be accomplished. Moran and Mugridge (1993) have also provided international perspectives on collaboration in their recent book.

The need for co-operation has been advocated in distance education for decades. Much has been made of the capacity of technologies to facilitate this co-operation. But judging by the literature surveyed for this chapter, there is some reluctance on the part of distance educators to publish their stories of collaboration in the journals. The importance of co-operation means we need to profit from one other's experiences.

Training

Training is defined as education that is directly linked to the workplace and is supplementary to the formal programs offered by institutions.

Although this is not one of the headings used by Calvert, training has begun to make more use of distance education. It is also a field that exemplifies the blurring of the lines between classroom and distance education as the application of technologies continues to bring the two into closer alignment. Studies by The Conference Board of Canada (1993) provide us with information on the policies, practices, and expenditures for training and development in Canadian business. Stahmer et al. (1991, 1992) extend this with information on the applications of technologies to distance education in business and other education and training settings. The *Training Technology Monitor* supplements and updates this information and provides an essential service, as the literature is almost mute on this topic. The articles surveyed in this chapter focus almost exclusively on university and college education, neglecting the private sector as an important field of distance education. Practitioners within training should be

encouraged to contribute to our journals, and institutional practitioners need to find ways to examine industrial practice for
mutual benefit.

A resource forthcoming from the federal government will help
us to understand the extent of distance and technology-based
training in Canada. For the first time, the *1994 Adult Education
and Training Survey* included a separate question on distance
education. Respondents were asked where any course/program
was taken (including home, community, centre, campus, work)
and how the program was provided (including classroom instruction; educational software; radio and TV broadcasting; cassettes,
tapes, or discs; reading materials). The follow-up question asks,
"Was any part of this program (course) taken by correspondence
or through some other form of distance education or open learning?" This separation acknowledges that technology no longer
equates with distance education, and that a variety of
teaching/learning methods are possible in any program.

Analysis

In each of the above research categories, our understanding of
the learners, the technologies, and the institutions has increased,
some more than others. The question remains whether the
research is enabling distance educators to shape the expansion
of their own field. In Thorpe's view (1994): "... the pioneering days
of distance education are over and its success poses difficulties
for the educator who welcomes its expansion in principle, but
discovers that what is expanded may not always offer more
choice and new opportunities to learners but a cut-down,
bargain-basement version of the idealistic visions of the early
pioneers of both open and distance learning" (p. 4). Some of the
strengths and the gaps in what we have learned and what we
need to learn have been suggested above. The next section will
look more closely at the convergence between distance education
development and the research.

In a recent review of distance education, Watkins and
Goulding (1993) state, "From our observations, we conclude that
the external forces of changing market demands, fast-paced

advances in technology and a depressed economic environment for education will drive the need and demand for distance education" (p. 5). Many have pushed this assessment further. Catchpole (1992) asserted that open learning, distance education, and classroom instruction are increasingly overlapping so that "one might speak more accurately of degrees of openness, structure, distance, and didactic methodology rather than attempt to maintain sharp lines between the three approaches" (p. 34).

Distance education (in the broader sense outlined above by Catchpole) is no longer relegated to the small department of a large university, a dedicated distance teaching institution, or even traditional education. Industry, business, and government have also "discovered" it, as the potential solution to their problems of training, the impetus to the reform of education, and the content for their expanded telecommunications networks. The necessity for distance educators to guide the development of the new services is apparent, if we want to see our positive experiences reflected in new approaches and uses.

The future for distance education holds immense promise for large-scale adoption of technologically based methods to serve diverse and large groups of educational consumers and learners. Distance educators can provide leadership for this change or, as some of the contributors to this volume have suggested (Pacey & Penney, Chapter 2; Paul, Chapter 7), they can be left behind. The research that we are undertaking is one indication of how well we are adapting to the new challenges before us.

As is evident in this review, researchers have continued to validate a number of Calvert's "cherished beliefs," related to the learner and learning: the appropriate use of technologies; the democratization of education through reaching new learners; and the need for interaction, flexibility, and collaboration in design, teaching, and support for students. These issues are of crucial and continuing importance for distance education practitioners. The research reviewed in this chapter has provided important guidance for improved practice. But other information needs continue to go unmet, for both experienced distance education practitioners and for newcomers to the field.

In criticizing a recent book for not including essays that reflected the new perspectives in distance education, Mugridge (1995) stated, "the problem is not the book but the field." His contention is that there has been remarkably little development in what we write about, and how we think about, distance education. In an editorial in *Research in Distance Education,* Rubin (1992) put forward his opinion that "the state of distance education research has not changed or improved significantly. If one looks at past reviews of distance education research (e.g., those of Jocelyn Calvert and Dan Coldeway), one might easily argue that things haven't changed much. We are still publishing primarily descriptive articles in the literature, with little systematic investigation of critical variables" (p. 1).

Of this chapter's review, which is admittedly not a comprehensive one, it can perhaps be said that "it's not the articles, it's the literature." Many of the individual articles are creative and insightful pieces of research. It is only in reading through the whole literature that a strong sense of *déjà vu* develops. It seems that the questions and challenges of 10 years ago are still being taken on, with only minor changes in theoretical constructs, languages, and technologies.

For example, the equivalency of distance education to conventional university teaching is still being measured; the effectiveness of one or another technology (not the instructional design used) is still being tested. In North America at this time, it is not the professor in the next office that has to be convinced that distance education is effective or equivalent. It is the owners of the telecom and cable companies, the educational and "edutainment" software developers, and the satellite systems operators who must be convinced that our theories and our methods not only work, but are essential for developing independent learners. They must also understand the importance of sharing this ultimate goal with us. The research simply has not reached a point of coherence or cohesion where this is possible. To quote Mugridge (1995) again, we have been "so concerned with examining and describing the bewildering variety of methods by which we teach and by which we organize ourselves to do it that we have focused on this rather than on the larger, more significant questions."

Education, at all levels, is under intense scrutiny at the moment because of economics, of dissatisfaction with graduates and the preparation they receive, and of the entry of new interests into the education field. What has been seen as a long-term monopoly has ended, but institutions and those working within them have been slow to respond (Hebenstreit, Tobin, & Winship, 1994, p. 113). Traditional education still has control of the accreditation and granting of credentials, but the means of delivery are being developed by other interests with far different values and goals than educators. As the convergence of technology brings us home delivery of education, as well as every other conceivable service, distance education practices could provide the point of entry that traditional educators will need. Institutions may find that their future does not look very much like their past and that distance educators will become their closest allies as they try to change. As distance educators, we need to ensure that we are ready for these partnerships. Research in distance education must become more aware of the era that it is living in and focus more effectively on the wider issues that have remained partially or wholly unresolved.

Statements on these issues have been consistent. The second edition of a booklet on distance education from the Canadian Studies Directorate (1994) presented the key questions for research as the real needs of the learners; the characteristics, capabilities, and limitations of the learning systems; and the quality of the learning systems and how effective they are in meeting stated goals and learner needs (p. 17). Evans and Nation (1992) stated that we need to emphasize how the learners take what is sent to them and turn it into knowledge (p. 5). Thorpe (1994) found that the emphasis on the development of materials functions as a default mode, taking energy away from the consideration of educational practices that include the social conditions and educational effects of the widening of our field. Finally, in a research agenda for Norway, Rekkedal (1993) included "intensive studies on methods of learning; organizational forms and forms of co-operation; and studies of the educational process, learning media and two-way communication" (p. 36). In effect, we are back to the basic questions of how learning happens, the role of teaching, and how these two are brought together in learning systems.

Answers to these questions are being developed but in a piecemeal fashion, partly because of the initial reasons for doing the research. Very few of us have the luxury of taking the long view. Instead, we are simultaneously explaining and assessing our projects for our institutions, developing a theory that we can apply within our own professional situation, communicating with our colleagues, and operating within funding restrictions that sit heavily on research.

An enormous percentage of the current research reflects the experience at universities, with a lesser focus on colleges or technical education and training. K–12 education receives the least attention. This also limits our responses to the wider questions as we focus on such specific populations that our research has limited applicability to the newer activities in distance education. This includes the societal context in which distance education operates. Our studies have to take into consideration factors that go far beyond the learners as individuals or as members of learning groups. We must continue to look at the cultural context for learning and the factors that operate outside the control of the learners, and establish ways of taking the learning to "where they live."

As educators who believe in what we do and in its broader application for learners, we need to look for ways to overcome the fragmented and repetitive nature of our research. A greater congruence between research and practice can ensure that learner-centred values and practices are addressed in our research studies and continue to be applied to the development and delivery of distance education.

Conclusions

This enhanced congruence can be encouraged through collaboration, exchange, and a commitment on the part of every researcher to keep focussed on the wider issues, even when investigating a very specific question. It is essential to remember that we are seeking to serve a wider audience with our research and that we must keep their needs and interests in mind.

Co-operation is the key word for the expansion of distance education research horizons. If one researcher or one institution cannot afford to do a more inclusive study, then maybe three can. If the emphasis is on the broader purpose and the learners' benefit, then institutional differences will have to be minimized.

The linking together of interprovincial institutions can perhaps improve access to national funding—whether governmental or industrial. In recognizing that the public monopoly on education is in the process of dissolving, it may be advantageous to work with some of our partners (or competitors) in education. This would probably represent our best chance of convincing them that our perspective and experience are crucial to their success.

In the past few years, the Council of Ministers of Education, Canada, the Human Resources Directorate, and Statistics Canada have turned their attention to distance education. They may prove to be advantageous partners for further research on learning and teaching questions, and in widening our scope beyond higher education.

The Commonwealth of Learning, working with the International Council for Distance Education, has established a bulletin board specifically for research. Its purpose is to facilitate co-operative development of research projects and the sharing of results. The initial communications appear to be more concerned with the issues themselves, but this could be developed as an excellent forum for linking together common interests and expanding the parameters of the studies.

Another recommendation is to build on what is known. This isn't meant in the traditional sense of consulting the appropriate sources in the development of our question. The challenge is to ensure that we are asking or answering questions that are in fact new in our research. Even when circumstances limit the purpose and scope of our studies, we can compel ourselves to add one really new element that relates to the broad needs of distance education research.

It is perhaps most important to remember why the research is being done. The immediate reason is to ensure that learners can be better served by distance education. As distance education takes on a more mainstream character, our research is no longer a conversation among traditional distance educators. At its best, it can be the guideline for the development of education for the next century. With this challenge in mind, researchers must ensure that they are addressing the crucial issues.

References

Bates, A.W. (1994, March). *Costing distance education technologies: Developing a methodology.* Preliminary Discussion Paper. Burnaby: Open Learning Agency.

Baynton, M. (1992). Dimensions of "control" in distance education: A factor analysis. *The American Journal of Distance Education, 6*(2), 17–31.

Beatty, E., & Morgan, A. (1992, November). *Developing skill in learning. Open Learning, 7*(3), 3–11.

Black, E.J. (1992). Faculty support for university distance education. *Journal of Distance Education, VII*(2), 5–29.

Brindley, J., & Fage, J. (1992, November). Counselling in open learning: Two institutions face the future. *Open Learning, 7*(3), 12–19.

Burge, E.J., Snow, J.E., & Howard, J.L. (1988). *Developing partnerships: An investigation of library-based relationships with students and educators participating in distance education in Northern Ontario.* Toronto: The Ontario Institute for Studies in Education, Distance Learning Office.

Butterworth, C., & Edwards, R. (1993, November). Accrediting prior learning at a distance. *Open Learning, 8*(3), 36–43.

Calvert, J. (1986). Research in Canadian distance education. In I. Mugridge & D. Kaufman (Eds), *Distance education in Canada* (pp. 94–110). London: Croom Helm.

Canadian Studies Directorate. (1994). *Open learning and distance education in Canada* (2nd ed.). Ottawa: Author.

Catchpole, M.J. (1992). Classroom, open and distance teaching: A faculty view. *The American Journal of Distance Education. 6*(3), 34–44.

Chacón, F. (1992, February). A taxonomy of computer media in distance education. *Open Learning, 7*(1), 12–27.

Clark, T. (1993). Attitudes of higher education faculty toward distance education: A national survey. *The American Journal of Distance Education, 7*(2), 19–33.

Conference Board of Canada. (1994). *Training and development 1993: Policies, practices and expenditures in Canadian business.* Ottawa: Author.

Council of Ministers of Education, Canada. (1993, October). *The impact of information and communications technologies on postsecondary education: Report presented to the CERI/OECD.* Toronto: Author.

Curran, C. (1993). *Scale, cost and quality in small distance teaching universities.* Paper delivered at COSTEL Workshop, Copenhagen.

Davie, L.E., & Inskip, R. (1992). Fantasy and structure in computer mediated courses. *Journal of Distance Education, VII*(2), 31–50.

Deschênes, A., Bourdages, L., Michaud, B., & Lebel, C. (1992). Les activités d'apprentissage dans les cours conçus pour l'enseignement à distance. *Journal of Distance Education, VII*(1), 53–81.

Dhanarajan, G., & Timmers, S. (1992, February). Transfer and adaptation of self-instructional materials. *Open Learning, 7*(1), 3–11.

Dillon, C.L., & Walsh, S.M. (1992). Faculty: The neglected resource in distance education. *The American Journal of Distance Education, 6*(3), 5–21.

Edwards, R. (1991, June). The inevitable future? post-Fordism and open learning. *Open Learning, 6*(2), 36–42.

Enoch, Y. (1994). Women as distance learners in Israel: A second look. *Open Praxis, 1*, 21–23.

Evans, T., & Nation, D. (Eds). (1989). *Critical reflections on distance education.* London: Routledge.

Evans, T., & Nation, D. (1992, June). Theorising open and distance education. *Open Learning, 7*(2), 3–13.

Faith, K. (Ed.).(1988). *Toward new horizons for women in distance education: International perspectives.* London: Routledge.

Farnes, N. (1993, February). Modes of production: Fordism and distance education. *Open Learning, 8*(1), 10–20.

Gibson, C.C., & Graff, A.O. (1992). Impact of adults' preferred learning styles and perceptions of barriers on the completion of external baccalaureate degree programs. *Journal of Distance Education, VII*(1), 39–51.

Hall, R., Greenglass, D., & Metcalfe, J. (1993, November). Independent learning in practice: An examination of student behaviour in the Open University, U.K. *Open Learning, 8*(3), 26–35.

Hebenstreit, J., Tobin, J., & Winship, J. (1994). The future of technology in post-secondary education. In Organization for Economic

Co-operation and Development/Centre for Educational Research & Innovation, *The future of post-secondary education and the role of technology: A clarifying report* (pp. 85–131). Working papers. Paris: OECD.

Henderikx, P. (1992, November). Management and promotion of quality in distance education. *Open Learning, 7*(3), 34–41.

Henri, F. (1993). Formation à distance, matérial pédagogique et théorie de l'éducation: La Cohérence du changement. *Journal of Distance Education, VIII*(1), 85-108.

Henri, F. (1992). Formation à distance et téléconference assistées par ordinateur: Interactivité, quasi-interactivité, ou monologue? *Journal of Distance Education, VII*(1), 5–24.

Hillman, D.C.A., Willis, D.J., & Gunawardena, C.N. (1994). Learner–interface interaction in distance education: An extension of contemporary models and strategies for practitioners. *The American Journal of Distance Education, 8*(2), 30–42.

Hotte, R. (1993). Encadrement assisté par ordinateur et formation à distance. *Journal of Distance Education, VIII*(2), 37–53.

Kascus, M.A. (1994). What library schools teach about library support to distant students: A survey. *The American Journal of Distance Education, 8*(1), 20–35.

King, B. (1993, November). Open learning in Australia: Government intervention and institutional response. *Open Learning, 8*(3), 13–25.

Kirby, D. (1993). Is it time to rid universities of distance education? *Journal of Distance Education, VIII*(2), 69–72.

Koumi, J. (1993). Types of co-production: Case studies from nine countries. *Open Praxis, 1,* 17–20.

Lauzon, A.C. (1992). Integrating computer-based instruction with computer conferencing: An evaluation of a model for designing on-line education. *The American Journal of Distance Education, 6*(2), 32–46.

Martin, E.D., & Rainey, L. (1993). Student achievement and attitude in a satellite-delivered high-school science course. *The American Journal of Distance Education, 7*(1), 54–61.

McGreal, R., & Simand, B. (1992). Problems in introducing distance education into northern Ontario secondary schools. *The American Journal of Distance Education, 6*(1), 51–61.

Moore, M.G. (1989). Three types of interaction. *The American Journal of Distance Education, 3*(2), 1–6.

Moran, L. (1993). Genesis of the Open Learning Institute of British Columbia. *Journal of Distance Education, VIII*(1), 43–70.

Moran, L., & Mugridge, I. (Eds). (1993). *Collaboration in distance education: International case studies.* London & New York: Routledge.

Morgan, C., & Morris, G. (1994, February). The student view of tutorial support: Report of a survey of Open University education students. *Open Learning, 9*(1), 22–33.

Mugridge, I. (Ed.). (1992). *Perspectives on distance education: Distance education in single and dual mode universities.* Vancouver: The Commonwealth of Learning.

Mugridge, I. (Ed.). (1994). *Perspectives on distance education: The funding of open universities.* Vancouver: The Commonwealth of Learning.

Mugridge, I. (Rev.).(1995). Harry, K., John, M., & Keegan, D. (Eds.), Distance education: New perspectives. *In Canadian Journal of Higher Education, 24*(3), 115ff.

Olcott, D.J., Jr. (1992). Policy issues in statewide delivery of university programs by telecommunications. *The American Journal of Distance Education, 6*(1), 14–26.

Organization for Economic Co-operation and Development/Centre for Educational Research & Innovation. (1994). *The future of post-secondary education and the role of technology: A clarifying report.* Working papers. Paris: Author.

Phillip, A. (1993, February). Problems for women in distance education at the University of Papua New Guinea. *Open Learning, 8*(1), 3–9.

Reilly, K.P., & Gulliver, K.M. (1992). Interstate authorization of distance higher education via telecommunications: The developing national consensus in policy and practice. *The American Journal of Higher Education, 6*(2), 3–16.

Rekkedal, T. (1993, February). Post-Fordism and distance education— A flexible strategy for change. *Open Learning, 8*(1), 32–37.

Rubin, E. (1992, July). A note from the editor. *Research in Distance Education, 4*(3), 1, 17.

Rumble, G. (1992, June). The competitive vulnerability of distance teaching universities. *Open Learning, 7*(2), 31–45.

Russell, T.L. (1992, October). Television's indelible impact on distance education: What we should have learned from comparative research. *Research in Distance Education, 4*(4), 2–4.

Sewart, D. (1993, November). Student support systems in distance education. *Open Learning, 8*(3), 3–12.

Schieman, E., Teare, S., & McLaren, J. (1992). Toward a course development model for graduate level distance education. *Journal of Distance Education, VII*(2), 51–65.

Stahmer, A. (1991). *Uses of technologies in Canadian business and industry.* Ottawa: Employment & Immigration Canada.

Stahmer, A., Bourdeau, J., & Zuckernick, A. (1992). *Technologies and lifelong learning* (Vols. I & II). Ottawa: Steering Group on Prosperity.

Stahmer, A., & Green, L. (Eds.).(1993–present). *The Training Technology Monitor.* Toronto.

Statistics Canada. (In preparation). *1994 Adult Education and Training Survey.* Ottawa: Author.

Sweet, R. (Ed.). (1993). *Perspectives on distance education: Student support services: Toward more responsive systems.* Report of a symposium on student support services in distance education convened by the Commonwealth of Learning in Delhi, June 21–27, 1992. Vancouver: The Commonwealth of Learning.

Tallman, F.D. (1994). Satisfaction and completion in correspondence study: The influence of instructional and student-support services. *The American Journal of Distance Education, 8*(2), 43–57.

Taylor, L., & Kirkup, G. (1994). From the local to the global: Wanting to see women's participation and progress at the OUUK in a wider context. *Open Praxis, 1,* 12–14.

Thompson, A.D., Simonson, M.R., & Hargrave, C.P. (1992). *Educational technology: A review of the research.* Washington, DC: Association for Educational Communications and Technology.

Thorpe, M. (1994, May). *The expansion of distance education: A cautionary tale.* Paper presented at the Canadian Association for Distance Education annual conference, Vancouver.

Tuckey, C.J. (1993). Computer conferencing and the electronic white board in the United Kingdom: A comparative analysis. *The American Journal of Distance Education, 7*(2), 58–72.

Va'a, R. (1994). Women and science at a distance at the University of The South Pacific. *Open Praxis, 1,* 19–20.

Watkins, A., & Goulding, P. (1993, December). *Distance education in Ontario: Planning growth in the '90s.* Toronto: George Brown College, Computer Assisted Learning Centre. The Metro Distance Education Project Final Report.

Wolcott, L.L. (1993). Faculty planning for distance teaching. *The American Journal of Distance Education, 7*(2), 26–36.

Worth, V. (1994, February). The same difference: Tutoring for the Open University in prison. *Open Learning, 9*(1), 34–43.

Situating Issues in an International Perspective

IAN MUGRIDGE

As I write this chapter in the fall of 1994, it is about ten years since the conversations began that ultimately led to the publication of *Distance Education in Canada* in 1986. That volume of essays attempted to describe, as fully as possible, the distance education scene in Canada in the mid-1980s, but it contained no contribution with a title or a theme similar to the one at the head of this page. So far as I recall, David Kaufman and I, in planning the subjects we wished to see covered, never discussed the inclusion of such a topic. In hindsight, this now seems a curious oversight.

Not long before the publication of that book, the International Council for Correspondence Education (ICCE) had, at its 1982 meeting in Vancouver, under the leadership of an incoming Canadian president, changed its name to the International Council for Distance Education (ICDE). The new name was intended to signify the changes that had already occurred, or were foreseen, in the practice of distance education. The conference was the first to be held in Canada since ICCE's founding meeting in Victoria in 1938 and the largest to that point. It brought to Canada large numbers of distance educators and led to many associations that have grown in strength and importance since. Many Canadian institutions were becoming involved in projects with developing nations and institutions overseas. For example, our own Open Learning Institute (OLI) was undertaking major projects in Malaysia and Indonesia by 1985. OLI was also beginning to look outward toward other institutions for such activities as collaborative development and use of distance teaching materials. (This organization no longer exists.)

However, no hint of these developments appeared in *Distance Education in Canada*. If this was a serious omission, it did not seem so at the time, either to the editors or to the contributors. Further, no review of the book, in Canada or overseas, pointed out that we had provided no international perspective on distance education in Canada. The explanation is, I believe, that we saw the practice of distance education very much from a national, even a provincial, perspective; we felt that this perspective was paramount and would probably remain so in the future. This is no longer the case, and hence, the inclusion of this chapter in this newest book on Canadian distance education.

Yet, it might be argued that, at least on the surface, little has changed in distance education in the last 10 years. It is true, of course, that a Canadian is once again president of ICDE and that Canada has played a significant part in establishing three major distance education agencies. Indeed, two of the other three have Canadian leaders: a Canadian is president of one; a Canadian heads the board of the other, which is headquartered in Canada (see Partnerships in Distance Education, below). But what evidence is there, for example, that federal and provincial governments regard the prominent place held by Canadian institutions as an asset to be encouraged and exploited? A recent study of distance education projects currently supported by the Canadian International Development Agency (CIDA) indicates that this is far from the case.

The study lists 20 such projects in progress through Canadian institutions or consortia. It also notes that, while projects funded by CIDA in distance education accounted for a mere one percent of bilateral and university and college linkage budgets in 1990, this figure had fallen by 1993 to an even more unfortunate 0.5% (Coldevin, 1993). Such a fact should lead to the conclusion that CIDA, at least, does not yet see distance education as an approach that might make a major contribution to its development work. Moreover, there is little evidence that provincial governments, while in many cases encouraging institutions to look for overseas contracts and students, have recognized the contribution that Canadian distance education might make to activities in other parts of the world.

The issue of government support and funding for international activities does not properly belong in a discussion like this. While this question is of paramount importance to Canadian institutions, it can be argued that it is the responsibility of the distance teaching institutions and their officials to make a more persuasive case for government funding. However, one comment about the type of project being funded is appropriate here. The findings of the Coldevin study cited above indicate that where support was given, it was primarily for conventional institution-to-institution projects. Thus, most of those listed are projects like the Intra-Jamaica Teleconference Network for the University of the West Indies, undertaken by Memorial University of Newfoundland, and the Open University Support Project for Universitas Terbuka, Indonesia, an initiative of the Open Learning Agency of British Columbia.

The two major collaborative projects mentioned earlier are, however, quite different in concept and nature from those discussed by Coldevin. They will be described below in a different context, but their continued presence as major recipients of CIDA support may perhaps be seen as a sign that the federal government's attitude toward the funding of distance education is changing.

Issues

While the question of funding does not figure prominently in the main body of this chapter, there are four separate but related questions that will provide the basis for the discussion of international perspectives on Canadian distance education. These are:

• The growing emphasis on institutional and other partnerships in distance education, not merely within countries but across national borders.

• The pragmatism that has characterized the Canadian approach to distance education, and the perspective that this attitude brings to international work.

• The growing worldwide concern with the welfare of the distance learner and the contribution that Canadian distance educators, particularly with their necessary attention to cross-cultural issues within their own country, can make.

• The ever-present and inescapable question of quality, and how to define and to achieve it.

Each of these questions, aspects of which have been raised in several of the preceding chapters of this book, will be addressed in the pages that follow with particular reference to examples of Canadian activity in the international arena.

Partnerships in Distance Education

Collaboration among distance teaching institutions in Canada is a well-established tradition. There exists a long and growing list of successful projects and continuing relationships at several levels. These include such major inter-institutional delivery arrangements as Ontario's Contact North (Croft, 1993), course-sharing agreements like that between Laurentian University and the B.C. Open Learning Agency (Croft, 1992; Davis, 1992) and collaborative degree programs such as those offered through OLA, which build on college and institute diplomas in other provincial institutions (Bottomley, 1993). Further, there is a growing tendency among Canadian institutions to enter into similar partnerships with overseas as well as domestic institutions. This trend does not reflect the kind of conventional institutional development projects noted above, though these continue to be important. The new aspect is that Canadian institutions are making arrangements with overseas partners that are often similar to those they made at home. Just as, for example, Laurentian and OLA share courses, the former institution now makes its own courses available to the University of Mauritius, while Athabasca University offers a nursing program in Sri Lanka.

Such bilateral arrangements are perhaps likely to be less significant in the long term than the kind of multilateral programs to which Canadian institutions and CIDA are now giving support. Two of these—the Consortio-red de educación a distancia (CREAD) and the Commonwealth of Learning (COL)—have already been mentioned in passing and will now be discussed in some detail. Both of these organizations have, apart from major Canadian funding, strong links to Canada, for the current president of the former is a Canadian and the latter agency has its headquarters in Vancouver.

The primary purpose of CREAD is "to facilitate distance education projects at all levels within Latin America and the Caribbean." The enterprise is managed by an inter-American consultative committee that includes members from all regions of Canada, from the United States and from Latin America. In its initial stages, the outputs for the project were seen as drawing up an action plan for establishing an electronic information network, a human resource development program, and a directory of existing distance education products and technical services for members (Coldevin, 1993, p. 59).

The Commonwealth of Learning has similar objectives on a Commonwealth-wide scale. It was established through an initiative approved by the Commonwealth Heads of Government meeting (CHOGM) held in Vancouver in September 1988, and began operations early in 1989. COL has benefitted from contributions by some 28 of the 50 Commonwealth countries, though by far the largest contribution in its first quinquennium came from the governments of Canada (through CIDA) and of British Columbia. COL "represents a major cooperative effort by Commonwealth countries to improve the quality and scope of distance education" (Coldevin, 1993, p. 51), particularly in the developing countries, and thus to increase access to education and training at all levels in these countries. COL has acted primarily as a facilitator in assisting development of distance education capacity rather than as a more conventional donor agency. In this respect, CREAD and COL are very much alike.

They also may be said to represent, or at least to presage, the increasing force of the argument for placing Canadian distance education in an international context. Through organizations of this sort and others like ICDE, distance education itself becomes more clearly an international activity as well as one of regional or national concern. The fact that countries other than Canada are adopting this international approach makes it more imperative that Canadian distance educators, and the policy makers to whom they are responsible, view their activities from an international perspective. The example of the United Kingdom Open University (UKOU) illustrates this point.

In the last few years, the UKOU has engaged in a major expansion into Europe and, in the years between 1990 and 1993, moved rapidly from a national open university (which could accept students only if they were resident within the United Kingdom) to become an international organization, accepting large numbers of students from continental Europe. These developments were described at a conference held in the summer of 1994 at Pennsylvania State University (Tait, 1994). At the same conference, other speakers talked of the increasing internationalization of the activities undertaken by distance educators (see, for example, Kinyanjui, 1994). Such evidence forces us to conclude that distance educators, indeed any educators, must increasingly take into account the developments that are occurring in other parts of the world in making their plans and developing their programs.

A Pragmatic Approach to Distance Education

Linked to this growing international focus is an important contribution to distance education that is particularly Canadian. Other chapters in this volume demonstrate that one of the most prominent characteristics of distance education in Canada has been and continues to be its pragmatism. Distance education institutions and practices have grown up across the country in various ways because they have been required to respond to a variety of needs and circumstances. One of the most enduring vehicles for the delivery of distance teaching in Canada has been the provincial correspondence branches, each of which developed differently (McKinnon, 1986). At the college level, a similar variety in intention and approach has long been evident (McWilliams, 1994). A recent collection of essays on models of distance education at the university level contained essays on four Canadian institutions— Athabasca University, the B.C. Open University, Laurentian University, and the University of Waterloo—which presented widely divergent approaches to the challenge of providing university education to dispersed populations (Mugridge, 1992).

Each approach, dictated at least in part by perceptions of the best way to meet student needs, provides insights into ways in which overseas institutions can meet their own students' needs. This has, in fact, been the case as many Canadian institutions have engaged in development projects related to new institutions. This is perhaps particularly apposite at a time when doubts are being expressed about the systems put in place by some of the major open universities of the world, doubts that draw attention to the difficulties of students studying in huge institutions in which systems must often, to remain functional, become less flexible and personal (see Evans & Nation, 1993, pp. 201–209). In such a situation, the approaches taken by the necessarily smaller Canadian institutions can be informative examples for reform of the mass teaching institutions of other countries.

In Chapter 7 of this book, Paul discusses the ever-present question of technology and its role in traditional and distance education. In arguing for some limits in its application (limits that might avoid at least some of the difficulties being encountered by the bigger, more mechanized distance teaching institutions), he urges that the major challenge for educators now and in the future is "to focus attention back where it belongs—on the individual learner and his or her learning needs." In doing this, his arguments are consistent with those advanced by Stahmer (Chapter 3) and Brindley (Chapter 6), as well as with those of Evans and Nation (1993, pp. 196–214) in their own concluding chapter. In it, they argue not merely for a more comprehensive definition of technology but also for an approach to its use that seeks to limit the size of the units that are developed to deliver instruction at a distance and to emphasize effective networks rather than very large institutions.

The Learner: Cross-Cultural Issues in Distance Education

Distance teaching institutions worldwide have become increasingly conscious of learners' concerns. The very imperatives to provide widespread access that led them to establish efficient and streamlined systems in the first place have too often meant that institutions have tended to move away from the equally strong need to be sensitive to student concerns. It would be hard to argue that Canadian institutions have been more or less successful than others in restoring a working balance between these two often conflicting requirements. However, the pragmatism discussed above and in many of the other chapters in this book point to the existence of at least proposed solutions to the dilemmas with which institutions are faced. Brindley, for example, argues strongly (and, in my view, correctly) for the centrality of student support issues in distance teaching institutions. If institutions lose sight of this function, the effectiveness of their teaching will be drastically diminished.

One area of student concern to which many Canadian institutions have paid particular attention is cross-cultural issues, a matter that has become increasingly central as distance education becomes more internationalized. At a very basic level, most of us have long been aware that the transfer of teaching materials from one country to another, even between two institutions in different parts of the same country, is by no means a simple matter. Some of the course-sharing agreements in existence in Canada have already been mentioned. Such agreements will undoubtedly proliferate and tend more toward the collaborative development of course materials because the means of producing materials collaboratively are becoming more widely available and cheaper; the means of moving materials from place to place are becoming simpler; the means of allowing students to study simultaneously at more than one institution are becoming more common; and the means of transferring credits among institutions are becoming more liberal and refined. As these factors come increasingly into play, institutions will almost inevitably come to see themselves as partners with others in providing education and training to increasingly diverse and widely separated groups of students.

In this context, the questions posed by Moore at the 1994 Penn State conference are just as relevant for Canadians as they are for Americans (Moore, 1994). Cultural difficulties always arise when institutions serve diverse groups of students. They can be problematic when students move from one country, or even one region, to another. There may be even more problems when distance education makes it possible for students to study abroad without actually travelling. In this situation, the Canadian experience may become particularly relevant.

Cross-cultural problems have always existed in Canadian education, and this has been as true for distance educators as it has for others. One particular example is Contact North in northern Ontario, whose mandate is to serve Anglophone, Francophone, and Aboriginal students spread in small groups over a wide area (Roberts, Burge, & White, 1990). These problems are not, of course, restricted to particular linguistic groups, as distance teaching institutions have been obliged to deal with the challenges of delivering instruction at all levels to a wide range of immigrant groups as well (Roberts, 1994).

The Question of Quality

The question of providing education and training of high quality is fundamental. The basic problem in this context is that of defining quality and how to achieve it. Quality assurance is becoming increasingly an international endeavour. For several years, there has been an annual conference on assessing quality in higher education. The papers presented to these meetings have added considerably to the literature on the subject. In 1991, the Hong Kong Council for Academic Accreditation (HKCAA) sponsored a conference on the subject, an event that has had two concrete results. First, the publication of the conference proceedings has provided one of the most widely cited collections in the field (Craft, 1992). Second, the meeting led to the formation of the International Network of Quality Assurance Agencies in Higher Education. Based at the HKCAA headquarters in Hong Kong, the Network has become actively involved in disseminating information about current practice and research in the field, including the publication of the Proceedings of the Network's Second Conference, held at Montréal in 1993 (Craft, 1994).

These events have led to a heightened and more informed interest in quality assurance in higher education in general, and thus institutions and governments have begun to pay increased attention to it. Concurrently, the question of quality assurance in distance education has come under closer scrutiny and discussion at a series of events that have published their results, thus giving them a wider currency.

For example, in 1991, the Australian and South Pacific External Studies Association devoted its biennial forum to the subject of quality assurance (Atkinson, McBeath, & Meacham, 1991). Two years later, a major conference at the UKOU was organized around a similar theme (Tait, 1993). Further, COL has encouraged the establishment of workable quality assurance mechanisms in distance teaching institutions. Through a major project to introduce such mechanisms into Indian open universities and correspondence institutes, it has begun an effort that should promote such developments, not merely in India, but also in other developing Commonwealth nations (Deshpande & Mugridge, 1994).

Although Canadian institutions have not been prominent in the debate over quality assurance in higher education, this does not mean that they are not sensitive to it. Canadian distance teaching institutions, however, have a historical stake in quality assurance: believing that the instruction they provide had to be seen to be as good as that of conventional institutions, they designed from the start procedures aimed at ensuring the quality of their course materials and teaching. They are thus well placed to participate in the continuing search for quality in distance education and, as the distinctions between distance and conventional education become increasingly blurred, in education in general.

Conclusions

The evidence presented in this chapter strongly suggests that distance education (like campus-based education) is becoming increasingly internationalized. In 1979, when the UKOU celebrated its 10th anniversary with a conference on teaching adults at a distance, the idea of collaboration among institutions was widely discussed and applauded, and generally regarded as beyond the capacity of most institutions. Today, it is hard to believe that this was the case such a short time ago. Several examples of important and successful collaboration have been quoted in this chapter. A recent collection of essays documents collaboration on a wider scale (Moran & Mugridge, 1993). Increasingly, institutions are seeing their own concerns within a wider context and recognizing that colleagues in other countries have important contributions to make to the solution of what were once seen as purely local problems.

An instructive example of this was a seminar on the funding and costing of open universities sponsored by ICDE and COL in conjunction with the annual conference of the Asian Association of Open Universities in Hong Kong in November 1993. This event spent a day discussing, on the basis of several pre-distributed case studies, common problems related to funding and costing and the possibility of devising a common solution. The discussion, in which a third of the participants were heads of institutions, led to a decision to publish the case studies and to pursue investigation of many of the problems identified. The first of these occurred early in the following year (Mugridge, 1994) and an international working group is being set up to begin further research.

Canadian distance teaching institutions, with the special skills and expertise derived from their own experience, have so far made major contributions to the internationalization of these activities. This has been done alone, in concert with other institutions, and through international consortia. While it is difficult to imagine a future in which Canadian institutions will no longer be required to place the interests of their own regions and students first in their planning, it is equally difficult to envisage one in which the trends that have been discussed here will be reversed. Although it is presumptuous to predict the precise form that this future will take, it is clear that, in their search to provide better and more accessible learning opportunities for their students, Canadian distance teaching institutions will continue along the course of internationalization on which they have firmly embarked.

References

Atkinson, R., McBeath, C., & Meacham, D. (Eds.).(1991). *Quality in distance education: ASPESA Forum 91*. Bathurst: Australian and South Pacific External Studies Organization.

Bottomley, J. (1993). Institutional cultures and their impact: "Laddered" studies in health sciences in British Columbia. In L. Moran & I. Mugridge (Eds.), *Collaboration in distance education: International case studies* (pp. 12–36). London: Routledge.

Coldevin, G. (1993). *Distance education and other alternative learning strategies: Opportunities and constraints for Canadian official development assistance*. Ottawa: Canadian International Development Agency.

Craft, A. (Ed.).(1992). *Quality assurance in higher education: Proceedings of an international conference, Hong Kong, 1991*. London: Falmer.

Craft, A. (Ed.).(1994). *International development in assuring quality in higher education.* London: Falmer.

Croft, M. (1992). Single or dual mode: Challenges and choices for the future of distance education. In I. Mugridge (Ed.), *Distance education in single and dual mode universities* (pp. 49–62). Vancouver: The Commonwealth of Learning.

Croft, M. (1993). The Contact North project: Collaborative project management in Ontario. In L. Moran & I. Mugridge (Eds.), *Collaboration in distance education: International case studies* (pp. 132–150). London: Routledge.

Davis, A. (1992). The Open University of British Columbia, Canada. In I. Mugridge (Ed.), *Distance education in single and dual mode universities* (pp. 63–78). Vancouver: The Commonwealth of Learning.

Deshpande, P., & Mugridge, I. (Eds.).(1994). *Quality assurance in higher education.* Vancouver: The Commonwealth of Learning.

Evans, T., & Nation, D. (Eds.).(1993). *Reforming open and distance education: Critical reflections from practice.* London: Kogan Page.

Kinyanjui, P. (1994). Recent developments in Africa. In *Conference Proceedings: International Distance Education Conference* (pp. 13–30). College Park: Penn State University.

McKinnon, N. (1986). Public elementary and secondary schools. In I. Mugridge & D. Kaufman (Eds.), *Distance education in Canada* (pp. 194–203). London: Croom Helm.

McWilliams, P. (Ed.).(1994). *Colleges reaching out.* Vancouver: The Commonwealth of Learning.

Moore, M. (1994). Is there a cultural problem in international distance education? In *Conference Proceedings: International Distance Education Conference* (pp. 62–65). College Park: Penn State University.

Moran, L., & Mugridge, I. (Eds.).(1993). *Collaboration in distance education: International case studies.* London: Routledge.

Mugridge, I., & Kaufman, D. (Eds.).(1986). *Distance education in Canada.* London: Croom Helm.

Mugridge, I. (Ed.).(1992). *Distance education in single and dual mode universities.* Vancouver: The Commonwealth of Learning.

Mugridge, I. (Ed.).(1994). *The funding of open universities.* Vancouver: The Commonwealth of Learning.

Roberts, J., Burge, E., & White, B. (1990). Distance education for minority groups: Issues confronting a delivery agency. In M. Croft, I. Mugridge, J. Daniel, & A. Hershfield (Eds.), *Distance education: Development and access* (pp. 43–45). Caracas: Universidad Nacional Abierta.

Roberts, J. (1994). Cross-cultural and international reflections: Francophone, Aboriginal and immigrant distance learners in Canada. In *Conference Proceedings: International Distance Education Conference* (pp. 66–105). College Park: Penn State University.

Tait, A. (Ed.).(1993). *Quality assurance in open and distance learning: European and international perspectives—Conference papers.* Cambridge: The Open University.

Tait, A. (1994). From a domestic to an international organization: The Open University UK and Europe. In *Conference Proceedings: International distance education conference* (pp. 31–41). College Park: Penn State University.

CHAPTER 13

Policy Approach for Distance and Open Learning in the Information Age

Erin M. Keough
Judith M. Roberts

Communications and education have always been priority policy areas for governments in Canada.

Communications has been important because Canada's population is relatively small compared to its geographic area: approximately 29 million people spread over 9 970 000 square kilometres (Council of Ministers of Education, Canada [CMEC], 1993, p. 1). Successive federal governments have strongly supported initiatives to unite the country geographically, such as the development of the Great Lakes waterways, the Canadian Pacific Railway, and the Trans-Canada Highway. Such policy objectives also focussed on social and economic goals such as promoting trade along the east–west axis to offset persistent north–south patterns. Similarly, after the invention of the telephone in 1874, the federal government also supported the application of telecommunications systems to achieve similar goals of enhanced trade, competitiveness, cultural vitality, and national sovereignty (Manley, 1994, p. 7).

Thus, although the Canadian Information Highway might seem to have suddenly appeared on the government's policy agenda, it actually has a robust history and tradition upon which to build. Canada's interest in communications has traditionally involved three major stakeholders: the federal government, provincial or territorial governments, and private sector companies. Policy has therefore evolved among them in a complex and dynamic interplay of forces and interests.

Education, while considered equally important to Canada's success, has had a simpler history. It has always been a provincial or territorial government responsibility, with minimal federal and private sector involvement. Since Queen's University launched distance education in Canada by offering a correspondence course in 1889, distance educators have traditionally dealt primarily with provincial ministries of education. As long as distance educators relied on stand-alone technologies such as print, audiocassettes, and videotapes, the policy environment remained essentially provincial. However, once they began experimenting with such technologies as the Hermes satellite in the 1970s (Kerr, 1993; Jelly, 1993), they gradually moved into the realm of federal policy. With each successive communications tool they adopted, distance educators have become increasingly implicated in a wider range of telecommunications and broadcast policy environments.

Traditionally, distance educators have had policy objectives similar to those expressed by the federal government when it built the railroad or established the Canadian Broadcasting Corporation: that is, equitable access to opportunities for all citizens. Now, however, government policy contexts are changing, and distance educators face some interesting new policy issues, particularly as they relate to this powerful new tool, the information highway.

Previous chapters in this book have described specific challenges at the interface of communications technology with such aspects of distance education as learner support or cultural sensitivity. This chapter's goal is to provide a framework within which specific issues can be situated: that is, to suggest a context that will facilitate systemic thought (see Pacey & Penney, Chapter 2) rather than ad hoc reaction. We will therefore briefly outline the structure of two sectors (telecommunications/information technology [IT] and education/distance education) and describe and apply a policy analysis framework. We will then examine these two sectors from the perspective of policy development, and conclude by analyzing issues that emerge for distance educators.

Table 13.1
Structure of Canada's telecommunications and broadcast industry.[1]

	Revenues ($ Millions)	Employment
Telecom manufacturing*	$ 3 644	22 572
Telecom services*	$ 16 236	107 248
Computer manufacturing*	$ 3 512	12 456
Computer services*	$ 6 076	61 631
Cable TV†	$ 1 968	9 112
Total	**$ 31 436**	**213 019**

* Industry, Science & Technology Canada (1993a), *Information Technologies Statistical Review.*
†Statistics Canada (1993b), *Advanced Statistics of Canada 1993/94.*

Issues/Context

Telecommunications

Canada has a strong record of innovation in telecommunications and broadcast technologies. The telephone was invented by a Canadian, Alexander Graham Bell, in 1874. The first trans-atlantic wireless radio telegraph was sent from England to Signal Hill, Newfoundland, in 1901. In 1972, Canada became the first country in the world to have its own domestic communications satellite service (Communications Canada, 1992).

Table 13.1 describes the structure of Canada's communications sector.

Nine of Canada's approximately 58 telecommunications carriers belong to Stentor, a consortium that permits them to collaborate on issues of mutual concern such as sharing of long-distance revenues. Some companies are private (e.g., Stentor), while others are government owned (e.g., Edmonton Telephone).

IT networks are also divided between the public and private sectors. Some services such as e-mail are provided by the private sector, but the fastest growing e-mail services are provided by public sector stakeholders such as Internet.

This, then, is the telecommunications (and IT) context in Canada in the mid-1990s—dominated by the federal and private sectors with little provincial involvement.

Education/Distance Education[2]

With some exceptions relating to Canada's Aboriginal populations and its armed forces, Canada's Constitution and associated statutes assign responsibility for education to the provincial and territorial governments. These governments have the power to delegate authority to local school boards or to other authorities recognized by the province.

The Council of Ministers of Education, Canada (CMEC) was established in 1967. In a context where each province and territory is responsible for its education system, CMEC offers ministries and departments an opportunity to work collectively, consult on matters of mutual interest, represent Canadian education internationally, provide liaison with various federal departments, and co-operate with other national educational organizations such as teachers' federations or the Canadian Association for Distance Education (CADE).

There are three levels of formal education in Canada: elementary/secondary, college, and university. Statistical information on enrolments and expenditures is given in Table 13.2.

In 1993–94, 54 percent of these universities were active in distance education (CMEC, 1995). Sixty-eight percent of colleges were reported to be involved in distance education in 1992–93 (McWilliams, 1994). Thirty-six percent of large and medium-sized companies use distance education techniques (Stahmer & Green, 1994). There are no equivalent statistics for the elementary/secondary school activity trends.

Elementary/Secondary Education

Public education in Canada is provided free up to the end of secondary school. A provincial ministry of education is responsible

Table 13.2
Canada's education and training systems, 1993–94*

Education Level	No. Institutions	Full-time Enrolment	Expenditures ($ Billion)
Elementary/ secondary	16 231	5 360 900	$35.0
College	203	365 065	4.1
University	69	585 200	11.1
Training†		262 891	5.3
Totals	**16 503**	**6 574 056**	**$55.5**

* Statistics Canada (1993b), *Advanced Statistics of Canada 1993/94*, Tables 1, 6, 7, 8, 9, 11.
† Statistics Canada (1993a), *Education in Canada 1991/92*, Table 8.

for education. Local school boards, established under provincial legislation, organize and administer the publicly funded school services, and have the authority to levy taxes. There are also private, fee-charging schools that generally follow closely the curriculum requirements of the province.

Post-Secondary Education

Colleges have different methods of governance and roles in various provinces. All offer diploma or certificate programs reflecting the interests and needs of the region they serve. Public colleges are supported primarily by government operating grants, as well as by tuition fees paid by individual students and other sources of revenue.[3] Private vocational and technical colleges generally do not receive government funding.

Universities offer three different levels of study leading to degrees and may offer diploma or certificate courses. Universities are generally established as separate legal entities, and have a high degree of autonomy. Overall, 74.9 percent of universities' general operating expenditures were covered by government

Table 13.3
Government policy instruments.

Low Coercion	Medium Coercion	High Coercion
• Advertising campaign	• Taxes	• Regulatory agency
• Speeches	• Expenditure	• Crown corporations
• Task forces	• Goverment model use	

funding in 1991–92 (Cansim Table 00590206),[3] with the balance of revenues coming from tuition fees, research grants, and other sources.

The public education context, then, is primarily provincial with little federal or private sector involvement.

Government Policy Instruments

Both provincial and federal governments have at their disposal a wide variety of policy instruments which they can and have applied to these two sectors, for example, laws, taxes, licences, regulatory agencies, commissions, and expenditures. A common approach to categorizing these instruments is to rank them on a continuum between low and high coercion.[4] Coercion refers to legitimate actions of an elected government in carrying out the wishes of its citizens. High-coercion instruments allow direct government involvement, such as the establishment of a regulatory agency or Crown corporation. Low-coercion instruments include such activities as advertising campaigns. In the middle are taxes, government expenditures, and some activities of the bureaucracy (Woodside, 1986; Pal, 1991). Table 13.3 summarizes the range of such instruments.

The type and mix of these instruments employed in any policy domain are of interest to those in a given community affected by the policies. Policy instruments used in the telecommunications and education fields are described below. Examples have been selected that highlight issues related to current distance education challenges.

Case Studies

Telecommunications and Broadcast

Both federal and provincial governments employ a variety of policy tools across the high- to low-coercion continuum in this area.

High coercion

Crown Corporations/Government Enterprises

The federal government created the Canadian Broadcasting Corporation in 1936 (Manley, 1994, p. 7). Its initial mandate in radio, extended to television in the 1950s, related to the support of regional and national cultural and social goals. In 1969, the federal government created Telesat. Jointly owned by the federal government and the major telecommunications providers, it was charged under federal legislation with the responsibility to provide all domestic satellite services. It served the government's policy objective of promoting reasonably priced, universal basic telecommunications service, particularly in Northern and remote areas of Canada. By 1991, however, the government had privatized Telesat completely. Teleglobe, a successor to the 1949 Canadian Overseas Telecommunications Company, was established in 1975. Vested with sole responsibility for international long-distance satellite service, it was privatized even sooner than Telesat, in 1987.

Provinces were also highly interventionist in telecommunications. Several provinces owned telephone companies at the turn of the century. In 1994, only Saskatchewan and Manitoba do.

Regulations

The Canadian Radio-television and Telecommunications Commission (CRTC), whose mandate is to regulate the broadcast and telecommunications industries in Canada, is another example of coercive government policy implementation. It was created by the federal government in 1976.[5] CRTC policies led to the privatization of Teleglobe and Telesat. In addition to fostering privatization, CRTC rulings affecting Canada's telephone companies have also encouraged competition. Since 1979, the CRTC has gradually lessened the monopoly position of the Stentor member companies in the long-distance market.[6]

Until the late 1980s, the provinces also maintained regulatory boards. In Newfoundland, for example, Terra Nova Telephone was regulated by the CRTC, while Newfoundland Telephone was regulated by the Newfoundland and Labrador Public Utilities Board. However, in 1989, the Supreme Court of Canada effectively eliminated provincial powers by giving the CRTC jurisdiction over all telephone companies.

Medium coercion

Taxation/Expenditure

Both levels of government employ tax policies to enhance the use of telecommunications networks. For example, Industry Canada grants research tax credits to companies that participate in trials of Canada's information highway, CANARIE Inc. (Canadian Network for the Advancement of Research, Industry and Education). Some provincial governments give tax credits for R&D, a substantial inducement considering that Ontario's telecommunications sector, for example, invests over $810 million in R&D annually.

The federal government has, in the past, allocated tax revenues both to the development of Canada's information and telecommunications infrastructure, and to the development of social, educational, and cultural applications using the infrastructure. In the 1970s, for example, the federal Department of Communications (DOC) supported social and educational trials with the Hermes and Anik satellites (Kerr, 1993; Jelly, 1993). More recently, Industry Canada has conducted a competition for the establishment of Networked Centres of Excellence, one of which is in tele-learning. Through CANARIE and the Social Science and Humanities Research Council, it has funded several pre-competitive research projects related to development of products for the information highway. CANARIE estimates that the $14.2 million it allocated to projects in February and May 1994 leveraged $36.8 million from other partners.

Provincial governments have also invested funds in infrastructure. For example, on June 17, 1994, the Ontario
Government announced that it was spending $5 million to create
the Ontario Education Highway, a link between elementary and
secondary schools similar to O*Net, the Ontario component of
CA*Net, which in turn is the Canadian component of the
Internet, used by the province's colleges and universities.

Government as Model User
Both federal and provincial governments are becoming model
users of telecommunications in their day-to-day business. The
federal government now places its announcements of Requests
for Proposals on a networked electronic database. In 1994, it created Radian, a cost-recovery business unit, whose mission is to
provide distance learning and business communications services
to the federal public service, and to any other public sector organization. Provincial governments have sometimes used their bulk
purchasing power to obtain preferential long-distance rates to
support distance education networks (e.g., TENB in New
Brunswick) and have intercity networks for administrative functions (GoNet in Ontario).

Public/Private Sector Partnerships
CANARIE represents a combined public/private investment of
$115 million in Phase 1, and in excess of $400 million in Phase
2. Its mission includes connecting researchers and educational
communities by 1999 with a high-speed broadband network and
upgrading the Canadian gateway to Internet. CANARIE argues that
achieving these educational goals will support long-term economic development and competitiveness.

Ontario's Sector Partnership Fund, a three-year $150 million
funding program launched in 1992, has placed a high priority on
the telecommunications sector.

Low coercion

**Task Forces, Roundtables, Commissions, Ministerial
Statements**
Recent ventures such as CANARIE and Radian have emerged in the
context of innumerable commissions, task forces, and inquiries

from both levels of government. The Prosperity Initiative Reports
(1991/92), *Public Service—2000* (Government of Canada, 1990),
and the ministerial position paper, *The Canadian Information
Highway* (Manley, 1994) are but a few examples.

The first three instruments give stakeholders in a particular
policy area the opportunity to provide input at the policy formulation stage. For example, the Prosperity Secretariat's Steering
Group consultation process was extensive. Its strong recommendations about distance education, the information highway, and
economic competitiveness had some effect on the establishment
of CANARIE and on the priority that CANARIE accords to distance
education as an applications area for its services.

In other initiatives at the low-coercion end of the scale,
provincial governments issue policy or ministerial statements.
Provincially, the Government of Newfoundland and Labrador's
(1992) Strategic Economic Plan (*Change and Challenge*) included
telecommunications and IT. In Ontario, the Report of the
Advisory Committee on a Telecommunications Strategy for the
Province of Ontario (1992) included economic renewal as a benefit of information infrastructure (*Telecommunications: Enabling
Ontario's Future*). In provinces such as New Brunswick, the
Premier has been a highly visible advocate of telecommunications
and IT.

Sector Strategies
Nine provinces have engaged consultants to develop strategic
plans for their telecommunications sector. All provided access
points for members of the provincial policy communities to have
input in the formulation of policy in this important new area
(Miller, 1994).

Bureaucracy
The bureaucracy plays an important role, not only in formulat-
ing, generating, and implementing policy, but also by reflecting
general government directions. Historically in the federal arena,
jurisdiction over telecommunications and information technologies became the exclusive responsibility of the Department of
Communications (DOC) when it was created in 1970. It represented Canada at international regulatory bodies such as the
International Telecommunication Union (ITU), conducted

research, enforced regulations, and controlled licences. However, in 1992, DOC became a component of Industry, Science and Technology Canada. In 1993, it became a division of Industry Canada. Government is clearly signalling its recognition of the importance of telecommunications and information technology to the industrial base of the country.

Similar trends can be seen in the provinces. Newfoundland recently incorporated the Division of Communications into its new Department of Industry, Trade and Technology. In 1992, the Advisory Committee on a Telecommunications Strategy for Ontario reported to the Minister of Culture and Communications. In 1994, the Council for an Ontario Information Infrastructure (1994) presented its first annual report (*Full Speed Ahead*) to the Minister of Economic Development and Trade. The Province of New Brunswick has taken a different approach by creating a Ministry of the Electronic Highway.

Education/Distance Education
High coercion

Government Agencies

Constitutionally, the federal government does not have responsibility for education, and thus exercises no high-coercion policy instruments in this domain. However, as distance educators make increasing use of telecommunications facilities, federal government intervention in that sector indirectly affects education. If government adopts a high-coercion instrument (e.g., Crown corporations such as Teleglobe), then options available to distance education for, say, international networking are, in effect, set by the federal government.

Provincial governments intervene directly in education in terms of the type of institutions they create. In the distance education sector, provincial initiatives range from creating distribution networks such as Contact North/Contact Nord and TENB to establishing, by statute or other means, single-mode universities such as Athabasca and Télé-Université and single-mode colleges such as Collège de l'Acadie and Centre collégial de formation à distance, in the Québec Ministry of Education. Moreover, at the elementary/secondary level, government ministries of education have been the primary source of correspondence courses ever since British Columbia decided to serve a lighthouse keeper in 1919.

Regulations

Before the advent of networked distance education tools, education was unaffected by CRTC decisions. Now, however, the rates that Stentor companies are allowed through the CRTC are quite pertinent to education. Increasingly so, if—as Paul (Chapter 7) and Pacey and Penney (Chapter 2) suggest—traditional institutions are employing distance education techniques and technologies. In the 1970s and early 1980s, the CRTC prohibited customers from owning their own telecommunications equipment. A change in that policy in the early 1980s permitted many major distance education networks to expand aggressively. DOC is the Canadian signatory to the international standards committee for telecommunications equipment, which vendors must meet to sell their products in Canada—another highly coercive policy instrument that affects, for example, the type of computer equipment in education, either for stand-alone or networked purposes. Copyright is also within federal jurisdiction. Provincial education departments are increasingly affected by copyright policy as they acquire or look to produce multimedia products whose copyright status is unclear.

Curriculum at the elementary/secondary level is tightly controlled by provincial ministries of education. Even private schools conform closely to provincial guidelines so as not to disadvantage their graduates. The degree of provincial control in the college system varies considerably from province to province. At the university level, government exerts very little control once it establishes a university by statute. This variation in the use of coercive government policy tools affects the pace at which change occurs. For example, developing a common science curriculum at the secondary school level could, in theory, be accomplished by 10 to 12 officials from the provinces and territories. Standardizing university science, on the other hand, could involve a minimum of 69 science professors from across the country.

Medium coercion

Taxation/Expenditures

The federal government's main, publicly acknowledged role in education has been to transfer federal tax dollars to the provinces to support education. In recent years, the federal government has been reducing its transfer payments as it struggles to control its deficit. This reduction in federal spending has had a material effect on the provinces.

Just as the federal government's transfer payments affect the provinces, so do the provinces' payments affect schools, colleges, and universities. When the provinces' tax revenues and grants to education decrease, school boards are faced with the option of increasing local taxes or cutting services to make up the short-fall. Similarly, post-secondary institutions must raise student tuition or become creative about finding other revenue sources.

Many provincial governments have policies that treat full-time and part-time learners differently in terms of how institutions can finance their services to these two types of learners. Both college and university distance educators report that they received far less base operating grant support for their distance students than for their on-campus students (CMEC, 1995).

Government as Model User

Provincial governments have traditionally not used distance education as a training technique for their employees, an interesting point in view of the recommendations of provincial task forces and commissions to increase distance education (see below).

As noted above, as part of the federal government's attempt to use telecommunications more systematically in its operations, Radian is also aggressively promoting distance education as a cost-effective tool for public servants further to policy reviews (Hossack, 1991).

Public/Private Sector Partnerships

As business has become concerned about the quality of graduates, it has begun to collaborate with various parts of the education system to address the problem. Sometimes, for example with technical college level programs, the issue is defining workplace job standards so that colleges know "what to offer" (Human Resources Development Canada, 1994). Sometimes, the issue is that universities, say, develop new financial templates in their relationship with the private sector. For example, the University of Waterloo and Bank of Montreal are developing training materials for software professionals. Another type of partnership is that of The Learning Partnership, founded in 1993 by a group of education and business leaders to create a learning culture by, among other things, bringing together key leaders in education, business, and the community so that educational resources and opportunities are maximized. It is self-funded by annual contributions of its members. Since more than 16 of its 64 members (as of 1994) are school boards, university and college public monies are being used in new ways by autonomous public institutions.

In distance education, such partnerships have often involved the donation of telecommunications equipment to support education. For example, Northern Telecom donated equipment to River Oaks School in Burlington, Ontario, and Electrohome provided hardware to the Waterloo/Guelph Electrohome Link.

Low coercion

Task Forces, Roundtables, Commissions, Ministerial Statements

The federal government has leveraged its role in telecommunications and industrial development to encourage distance education in reports made by task forces such as that on prosperity (1993) and by advisory bodies such as the Economic Council of Canada (1992). Generally, these reports are not written from the perspective of the pedagogical issues but from the economic interest: that is, distance education will enhance prosperity by delivering training and education more flexibly and, often, more cost effectively.

Government has also funded a broad series of tools to support the development of the training sector in Canada, and the use of technology. For example, the Canadian Consulate General in Boston has produced *Multimedia in Canada and New England: A Strategic Alliance Directory*. Industry Canada has produced a *Directory of Canadian Suppliers of Commercial Education and*

Training Services. While these do not seem to affect the provinces' public education sectors, the Canadian reality is that there is overlap. For example, publicly funded post-secondary institutions are using multimedia and are able to seek contracts as adjunct revenues. Thus, federal support of Canadian suppliers of commercial education inevitably includes some colleges and universities.

As noted above, there have been many provincial royal commissions and task forces on education in recent years. Some, such as in Saskatchewan and Manitoba, have addressed distance education exclusively. Others, such as in Newfoundland, have treated distance education as a component of a larger study (Government of Newfoundland and Labrador, 1992). Nevertheless, the fact remains that distance education is now on the educational agenda.

Regional co-operation is important in the education sector, just as it was in telecommunications/economic development. For example, the Western Ministers of Education and Advanced Education prepared a *Report of Western Canadian Distance Learning in Post-Secondary Education* in the four provinces and two territories (Alberta Advanced Education & Career Development, 1993). The Maritime Provinces Education Foundation has political support from the Conference of Atlantic Premiers for its *Common Core Curriculum for Atlantic Canada* project (CMEC, 1995).

Bureaucracy
The federal bureaucracy has had a significant effect on distance education since the mid-1970s. For example, by making the technology of the Hermes and Anik satellites available for education applications, DOC materially affected the formation of the Telemedicine Project in Newfoundland and the Knowledge Network in British Columbia. Industry Canada has formed labour/management/government councils to examine human resource needs in certain industrial sectors deemed key to the Canadian economy, and is beginning to fund distance education applications. Foreign Affairs has funded a market survey of distance education opportunities in Australia and New Zealand.

Bureaucrats have a high degree of influence over the content of elementary/secondary education, but not over the delivery process, which is a local school board responsibility. Thus, developing curricula for the information highway could be accomplished fairly readily by a few people, but resolving the scheduling of networked virtual schoolrooms when schedules vary is a much larger challenge and one which the provincial ministries of education do not control.

Some governments have signalled their increasing interest in distance education in their organizational structure. Ontario, for example, created an Open Learning and Training Division when it consolidated its ministries of education and colleges/universities in 1993. The Division is beginning a number of research studies designed to accelerate the use of distance education and open learning in Ontario. It is a medium/low-coercion tool, however, as it has no line responsibility over the institutions.

Analysis

Four trends emerge from this review of government policy instruments in telecommunications and education/distance education.

The first is that the Canadian federal government is privatizing telecommunications and using a full range of high- to low-coercion instruments to do so. It is withdrawing from the direct operation or ownership of telecommunications companies and agencies and is reorganizing telecommunications departments to integrate telecommunications with economic development. This increasing privatization of telecommunications may mean social policy goals are endangered since companies, of necessity, make decisions on the basis of cost, not social value.

For example, Stentor companies plan to serve only 80 to 90 percent of Canadian homes and businesses by the year 2005 with broadband multimedia service, an understandable goal when CRTC decisions continue to encourage deregulation, privatization, and competition in service delivery, but a significant departure from previous government policy with respect to universality. Educators may therefore have to apply a business planning perspective to their telecommunications needs. Such a perspective challenges distance educators to find creative ways to address issues related to access.

Second, there is a trend for telecommunications to migrate from provincial to federal control. When provincial governments had some regulatory power, they could potentially influence integration, say at the Cabinet level, decisions affecting telecommunications and education. In theory, therefore, distance educators needed to be knowledgeable not only about provincial, but also federal policies. Since all telecommunications decisions are being made at the federal level, distance educators at individual universities, colleges, and school boards have to take collective action and seek national consensus to get provincial issues resolved to their satisfaction. They must be aware and take advantage of all the access points mentioned above to ensure that their concerns are on the policy agenda. National bodies such as CADE, CMEC, AUCC and ACCC are beginning to take a greater interest in telecommunications in order to serve their stakeholders.

A third issue is that the convergence of technologies such as telecommunications and broadcasting, recently encouraged by the CRTC, will further complicate the policy environment for distance educators. For example, content is a provincial issue (education), network is federal (telecommunications and broadcasting), and trade overlaps. To achieve their policy goals, distance educators will have to become knowledgeable about the content, process, and stakeholders involved in all these areas. Being knowledgeable about learner needs will be only a small component of a much larger, more complex environment.

A fourth issue is the increasing focus on distance education as a cost-effective alternative to classroom teaching. Impressive cost savings can be cited when distance education is used in the private sector, as travel costs and employee wages are direct expenses that are reduced when technology is used (Stahmer & Green, 1994). However, there are no such learner wages to be saved by full-time school, college, or university learners. Teachers and faculty are concerned that the savings will be effected by treating self-study and virtual classrooms as ways in which one teacher can do the job that two formerly did. In this view, distance education will be cheap, because teaching positions will be eliminated. From another perspective, some distance education programs (such as those offered to small rural high schools) make programs available that were not previously so. While they deliver significant benefits, they are not without costs.

Given this context, the fact that provincial government funding policies do not yet fund distance education in the same way as on-campus education can be either an opportunity or a barrier. Because part-time (i.e., usually distance) students are sometimes ineligible for the same base operating funding as full-time learners, distance education programs, while receiving much "hype" and publicity, are not receiving funding commensurate with expectations. The convergence of technologies and the convergence of classroom and distance teaching could mean that distance education will get access to the tax revenues it needs, or that classroom education will be expected to function on the kind of cost recovery that distance education is seen to have pioneered.

Another reality is that, in spite of the hype about distance education, probably no more than 10 percent of institutional enrolments (even part-time) come from that domain. For example, McWilliams reported 63 000 part-time distance learners in colleges across Canada. She included single-mode colleges, which account for 26 000 of that total, leaving 36 000 from dual-mode institutions. Given that colleges claim there are as many as 1.5 million part-time learners in the system, distance education is still a very small activity (CMEC, 1993).[7]

Conclusion

This chapter has described changing policy environments in telecommunications and education, which have direct impact on distance education. Some impacts will be positive opportunities; others will provide challenges. This chapter may contribute to making the case that models are needed.

Education stakeholders must interface increasingly with private sector providers of a service—telecommunications—that is increasingly important to education, yet is being increasingly deregulated and privatized. Distance educators are caught between low-coercion government approaches to the delivery mechanisms they use in their work, and high-coercion approaches to the content aspect of their work.

This chapter has discussed reduced government interest in the social policy functions of telecommunications, the loss of local influence over telecommunications, and the leveraging of policy tools in this new environment. Many features of open learning are under institutional control at the college and university level, but are issues for provincial ministries at the elementary/secondary levels. No model exists for policy development across these administrative boundaries.

Many educational administrators are aware of the range of tools outlined in this chapter. However, these tools have not received attention in the literature. If distance educators are to control the information highway, they need an analytical framework to enhance their capability to do so.

Endnotes

1. Taken from data compiled in November 1993 by the Ontario government.

2. Taken from CMEC (1992), *Education in Canada 1988–92.*

3. In 1991/92, 87.9 percent of colleges' operating expenditures were supported with government funding (Statistics Canada, Cansim Table 00590203).

4. There is extensive literature related to categorization of policy instruments. Needless to say, there is no easy way to relate comprehensively the wide array of instruments in use by various governments. Each categorization has its strengths. The one used in this analysis, based on the degree of coercion, is considered one of the best acknowledged of the scales. It was originally presented by Theodore J. Lowi in such writings as "American Business: Public Policy, Case Studies, and · Political Theory," *World Politics 16* (1964), 677–715 and "Four Systems of Policy, Politics and Choice," *Public Administration Review 22* (1972), 298–310. It was then expanded by G.B. Doern & V. Seymore Wilson (Eds.), *Issues in Canadian Public Policy* (pp. 8–35, 337–345).

5. Given its origins, the activities of the telecommunications industry were first governed by the *Railway Act,* the *National Transport Act, The Canadian Radio Television and Telecommunications Act,* the *Telecommunications Act* (1979), and most recently, the new *Telecommunications Act* bill (1992). There have been complementary federal regulatory agencies: the Railway Commission, the Telecommunications Committee of the Transport Commission, the Canadian Radio-Television Commission, and a merger of the last two in 1976 into the Canadian Radio-television and Telecommunications Commission.

6. In 1994, there are three major competitors to Stentor: i.e., Unitel, Sprint, and ACC, each of which has annual long-distance revenues in excess of $80 million. There are several other smaller competitors. The total non-Stentor long-distance business probably represents about 6 to 10 percent of the Canadian market at this point. If Canada follows the U.S. trend, and if the CRTC does not change its policy direction, Stentor companies could expect to retain 65 percent of the long-distance market in the long term.

7. As Statistics Canada reports only 200 000 part-time college learners, lack of reliable data is a challenge in analyzing government and institutional policies in terms of institutional activity.

References

Advisory Committee on a Telecommunications Strategy for the Province of Ontario. (1992). *Telecommunications: Enabling Ontario's future.* Toronto: Author.

Alberta Advanced Education and Career Development. (1993, November). *Report on Western Canadian distance learning in post-secondary education.* Report prepared for the Western Ministers of Education and Advanced Education. Edmonton: Author.

Communications Canada. (1992). *New media, new choices.* Ottawa: Ministry of Supply & Services.

Council for an Ontario Information Infrastructure. (1994, June). *Full speed ahead.* Toronto: Ministry of Economic Development & Trade.

Council of Ministers of Education, Canada (CMEC). (1992). *Education in Canada 1988–1992.* Toronto: Author.

Council of Ministers of Education, Canada (1993, October). *The impact of information and communications technologies on postsecondary education: Report presented to the CERI/OECD.* Toronto: Author.

Council of Ministers of Education, Canada (1995). *Distance education and open learning in Canada.* Toronto: Author.

Doern, G.B., & Wilson, V.S. (Eds.).(1974). *Issues in Canadian public policy.* Toronto: Macmillan.

Economic Council of Canada. (1992). *A lot to learn: Education and training in Canada.* Ottawa: Author.

Government of Canada. (1990). *Public service 2000.* Ottawa: Minister of Supply & Services Canada.

Government of Newfoundland & Labrador. (1992, March). *Our children, our future.* St. John's: Queen's Printer.

Government of Newfoundland & Labrador. (1991, June). *Change and challenge.* St. John's: Queen's Printer.

Hossack, E.P. (1991, August). *Training and technology... A winning combination.* Ottawa: The Public Service 2000 Task Force on Staff Training and Development.

Human Resources Development Canada. (1994, April). *Sectoral activities update report.* Hull: Author.

Industry, Science & Technology Canada. (1993). *Information technologies statistical review.* Ottawa: Author.

Jelly, D.H. (1993). Canada in space. *Journal of Distance Education/Revue de l'éducation à distance, VIII*(1), 15–26.

Kerr, W.T. (1993). Applications development for education: Using communications satellites. *Journal of Distance Education VIII*(1), 27–33.

Manitoba Task Force on Distance Education and Technology. (1993, October). *Final report.* Winnipeg: Manitoba Education and Training.

Manley, J. (1994, April). *The Canadian Information Highway.* Ottawa: Industry Canada.

Miller, B.H. (1994, March). *Analysis and strategic business plan for an Alberta regional network.* Edmonton: Alberta Economic Development and Tourism.

Pal, L.A. (1991). *Public policy analysis.* Toronto: Nelson Canada.

Prosperity Initiative. (1993, May). *The prosperity action plan: A progress report.* Hull: Canadian Communications Group.

Saskatchewan Education. (1991, April). *Distance education in Saskatchewan.* Discussion paper. Regina: Author.

Saskatchewan Education. (1992, June). *Response to the distance education discussion paper.* Regina: Author.

Stahmer, A. & Green, L. (1994, January). Developing a cost-benefit picture for CBT. *The Training Technology Monitor, 1*(4), 6–7.

Stahmer, A. & Green, L. (1994, April). Conference Board surveys training and development. *The Training Technology Monitor, 1*(6), 7.

Statistics Canada (1993). *Education in Canada 1991/92.* Ottawa: Author. Catalogue No. 81–229.

Statistics Canada (1993, September). *Advanced Statistics of Canada. 1993/94.* Ottawa: Author. Catalogue No. 81–220.

Woodside, K. (1986). Policy instruments and the study of public policy. *Canadian Journal of Political Science, XIX*(1), 775–793.

About the Contributors

Jane E. Brindley is a psychologist and distant education consultant who has worked with institutions in Canada, New Zealand, South and Central America, China, and the United Kingdom. Counsellor, Regional Director and Director of Student Services at Athabasca University in Alberta from 1971 to 1991, she was Co-ordinator of Program Development and Review at Cambrian College in Sudbury from 1991 to 1993. She is currently completing doctoral studies in Clinical Psychology at the University of Ottawa.

Margaret Haughey, a past president of the Canadian Association for Distance Education, has worked as an instructional designer, content expert, producer and administrator in distance education. She is a Professor in the Faculty of Education at the University of Alberta. Her major research interests are in the implementation of distance education and open learning in the schooling and post-secondary areas. She is also involved in exploring the potential of telecommunications in these sectors. Most recently, she has been a member of the research team assembled by the Canadian Education Association to examine the strategies for student success used in exemplary secondary schools in Canada.

Erin M. Keough, another past president of the Canadian Association for Distance Education, has taken up a new post as Executive Director of the Open Learning and Information Network of Newfoundland and Labrador, a collaborative venture of universities, colleges, schools, and the private sector in that province, after serving for several years as the Director of Memorial University's Telemedicine Centre. She has consulted widely in Canada and in international venues such as the West Indies, the Philippines, and Africa.

Thérèse Lamy is just completing her presidential cycle on the Canadian Association for Distance Education board and will resume a full-time consulting career as principal of SED enr., a company specializing in training, educational communication, and the design of learning environments. Some of her clients include Heritage Canada, the Institute of Canadian Bankers, and colleges and universities across Canada.

Daniel L. Larocque is a consultant in instructional design and distance education. His clients are mainly from the public sector, such as community health centres, literacy centres, schools, and colleges. He is presently involved in establishing various services for the newly created Collège des Grands Lacs in Ontario, a community college specializing in distance education. Daniel has recently completed a graduate degree at the Ontario Institute for Studies in Education, where he researched collaboration among institutions offering distance education.

Donald J. McDonell, Ph.D., taught philosophy before assuming responsibility for Distance Education at the University of Ottawa. He is responsible for the development and operation of a distance education network that has sites throughout Ontario and across Canada. He is a member of the board of directors of the International Teleconferencing Association. He has established a distance education network in six countries of Central America and Jamaica. His major interest is the pedagogical implications of distance education.

Norman C. McKinnon is the Director of NCM Consulting and an Associate of the Delta Centre in Guelph, Ontario. His specialty is advising clients on technology-assisted learning systems and distance education. After a teaching and administrative career in Ontario's elementary and secondary school systems, Norm moved to the Ontario Ministry of Education's Independent Learning Centre and obtained his Doctorate in Education with a concentration on the use of technology in distance education. His consulting practice, founded in 1993, has served clients in school boards, community colleges, government, and the private sector. Initial work in Mexico is being expanded to Latin America. He was President of the Canadian Association for Distance Education in 1991–92.

Ian Mugridge is Senior Consultant, Higher Education, at the Commonwealth of Learning in Vancouver and works in policy and program development at the Open Learning Agency, British Columbia. A member of the Governing Council of the Open Learning Institute of Hong Kong and of the executive of the International Council for Distance Education, Ian has worked around the world on projects principally related to institutional development.

Lucille M. Pacey is Vice-President, Education and Television at British Columbia's Open Learning Agency and a past president of the Canadian Association for Distance Education. Often in demand as a keynote speaker in Canada, the United States and abroad, Lucille's experience and interests lie in the corporate planning and administration of complex organizations, with a particular focus on new approaches to education and training.

Denise V. Pacquette-Frenette, a long-time active participant in various community, provincial and national organizations, has worked in educational television as manager of planning and utilization and, for several years, was training co-ordinator for the Forma-Distance program. She is a founding member of the Collège des Grands Lacs, a French-language community college operating mostly at a distance. She is presently completing a doctorate at the Université de Montréal while maintaining her consulting practice in adult and distance education, working with a variety of institutions at the elementary, secondary, college, and university levels.

Ross H. Paul is President of Laurentian University in Sudbury, Ontario and of CREAD, the quadrilingual Inter-American Distance Education Consortium. Formerly Vice-Present, Academic of Alberta's Athabasca University, Ross has written and consulted extensively in many countries on the management of open learning and distance education.

Pierre R. Pelletier is Director of Continuing Education at the University of Ottawa, and president of the Réseau d'enseignement francophone à distance du Canada, an institutionally based consortium of colleges, universities and other institutions involved in distance education in French.

Wayne P. Penney is Vice-Present of Pacific Leadership Inc., a west coast firm specializing in strategic thinking, management of change, leadership development and values management. Recent contracts include a human resource study of the consulting engineering industry in Canada; a similar study of the telecommunications industry is currently underway. Wayne works with a wide variety of public and private sector clients.

Judith M. Roberts, principal of Roberts & Associates/Associés, specializes in project design, management, and planning related to distance education, open learning, and telemedicine. Her clients range widely from the insurance industry to The Commonwealth of Learning, and include the Government of New Brunswick and Industry Canada's Information Highway Advisory Council's Working Group on Learning and Training.

Barbara J. Spronk, President-Elect of the Canadian Association for Distance Education and Associate Professor, Anthropology at Athabasca University, has just completed a project in Thailand and is resuming her special interests in women's and Aboriginal education in Canada. She is a Board member of Frontier College, one of Canada's pre-eminent literacy organizations, and serves also on several national committees such as selection panels for international partnership projects funded by the Canadian International Development Agency. She works closely with the International Centre of the University of Calgary and is a consultant in distance learning and participatory education to institutions in the Philippines, Bangladesh, and the West Indies.

Anna E. Stahmer is principal of Anna Stahmer and Associates, and co-publisher of *The Training Technology Monitor,* an independent source of information on how technology works and can be applied to education and training—from the user's point of view. As Vice-President for Telecommunications at the Academy for Educational Development in Washington, DC, Anna managed training technology projects on a worldwide basis, and continues to consult with agencies such as the World Bank.

Noël A. Thomas is President of Réseau Interaction Network Inc., an Ottawa-based company that specializes in computer applications in distance education through its Electronic Village Électronique service. Its largest project involves linking all teachers, schools, and boards in Ontario in the Creating the Culture for Change project sponsored by a consortium headed by the Ontario Teachers' Federation. Noël has presented at conferences in Belgium and France, and is positioning the Network for the export market.

Judith M. Tobin, Director, Strategic Issues, TVOntario has a strong background in policy and education research, with a specialty in the application of educational television. Her work has ranged from the elementary to the private, and includes consulting to the French government on the establishment of their educational television network, and work with UNESCO and the OECD.

Glossary

ACCC. (Association of Canadian Community Colleges.) A national organization of college-level education institutions from provinces and territories across Canada.

AFN. (Assembly of First Nations.) The national body representing provincial and territorial associations of registered Indians in Canada, which grew out of and, in 1982, succeeded the National Indian Brotherhood, Canada's first national Indian body, which was formed in 1968.

AUCC. (Association of Universities and Colleges of Canada.) A non-profit organization established in 1911, representing Canadian universities at home and abroad. Its mandate is to foster and promote the interests of higher education.

Audioconferencing. Two-way voice communication (usually by telephone) between or among two or more groups, or three or more individuals, who are all connected at the same time from different places.

Bridge. A telecommunications device that links multiple telephone, computer, or video terminals so that all participants can communicate.

CADE. (Canadian Association for Distance Education.) A national association founded in June, 1983, of professionals committed to excellence in the provision of distance education in Canada that advances distance education through a variety of publications, conferences, and related activities.

CANARIE Inc. (Canadian Network for the Advancement of Research, Industry & Education, Inc.) an industry-led and -managed consortium of 140 private and public sector members. It was created in 1993 as an innovative way for the federal government and private sector to collaborate in stimulating the development of Canada's Information Highway.

Ca*Net. Canada's national computer network and constituent of Internet, both of which historically linked primarily post-secondary institutions for research purposes. Ca*Net comprises a number of regional networks based in the provinces (e.g., O*Net, NBNet, NLNet).

CD-i. (Compact-disk interactive.) A technology developed and launched in 1993 jointly by Phillips and Sony, and available in both consumer and professional models. It plays digital data stored on a compact disk using a CD player and a television set or high-end colour computer monitor.

CD-ROM. (Compact-disk read-only memory.) A disk that stores information in digital form and requires that a computer, monitor, and CD-ROM drive are interconnected. Colour capacity and audio are also increasingly required features of this technology, which is used primarily for storage of reference or teaching materials.

CIDA. (Canadian International Development Agency.) A federal government agency that distributes a significant portion of Canada's foreign aid to developing countries with the goal of enabling them to build sustainable capacities in such areas as education and training.

CMEC. (Council of Ministers of Education, Canada.) A council established in 1967 by the various provinicial and territorial ministries of education to facilitate interjurisdictional collaboration on matters of mutual interest.

Codec. (Coder/decoder.) An electronic device that performs a specific analogue to digital conversion (e.g., television signal to digital format), usually incorporating an algorithm for compression.

COL. (Commonwealth of Learning.) An organization established in 1988–89 by the Commonwealth heads of government to promote and support distance education throughout the Commonwealth. Its head office is located in Vancouver, British Columbia.

Computer conferencing. Two-way communication through computer text between or among groups or individuals who contribute to the conference from different places at different times.

Conferencing technologies. *See* audioconferencing, bridge, computer conferencing, videoconferencing.

CREAD. (Consortio-red de educación a distancia.) A quadilingual membership-based organization founded in 1990 that creates new partnerships in support of distance education throughout North, Central and South America and the Caribbean.

CRTC. (Canadian Radio-television & Telecommunications Commission.) The federal government agency that regulates Canadian telephone and cable broadcasting companies.

Distance Education. Educational opportunities that are made available to a student who is separated from the institution offering the learning opportunity.

DOC. (Department of Communications.) Formerly, a separate federal government department; now part of a larger federal government department called Industry, Science & Technology Canada.

E-mail. (Electronic mail.) The exchange of short messages by computer using software packages designed to store and forward messages sent and received.

ENO. (Educational Network of Ontario.) A co-operative of education organizations headed by the Ontario Teachers' Federation that is developing computer conferencing applications in a project called Creating a Culture for Change.

EPSS. (Electronic Performance Support Systems.) Systems that provide job aides to workers using computers. EPSS can act as librarian, advisor, or instructor through various types of computer databases, expert systems, or on-demand training programs. They can also perform routine work, thus freeing employees for more creative tasks.

GoNet. The Ontario government's internal information and tele-communications network, which supports a wide variety of government operations and agencies.

ICCE. (International Council for Correspondence Education.) The initial organization of distance educators, which held its founding meeting in 1938. It changed its name to ICDE in 1982.

ICDE. (International Council for Distance Education.) A membership-based organization headquartered in Oslo, Norway, whose essential goal is to promote knowledge and improvement of distance education worldwide through such tools as publications, conferences, training seminars, and through developing regional and national associations.

Information Highway. Canada's information and communications network, a "network of networks" creating vital communications links among all public and private stakeholders in the knowledge-based society.

Internet. The worldwide network of computers linking some 80 countries and 20 million users. It is both a communications tool and an information tool.

IT. (Information and telecommunications technologies.) All computer, cable, and telecommunications technologies available to distance education and open learning.

ITFS. (Instructional Television Fixed Services.) A term used in the United States for microwave installations that transmit full-motion video signals in one direction and permit interaction by return microwave or telephone calls.

LAN. (Local Area Network.) A special data communications arrangement (usually high-speed) that connects computers and other communications devices for use inside a single building or confined area (e.g., a campus).

LEOS. (Low Earth Orbiting Satellite.) A relatively inexpensive communications satellite that orbits the earth and delivers messages in a store and forward manner.

Open Learning. An instructional system that places many aspects of the learning process under the control of the learner so that (s)he can choose when and how to study.

OECD. (Organization for Economic Co-operation & Development.) An international organization of some 24 countries which co-operates in areas that pertain to economic and sustainable development.

OLA. (Open Learning Agency.) A single-mode distance education institution based in British Columbia, Canada, which consists of an open university, an open college, and the Knowledge Network.

OLI. (Open Learning Institute.) A branch of the Ministry of Education in Ontario, Canada which offers distance education courses at the kindergarten to Grade 13 level.

PARENT. (Parents Against Reduction in Educational Quality Network Together.) A Canadian advocacy and lobbying group which seeks to improve the overall quality of primary and secondary educational programs.

PLS. (Prudential Learning System.) An open learning system employed by Prudential Insurance and Financial Services. Courses are available on a portable platform so that employees can train at work or at home.

R&D. Common short form for "research and development" activities.

REFAD. (Réseau d'enseignment francophone à distance du Canada.) A non-profit association founded in 1988; a national organization of institutions and individuals that promotes French-language distance education in Canada.

RUISSO. (Réseau unifié interactif scolaire du centre-sud de l'Ontario.) A consortium in south-central Ontario that offers, through distance education, secondary-level courses to students and professional development sessions for teachers.

SSHRC. (Social Sciences & Humanities Research Council.) One of three major Canadian councils that fund university-based research. As the name suggests, this one concentrates on the social sciences and humanities.

TEFL. (Teaching English as a Foreign Language.) Programs and approaches for teaching English to persons whose mother tongue is not English. These activities are frequently, but not exclusively, targetted at immigrants.

UKOU. (United Kingdom Open University.) The first of the single-mode universities. Based in Milton Keynes, England; sometimes referred to as the British Open University.

Videoconferencing. Two-way video communication between or among two or more groups or individuals; historically, the term referred to such technologies as two-way broadcast television, but now usually reFers to (compressed) television technology that can function on two data lines per site.

WAN. (Wide Area Network.) A special data communications arrangement that connects computers and other communications devices that are used over a dispersed geographic area, e.g., a city, province, or state.

Index

This index includes the names of authors whose work is quoted or discussed in the text. The works of many other writers, often equally important but too numerous to list here, are cited in the book and acknowledged in the references at the end of each chapter.